# SOVIET SOCIALISM

By the same author

*Contemporary Soviet Government*
*The Soviet Intelligentsia*

# SOVIET SOCIALISM
## SOCIAL AND POLITICAL ESSAYS

L.G. CHURCHWARD

ROUTLEDGE & KEGAN PAUL
LONDON AND NEW YORK

First published in 1987 by
Routledge & Kegan Paul Ltd
11 New Fetter Lane, London EC4P 4EE

Published in the USA by
Routledge & Kegan Paul Inc.
in association with Methuen Inc.
29 West 35th Street, New York, NY 10001

Set in 10/11pt Sabon
by Inforum Ltd, Portsmouth
and printed in Great Britain
by Billings, Worcester

Library of Congress Cataloging in Publication Data

Churchward, L.G.
  Soviet Socialism.

  Bibliography: p.
  Includes index.
  1. Soviet Union——Social conditions——1945–
2. Soviet Union——Politics and government——1945–
I. Title.
HN523.5.C48   1987        306'.0947        87–9733

British Library CIP Data also available

ISBN 0–7102–1166–X

6-16-89 sam

# CONTENTS

# TABLES

# PREFACE

The essays in this book were written at various times between April 1983 and September 1984. They were written on themes on which I had lectured and done research in earlier years but which seemed of continuing interest. They were written in retirement but not in isolation from the stimulus of students and colleagues. I have found it interesting to retrace footsteps and I hope that readers will share my interest.

The book was not written as a textbook but as a series of essays – afterthoughts. As such it should be useful for reference purposes in university teaching and in research. It should also be of interest to the wider circle of readers who are interested in the Soviet Union. The essays do not present a full coverage of Soviet society and politics but merely a selection of interrelated themes dealing mainly with the domestic scene. Yet as the essays were all written by myself and all written over a short space of time they should prove more integrated than the normal essay collection.

I should like to thank all those who have assisted in one way or another in the preparation of this book. In particular, I should like to thank Leslie Holmes and Harry Rigby who read through the manuscript and gave helpful advice, and other colleagues in the Department of Political Science at the University of Melbourne who offered encouragement throughout. I should like to thank the Chairman of the Department, Arthur Huck, for providing me with a room and other resources in my old Department. Finally, I must thank my wife and family for their tolerance and support for one who had the temerity to write a book when almost blind. I am especially indebted to my daughter Alison, who helped prepare the final text.

UNIVERSITY OF MELBOURNE

L.G. Churchward
*September, 1986*

# ACKNOWLEDGEMENTS

I wish to thank the editors of the Melbourne journal *Arena* for permission to reprint in Chapters 6 and 7 parts of an article originally published in *Arena*, no. 12, 1967.

To those who helped with the proof reading – my wife Mary, my daughter Dorothy, and colleagues Patrick Wolfe, Paul James and Stephen Wheatcroft – I extend my warmest thanks.

L.G.C.

# Glossary

**Aktiv**  The leading cadres and most active members of a particular organization or society. The Party *aktiv* – the cadres and most active members right down to the Primary Party Organizations.

**Apparat**  Organizational structure: the paid staff. Typically the paid officials of the Party or state.

**Apparatchik**  Typically a Party or state official. The term is not used in official descriptions of the CPSU.

**ASSR**  Autonomous Soviet Socialist Republic.

**AUCCTU**  All-Union Central Committee of Trade Unions.

**BAM**  (*Baikalo-Amurskaya-Magistral*) Baikal-Amur Trunk Railway – total length over 3,500 km. Built between 1967 and 1984.

**Bich**  From *byvshii intelligentnyi chelovek*. A dissident intellectual in temporary exile in remote places such as Siberia.

**Byurokratia**  Bureaucracy.

**Byurokratizm**  Bureaucratism: The undesirable behaviour of (some) office-holders.

**COMECON**  Council of Mutual Economic Assistance. Formed 1949.

**CPSU**  Communist Party of the Soviet Union.

**Demokratichesky tsentralizm**  Democratic centralism.

**Glavki**  Main Departments (of ministries).

**Gosplan**  State Planning Committee.

**Gossnab**  State Committee on Material-Technical Supplies.

**Gosudarstvo**  State.

**ITRs**  (*Inzhenerno-tekhnicheskie rabotniki*) Engineering-technical workers.

**Kantselyarshchina** Red-tapism, bureaucratism.

**Komsomol** All-Union League of Communist Youth.

**Kolkhoz** Collective farm.

**Krai** Territory.

**Kulak** A rich peasant. From the Russian for 'fist'.

**Kustar** A small-scale industrialist.

**MTS** Machine Tractor Station. Abolished 1958.

**Nachalnik** A person holding an official position – Party, state, or other.

**Nachalstvo** Authorities, officials.

**Nakazy izbiratelei** Electors' mandates.

**NEP** (*Novaya ekonomicheskaya politika*) New economic policy – introduced March 1921.

**NKVD** Commissariat of Internal Affairs.

**Nomenklatura** A list of official positions and also a list of those entitled to hold them.

**Obkom** Oblast (regional) Party Committee.

**Oblast** Province (region).

**Obshchenarodnoe gosudarstvo** State of the whole people.

**Okrug** Area. The Autonomous Area is the smallest national group given administrative recognition.

**Orgburo** Organizational Bureau of the CC of the CPSU.

**Podmena** Subordination: normally meaning the tendency for Party committees to supplant government agencies.

**Politburo** Political Bureau of the CC of the CPSU.

**Rabfak** A workers' faculty – a factory-based educational establishment to qualify workers for professional careers.

**Rabkrin** Workers and Peasants Inspectorate (1918–21).

**Raiispolkom** Executive Committee of a District Soviet.

**Raikom** District Party Committee.

**Raion** District. An administrative area in rural and (large) urban areas.

**Razvitoi sotsializm** Developed socialism.

**Sblizhenie** Drawing together.

**Shabashnik** A worker who does private contract work (after hours).

**Sluzhashchie** Employees (white-collar workers). The category often includes the intelligentsia.

**Sovkhoz** State farm.

**Sovnarkhoz** Regional Economic Council. Most recently established by Khrushchev in 1957. Abolished 1965.

**Union Republic** A constituent state in the USSR. There are fifteen of them at present of which the largest is the RSFSR, the Russian Soviet Federal Socialist Republic.

**USSR** Union of Soviet Socialist Republics.

**Utverzhdenie** Confirmation (of appointments).

**Volokita** Red tape.

**Vozhd** Leader: a term used to describe Lenin, Stalin, and occasionally, Brezhnev.

**VUZ** (*Vysshoe uchebnoe zavedenie*) Tertiary educational establishment (Plural: VUZy).

**Yezhovshchina** The height of the Stalin terror under the direction of Yezhov.

**Zek** A person undergoing forced (corrective) labour.

**Zemlyachestvo** An urban group consisting of migrants from the same rural district.

**Zhenotdel** Women's department of the Central Committee and lower Party committees. Established 1919.

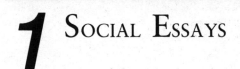

PART

1 SOCIAL ESSAYS

# 1 THE SOVIET APPROACH TO SOCIALISM AND ITS MARXIST CRITICS

Socialism reached Russia in the 1860s. While main sources were West European, chiefly French, German and English, Russian socialism was not simply a carbon-copy of any imported socialism. From 1861 up to the first Russian Revolution in 1905 the dominant revolutionary tradition was Populism, which while it drew some inspiration from Marx, was not a socialist movement in the Marxist sense. The Populists envisaged a rural socialism based on the survival of the peasant commune. The revolutionary movement was to be led by the intelligentsia with the support of the peasantry and the proletariat. Industrialization and urbanization were to be avoided.

Marxism began in Russia in the early 1880s as a breakaway from Populism and in opposition to it. It was led largely by Russian emigrés in Switzerland and London, the most important of whom was Plekhanov. From the outset the Russian Marxists challenged the basic propositions of Populism. They denied that Russia could avoid capitalism and industrialization. On the contrary, Russia was already well advanced on the path of capitalist development. They argued that the peasantry was not a revolutionary class in the full sense of the term, but only in their opposition to the landed aristocracy. The main revolutionary class, the class that would lead Russia beyond capitalism to socialism was the proletariat. While this class was still a small minority of the population it would grow in numbers and experience with the further growth of capitalism. Socialism was a promise for the future; it could come only after the overthrow of autocracy and the success and consolidation of a bourgeois revolution. Finally, the Russian socialists challenged the preferred strategy and tactics of the radical wing of Populism. They condemned terror and assassination as revolutionary methods. Their emphasis was on education, agitation, organization, mobilization and struggle of the entire working class.

Russian backwardness was a perennial problem for Russian socialists. Generally speaking, the more rigid and inflexible their Marxism, the less likely they were to support an early socialist revolution. But the pressure of events could force even the most rigid and 'orthodox' Marxist to flirt with the prospect of an early proletarian revolution. Witness the writings and speeches of Akselrod and other Menshevik leaders during the 1905 Revolution.

Of the two wings of Russian Social Democracy it was the Bolsheviks rather than the Mensheviks who made the greater adjustments to orthodox Marxism. This fact was noted by their rivals just as it has been by many Western critics of Lenin and Bolshevism. Thus Plamenatz considered Bolshevism as 'the distorted Marxism of a backward society exposed to the impact of the West'. But this is no more than a half-truth. Marxism for Plamenatz was economic determinism, but Marxism for Lenin was anything but determinist. From his first published work in 1894 Lenin demanded that Russian socialists should study the concrete reality of Russian society and not abstractions. In commenting on the aims of the newly formed Russian Social Democratic Labour Party (in *Our Program*) he declared that Marx's analysis was not to be regarded as 'something final or inviolable' but rather as 'general guiding principles' that 'had to be applied differently to England than to France, differently to France than to Germany, differently to Germany than to Russia.' In 1899 Lenin published his *Development of Capitalism in Russia*, a book comparable in some respects with *Capital*, Volume I. Lenin showed not only the rapid growth of capitalism since 1861 but the unevenness of that development. He discussed the development of large factories in key areas, the growth of *kustar* industry in the provinces and the growing class differences amongst the peasantry associated with the move from subsistence farming to production for the market. This book was followed in the early years of the twentieth century by the detailed analysis of Russian agriculture after the Stolypin reforms. These analyses made it possible for Lenin to make a re-evaluation of earlier Russian Marxist policies towards the peasantry. From this came, in September 1905, Lenin's call for an alliance of revolutionary workers and revolutionary peasants, especially of the poor and landless peasants. On this new appreciation of the class basis of the Russian revolution Lenin evolved his theory of the uninterrupted revolution, just as Trotsky, on a slightly different reading of the evidence, developed his theory of permanent revolution. Lenin and Trotsky were brilliant revolutionary leaders because they understood that Marx's theories could not be applied automatically to Russia. This lesson was generally understood by the entire Bolshevik leadership by 1917. This is not to suggest that the Bolsheviks did not frequently make inaccurate assessments and predictions and consequently make wrong policy decisions. Thus Lenin's insistence on the seizure of power in October 1917 was based not only on an assessment of the revolutionary situation in Russia but on the strength of revolutionary and anti-war feelings abroad. His evaluation of the former was undoubtedly more accurate than it was of the latter. Lenin's confidence in November 1917 that the Russian proletariat could build the 'lofty, towering edifice of socialism' was based on the assumption that proletarian revolutions would occur almost immediately in Germany and other advanced capitalist countries and lend support and material aid to the Soviets. The possibility of building socialism in Russia alone did not occur to Lenin until several years after 1917. But the necessity of formulating such an objective was evident as early as 1921.

Bolshevism, like many revolutionary movements suffered from the fetishism of concepts and slogans. Concepts like 'proletarian revolution', 'the worker and peasant alliance', 'socialism in one country', 'mature socialism', 'developed socialism' and 'the state of the whole people' assumed a mystique that obscured reality. But these concepts themselves are the result of adherence to the objective of building a communist society.

The purpose of this chapter is two-fold: first, to provide an historical account of Bolshevik theorizing about the building of socialism, and, second, to review some of the main Marxist critics of the Soviet achievement. It does not attempt to justify either the Russian Revolution or the Soviet achievement but merely to aid the understanding of these events.

## Building socialism

The Russian Revolution of November 1917 was planned to be a socialist revolution. Kerensky's Provisional Government had to be overthrown because it did not represent the interests of the Russian masses, of the workers and the peasants. The March Revolution, which had brought the Provisional Government to power, was regarded as an unfinished bourgeois revolution which had neither completely overthrown the old order nor fully established a democratic order. It had failed most abjectly in its refusal to abolish the landed aristocracy and to strengthen the peasantry and in its continuation of the War. Lenin's Bolshevik Government was pledged to peace and land reform, to achieving greater democracy, and at the same time to beginning to build socialism. Thus Lenin, while the fighting for the Winter Palace was still in progress, in an address to the Second All-Russian Congress of Soviets, declared enthusiastically:

We shall now proceed to build, on the space cleared of historical rubbish, the airy, towering edifice of socialist society. A new type of state power is being created for the first time in history, a power that the will of the revolution has called upon to wipe out all exploitation, oppression and misery, the world over . . . From now on all the marvels of science and the gains of culture belong to the nation as a whole, and never again will man's brain and human genius be used for oppression and exploitation.[1]

The Bolshevik Government acted quickly to destroy the last remnants of Tsarism and feudalism. Within a month of taking power Lenin's Government had abolished landed estates, confirmed the peasant seizures of land, withdrawn Russia from the War, abolished titles and the classification of the population into estates, abolished the old courts, police, ministerial structure and even the dumas. It had also declared its support for the liberation of the oppressed nations of Russia and commenced to dismantle the Tsarist Empire. New governmental agencies replaced the old ones – a Council of People's Commissars responsible to the All-Russian Congress of Soviets replaced the Provisional Government, Workers and Peasants Soviets replaced the municipal dumas, elected People's Courts replaced the old courts, and soon a new police and army replaced the Tsarist agencies.

The honeymoon period lasted only until February 1918. Opposition to the Brest-Litovsk Treaty with Germany resulted in the withdrawal of the Left Socialist Revolutionaries and of some Bolsheviks from the government. Growing resistance to Bolshevik social and economic policies and methods produced open opposition and in July the outbreak of Civil War. Civil War combined with foreign intervention caused a rapid acceleration of military and police agencies and a reduction of popular participation in all areas of public life. During 1918 the early experiments with workers' control of factories and other economic agencies gave way to one-man management under the control of central bureaucratic agencies – War Communism. Most of the industry became nationalized and extensive rationing and control over the distribution of supplies and services produced an illusion of early achievement of communist equality. Towards the end of the Civil War mounting popular resistance to government economic policy caused the Bolshevik leadership to alter course and introduce the New Economic Policy in March 1921. This replaced the compulsory acquisition of grain surpluses by a tax in kind. Surplus grain could then be sold on the market. There was a partial return to private trading and small-scale manufacturing, a temporary retreat in economic policy. Despite the partial restoration of capitalism the state continued to control the

'commanding heights' of the economy – mining, large-scale manufacturing, banking, foreign trade, most transport and communications. And the government apparatus continued to grow. By 1923
Bolshevik leaders such as Lenin and Trotsky were becoming increasingly critical of Soviet bureaucracy and bureaucratism.[2] Lenin
was particularly critical of the poor quality of Soviet officials and
declared in 1923 that:

> Our state apparatus, with the exception of the People's
> Commissariat for Foreign Affairs, represents in the highest
> degree a hang-over of the old one, subjected to only the slightest
> extent to any serious change.[3]

Did Lenin change his mind then about the possibility of building a
socialist society in Russia? It seems unlikely, even though he became
increasingly realistic about the difficulties of the task. Like most
Russian socialists in 1917 he believed that bureaucracy was alien to
socialism. In his work, *State and Revolution*, written in the autumn
of 1917, Lenin had argued that the revolutionary workers could rule
without the need for a special apparatus of repression, with only a
very simple machinery of government. This belief was quickly
modified. Thus in January 1921 in writing on 'The Party Crisis'
Lenin conceded that:

> A workers' state is an abstraction. What we actually have is a
> workers' state with this peculiarity, firstly, that it is not the
> working class but the peasant population that predominates in
> the country, and, secondly, that it is a workers' state with
> bureaucratic distortions.

But although this admission was followed by the partial retreat of the
NEP, Lenin never ever conceded that the Mensheviks had been right
in denying the possibility of building socialism in a backward and
largely agrarian country. While the delay to the world revolution
would cause a slowing down of the socialist revolution in Russia, it
would not cause its abandonment. From early 1922 Lenin began to
urge on the party the need to challenge the advance of capitalism in
agriculture by pushing rapidly ahead with cooperative peasant
farming and with state farms. He made his underlying confidence
quite explicit in his article 'On Cooperation' in January 1923 when
he wrote that:

> As a matter of fact, the power of state over all large-scale means
> of production, the power of state in the hands of the proletariat,

the alliance of the proletariat with the many millions of small and
very small peasants, the assured leadership of the peasantry by
the proletariat, etc.; is not this all that is necessary in order from
the cooperatives alone . . . to build complete Socialist society?
This is not yet the building of Socialist society, but it is all that is
necessary and sufficient for this building.[4]

Lenin's confidence in the possibility of building socialism in
backward Russia was given a clearer and more dogmatic formulation by Stalin and Bukharin over the years 1924–26. In so far as
'Socialism in One Country' had a clear theoretical basis it was to be
found in two theoretical propositions of Lenin. Lenin's 'law of
uneven development of Capitalism' (since its original enunciation in
August 1915) had been extended after 1917 to explain both the
initial outbreak of a proletarian revolution in Russia as well as the
survival of the revolution in Russia aione. Henceforth socialist
revolution, like capitalist revolution, was seen to be an uneven
development proceeding first in some countries and then in others.
Lenin's explanation of the class basis for the Russian Revolution, the
alliance of the revolutionary proletariat and the revolutionary
peasantry, under the leadership of the proletariat, had been extended
to explain the survival of the Russian Revolution and to justify its
continued progress towards socialism. By the time the theory of
Socialism in One Country was advanced the Russian Revolution had
survived for over six years and seemed likely to continue. However it
was still claimed that the complete guarantee against the revival of
capitalism in Russia required the ending of the capitalist encirclement and the extension of the socialist revolution to other countries.*

Stalin's justification of the thesis of Socialism in One Country
went through several stages. In April 1924 in 'Foundations of
Leninism' Stalin argued that while a socialist revolution could occur
and succeed in one country, the development of a socialist economy
required an international revolution. Between December 1924 and
the end of 1925 Stalin argued that the revolutionary forces of Russia
could develop a socialist economy in isolation, without the aid of the
world revolution, but they could not guarantee the survival of that
system until the socialist revolution had succeeded in one or more
capitalist countries. Only in February 1926 in 'On the Problems of
Leninism' did Stalin argue that the victory of socialism in one

---

* Trotsky extended Lenin's theory by formulating 'the law of uneven and
combined development'. See his *History of the Russian Revolution*.

country was possible. Even then he kept a symbolic toe on socialist internationalism by asserting that the 'final victory of socialism' required the spread of the socialist revolution.[5] Stalin justified this movement from the second to the third formulation in terms of the state of the inner-party struggle rather than in terms of a growth in the productive forces between 1924 and 1926. In February 1926 he stated:

> Subsequently, however, when the criticism of Leninism in this sphere had already been overcome in the Party, and when a new question had come to the fore – the question of the possibility of building a complete socialist society by the efforts of our country, without help from outside – the second formulation became obviously inadequate, and therefore incorrect.[6]

Trotsky's quarrel with the concept of Socialism in One Country was not over the claim that a start could be made to the building of socialism in Russia, but to the eventual claim that it could be built in isolation. To transform society in a socialist direction required the internationalizing of the revolution. Against the theory of Socialism in One Country Trotsky posed his theory of Permanent Revolution which comprised the movement from a democratic revolution to a socialist revolution, the continued revolutionizing of the entire society and not merely the economy, and the international spread of the revolution. The following passages bring out the crucial import-ance of the third of these aspects:

> The completion of a socialist revolution within national boundaries is unthinkable.

> Left to itself, the working class of Russia will inevitably be crushed by the counter-revolution at the moment when the peasantry turns its back on the proletariat.

> Backward countries, under certain conditions can arrive at the dictatorship of the proletariat sooner than the advanced countries, but they come later than the latter to socialism.[7]

These formulations were based on the Marxist belief that socialism, like capitalism, was international and on the recognition that the higher stage of socialism, communism, could only be achieved on the basis of material abundance.

Despite the factional struggles of the 1920s the Bolshevik leaders remained united in their determination to maintain the dictatorship of the proletariat, which meant in effect the maintenance of the Party monopoly of power. They were also united in their determination to keep the peasantry subordinate to the proletariat and in their recognition of the need to replace peasant farming by co-operative or socialist agriculture as soon as possible. The survival of peasant agriculture required frequent concessions to the peasants, uncertainties of food supplies for the towns and the army, and limited capital for industrial development. It is no accident that the eventual strategy finally adopted – accelerated industrial development combined with forced collectivization of agriculture – coincided with Stalin's emergence as undisputed leader of the Party.

The 'revolution from above' carried out over the years 1929–36 brought about a profound change to the Soviet economy and to Soviet society. There was a startling development of heavy industry and especially of coal, iron and steel. Between 1928 and 1937 coal production rose from 33.4 million tonnes to 128 million tonnes, while steel production rose from 4.3 million tonnes to 17.7 million tonnes. According to the revised 1956 Soviet estimates the First Five Year Plan achieved an annual average increase in industrial production of 19.2 per cent while the Second Five Year Plan achieved one of 17.8 per cent.[8] While agricultural production declined during the early years of collectivization the government increased its grain acquisitions, for it was easier to collect grain from a quarter of a million collective farms than it was from twenty-four million individual peasant farmers.

The accelerated industrialization meant accelerated urbanization of society. The class structure changed rapidly. Thus the working class increased from 17.6 per cent of the population in 1928 to 50.2 per cent in 1939, collective farmers increased from 2.9 to 47.2 per cent over the same period, while individual peasants dropped from 74.9 per cent to 2.6 per cent.[9] Over the same period bourgeois and petty-bourgeois elements in society dropped from 4.6 per cent to nil.

It was on the basis of this transformation of the social structure and the early success of the industrialization drive that Stalin was able to announce the achievement of socialism in the USSR and to have it written into the 1936 Constitution that the USSR was 'a socialist state of workers and peasants'. When some academic critics began to suggest that since socialism had been achieved the state should begin to wither away, Stalin was quick to reply that the withering away of the state which Engels had posited, could not happen while the Soviet Union remained encircled by hostile capitalist powers.[10] As late as 1950 Stalin continued to argue that the Soviet state would remain even under communism while the capitalist encirclement remained.[11] This was a surprising lack of adjustment to the emergence of the Soviet satellites in Eastern Europe in 1945 and of the People's Republic of China in 1949.

Stalin's heirs have not seen fit to change drastically the claim that socialism has been achieved in the USSR. In February 1955 V.M. Molotov referred to 'the basis of socialism having been attained in the Soviet Union' but he abandoned this position a few months later. Some adjustments were made to Stalin's dogmas about the role of the Soviet state at different stages in its development, mainly in the years 1956–9, but these adjustments did not challenge the underlying Stalinist theory.[12] It was only in 1959 that N.S. Khrushchev (then First Secretary of the CPSU and Chairman of the USSR Council of Ministers) began to talk frequently about the accelerated development towards communism ('the all-round development of Communism'). Under the stimulus of Chinese and Yugoslav challenges to Soviet leadership in the movement towards communism and the drafting of the new Program of the CPSU in 1961 Khrushchev sanctioned further modifications to the theory. What emerged was an over-optimistic assertion that 'the basis of communism' would be achieved by 1980. A new concept of 'mature socialism' (*zrelyi sotsializm*) was developed to cover the period of rapid approach to communism. Not only the economy but the state was expected to undergo rapid transformation. It would not wither away suddenly but would be gradually transformed into communist self-administration as more and more state functions were transferred to public non-state agencies. Although seen as a development of the 'dictatorship of the proletariat' the new state was gradually outgrowing this proletarian basis as it became a 'State of the Entire People', an *obshchenarodnoe gosudarstvo*.

The Brezhnev regime tended to play down these optimistic concepts in its early years but it did not abandon them.[13] They were revived in the early 1970s and given renewed emphasis in the final stages of the drafting of the new 1977 Constitution. The preamble to the 1977 Constitution makes clear the continuity of the theory from the 1961 Party Program:

> Socio-political and ideological unity of Soviet society, in which the working class is the leading force, has been achieved. The aims of the dictatorship of the proletariat having been fulfilled, the Soviet state has become a state of the whole people. The leading role of the Communist Party, the vanguard of all the people, has grown.
>
> In the USSR a developed socialist society has been built . . .
>
> It is a society in which powerful productive forces and progressive science and culture have been created, in which the well-being of the people is constantly rising, and more and more

favourable conditions are being provided for the all-round development of the individual.

It is a society of mature socialist social relations, in which, on the basis of the drawing together of all classes and social strata, and of the juridical and factual equality of all its nations and nationalities and their fraternal co-operation, a new historical community of people has been formed – the Soviet people.

It is a society of true democracy, the political system of which ensures effective arrangement of all public affairs, ever more active participation of the working people in the running of the state, and the combining of citizens' real rights and freedoms with their obligations and responsibilities to society.[14]

In this passage we find repeated key concepts of the Khrushchev era: 'mature' or 'developed' socialism (*razvitoi sotsializm*), 'the drawing together' (*sblizhenie*)* of classes and nations, and 'the state of the whole people'. To bring institutional titles into conformity with this new theory 'Soviets of Working People's Deputies' were renamed 'Soviets of People's Deputies'.

While there was no essential difference between Brezhnev's and Khrushchev's understanding of the nature of Soviet socialism there continued to be a difference about the time required to achieve even the basis of communism. Discussions of this problem in Soviet journals in the seventies invariably stressed the immensity and the slowness of the process.[15] The following preconditions for achieving communism were regularly emphasized:

• The need for a much higher material-technical basis and a much higher level of production of all kinds of goods so that the Soviet Union would overtake the most advanced capitalist countries.
• The changing of the basis for distributing individual income from payment according to the amount and value of the work performed to one based on the principle of 'From each according to his ability, to each according to his need'.
• The abolition of the distinctions between town and country and between manual and mental labour.
• The withering away of the State as an agency of coercion.
• The raising of the level of political consciousness of the entire adult population to the level of its vanguard.

Despite some suggestions by Western observers that the concept of 'developed socialism' was about to be abandoned, the Twenty-

---

* The term was dropped at the Twenty-Seventh Congress.

Seventh Congress of the CPSU in early 1986 retained it. It was however re-examined and recent tendencies towards mystification of the concept were sharply criticized. This re-working of the concept emphasized even more than before the need for accelerated socio-economic development. However this development was not to be technocratic but to be based on response to human needs. The concept of 'developed socialism' was enshrined in the preamble to the Rules of the CPSU adopted in March 1986.

From the above summary of the development of official Soviet theory about the quest for socialism in the USSR it is clear that socialism has been defined mainly in terms of class and property relations. It is further assumed that the political system is a reflection of the economic base. Applying this approach to the Soviet Union four things have been and are asserted. These are: that exploiting classes (capitalists, landlords and petty-bourgeoisie) have been abolished and productive property socialized; that working class political power has been established and extended; that a planned socialist economy has been established; and that a steadily improving and extending socialist democracy has been established. All these claims are open to question and indeed have been questioned both within and without the Soviet Union since its inception. The remainder of this chapter will consider some of the chief lines of criticism that have been directed against the proposition that the USSR is a socialist society.

## Marxist criticism of Soviet society

Marxist criticism of the Bolshevik approach to building socialism in Russia predates the Russian Revolution. The Bolshevik Revolution increased this criticism which came from German, British, French and American Marxists as well as from Mensheviks and Socialist Revolutionaries in Russia. These criticisms covered all aspects of Bolshevik strategy and tactics, policies and theories. Stalin's 'revolution from above' and his 1936 claim to have established socialism in the USSR vastly increased this criticism.

By far the most important work of criticism of the Soviet Union was Trotsky's *The Revolution Betrayed* which was written by this former leader of the Russian Revolution while in exile and completed in August 1936. Since this book has formed the basis of most subsequent Marxist criticism of Soviet society it will be discussed at greater length than later works.

Trotsky did not deny the validity of the Russian Revolution, he merely thought that the workers' cause had been betrayed by the bureaucracy. Whereas he had attacked the Mensheviks in the 1920s for arguing that the Russian Revolution would provoke a Thermidorian Reaction he accepted this thesis, in a modified form, in the 1930s. He saw Stalin as at once the offspring of the bureaucracy and the creator of the bureaucracy. He regarded both the contradictory social structure of the Soviet Union and the ultra-bureaucratic character of its state as a direct consequence of the failure of the international revolution and the attempt to carry out the proletarian revolution in a backward and isolated country. The bureaucracy was not just a legacy of the past, but was a result of the determination to force the pace of economic development while social contradictions remained and a continued shortage of consumer goods prevailed. The Soviet economy was basically socialist but it was directed by the bureaucracy against the interests of the workers and the peasants. The bureaucracy imposed a bourgeois system of distribution, an inequitable distribution of goods and services where the main emphasis went into securing the major share of these scarce resources for themselves. The Soviet Union was not yet a socialist society but was a contradictory or transitional society, halfway between capitalism and socialism. The bureaucracy was not a class in the Marxist sense because it did not occupy any special position in the production process. It did not own the means of production as did the bourgeoisie under capitalism. It was therefore a social stratum and a privileged and uncontrolled caste but not a class. Nor was the transitional society necessarily moving towards socialism. It could revert to capitalism. The only guarantee of its socialist future lay in another social revolution in which the workers would overthrow the bureaucracy and operate socialist property for the benefit of the masses, democratically. This, in summary form, is how Trotsky answered his own question, 'What is the USSR and where is it going?'

It was predictable that other Marxists would follow and amend Trotsky's analysis of Stalinist Russia. This was particularly so amongst Trotskyists. Differences soon emerged over the class character of Soviet society, over whether it was socialist-based and whether the Soviet Union was worth defending if war broke out. One of the most influential books to appear at this time was James Burnham's *The Managerial Revolution* (1945). Burnham, a former American Trotskyist, revised not only Trotsky but Marx. He argued that Marx's predictions about socialism emerging through the overthrow of capitalism had been proved incorrect and that capitalism, whether or not it was upset by a proletarian revolution, was being replaced by a managerial revolution. Burnham saw this as a universal trend in modern industrial societies and his book emphasized the similarities in this respect between New Deal America, Nazi Germany and Stalinist Russia. In all cases the managers were defined as the new ruling class. The managerial class was defined rather differently for each society and the Russian managerial class even more broadly than Trotsky defined his 'bureaucratic caste'.[16]

In 1957 Milovan Djilas, a former member of the League of Yugoslav Communists, published his book, *The New Class*. This book had echoes of earlier books by Trotsky, Rizzi and Burnham but its analysis was confined to the Communist world and particularly to the Communist states of Eastern Europe. In this respect it was the forerunner of subsequent books written by East Europeans. The core of Djilas's argument is contained in the following quotations:

> For a long time the communist revolution and the Communist system have been concealing their real nature. The emergence of the new class has been concealed under socialist phraseology and, more importantly, under the new collective form of property ownership. The so-called socialist ownership is a disguise for the real ownership by the political bureaucracy.
>
> Contemporary Communism is not only a party of a certain type or a bureaucracy . . . More than anything else the essential aspect of contemporary Communism is the new class of owners and exploiters.
>
> . . . after having come into power in underdeveloped areas, it became something entirely different – an exploiting system opposed to most of the interests of the proletariat itself.[17]

The Trotskyist tradition is still a very strong influence on contemporary Marxist writers on the Soviet Union. This is clear in the writings of Ernest Mandel and Hillel Ticktin. Mandel has long been a secretary of the Fourth International, the orthodox wing of Trotskyism. He is best known as a Marxist economist with an international reputation but he has also written extensively on the Soviet Union. The following discussion is based largely on his 'Marxist Economic Theory' (1968), 'Ten Theses on the Social and Economic Laws Governing the Society Transitional Between Capitalism and Socialism' (1974), and 'On the Nature of the Soviet State' (1978). Mandel discusses the Soviet Union mainly from the fixed positions established by Trotsky in 1936. Thus the basic feature of the Soviet Union is 'bureaucratic deformation or degeneration', making it 'a bureaucratically deformed workers' state'. Like Trotsky he rejects the claim that the bureaucracy is a ruling class:

> The bureaucracy is neither in the juridical nor in the economic sense of the word the owner of the means of production. It

cannot use the control over the means of production which it
monopolizes, for the acquisition of private property, nor for any
other specific economic purpose outside the consumption sphere.
Its privileges are limited to the extension or conservation of
advantages in income and direct acquisition in the consumer
goods sector.[18]

And like Trotsky, Mandel considers that a pre-condition for a
transitional society such as the Soviet Union becoming socialist is the
collapse or overthrow of the privileged bureaucracy monopolizing
power and management. Despite his arguing from fixed positions
Mandel has made some adjustments to his evaluation of the Soviet
Union and by 1978 was admitting that the Soviet bureaucracy was a
large segment of the Soviet population (ten million or more), that it
had close ties with the Soviet workers, that there had been a
remarkable rise in the living standards of Soviet workers over the
past twenty-five years, and that the workers were basically reformist
and unlikely to rebel.

One of the problems of Mandel's analysis of Soviet society is that
he does not have a consistent definition of bureaucracy. He alter-
nates between a broad and a narrow definition, depending on
whether he wishes to concede their links with the working class or
their antagonism to it. What tends to preserve the narrower definition is his insistence that the modern Soviet bureaucrats are primarily
concerned with exploiting the workers in order to maintain and
extend their social advantages. It is much easier to argue this thesis if
the bureaucracy is defined as a relatively small social stratum. But if
he insists on defining the bureaucracy as 'all those who exercise
management (leadership) functions in any sector of social life' he will
soon end up with a figure of more than ten million, a large minority
group.

Mandel, like Trotsky before him, refuses to recognize that the
Soviet bureaucracy has any *general social role*. He does recognize
that the bureaucracy does plan and administer the economy, albeit
imperfectly, but he still insists that the bureaucracy has no general
rationale and that individual bureaucrats are concerned solely with
maximizing their share of income, power and privileges. I find David
Lane's evaluation more perceptive:

> The dynamics of Soviet society cannot be explained by the
> bureaucracy seeking to exploit the working class and to promote
> its own wealth, privilege and political power. The overriding
> values are derived from Marxist theory, which provides an
> ideological motivation to build an industrial society leading to a
> classless society.[19]

It is doubtful whether the Marxist critique of bureaucracy is adequate for the explanation of Soviet or any other bureaucracy. Marx and Engels certainly thought that communist society would be free of bureaucracy, although they did concede that there would be economic planning and 'the administration of things' even under communism. The avoidance of bureaucracy would be possible through the ending of coercion and the overcoming of the division of labour which kept some as workers and others as rulers and administrators in earlier societies. Lenin, and Trotsky to an even greater degree, tended to compact the two stages of the future post-capitalist society, socialism and communism. The same tendency is inherent in the critiques of Mandel and Ticktin. Thus Mandel cannot consider the USSR to be socialist because it employs a regular and professional bureaucracy while Ticktin does not consider the Soviet Union to be socialist because it does not have the non-bureaucratic planning such as would characterize communist society.[20]

The following propositions about Soviet bureaucracy are offered as an extension of the argument provided by David Lane in *The Socialist Industrial State* (1976):

1  Socialism promotes bureaucracy and it would do so even if the socialist revolution occurred in an advanced capitalist country or in a number of such countries. Under conditions of backwardness and underdevelopment and in a country as extensive and diverse as the Soviet Union bureaucracy was clearly unavoidable. Direct control by the working class will always generate bureaucracy if the workers' regime is intent on planned economic development of the entire society. Without centralized planning there might be less bureaucracy but material production would remain at a low level making advance towards communism impossible.
2  The Soviet bureaucracy is not a parasitic caste, stratum or class but is an essential factor in the economic and social development of the country. Even Trotsky recognized this in 1936 when he wrote that:

> The present Soviet society cannot get along without a state, not even – within limits – without a bureaucracy. But the cause of this is by no means the pitiful remnants of the past, but the mighty forces and tendencies of the present.[21]

The Soviet workers unaided and undirected would not have achieved the industrialization of the Soviet economy, the mechanization of agriculture, the vast hydro-electrical undertakings, the building of new cities, the development of universal primary and secondary education, the vast expansion of higher education, science and technology, of health and other social services. Mandel is right to describe these as the achievements of the Soviet workers but is clearly wrong to exclude the bureaucracy from this achievement.

3  The Soviet bureaucracy continues to exercise this positive role. The 'heroic age' of Soviet achievement did not end with the Second Five Year Plan nor even with the death of Stalin in 1953. The rate of economic growth in the Soviet Union has slowed down but the economy is still expanding and some notable construction works such as the BAM railway in Eastern Siberia are still going on. New policies are still being implemented in every aspect of the economy as well as in education, research and development, social and cultural services. And all these developments involve the bureaucracy. Few such developments are really radical and some are not even progressive but most engender considerable support amongst ordinary people. One cannot blame the bureaucracy as a whole for the limited success of the economic reforms of 1965, 1973 and 1979; for the resistance to such reforms has come from particular sections of the state bureaucracy (chiefly Gosplan and the industrial ministries) and from the manual working class rather than from the Party leadership.

4  The relations between the bureaucracy and the working class are not purely exploitative. This is recognized much more clearly by Ticktin than by Mandel. Ticktin recognizes that the bureaucracy, under pressure from the working class, has had to steadily increase the wages of manual workers at the expense of some groupings within the intelligentsia, white-collar workers and some elements of the bureaucracy itself. The same could be said of recent housing and health policy and even of educational policy with the increased emphasis since 1970 on the access of working class and peasant youth to higher education.[22] This collaboration between bureaucracy and workers is also frequent at the factory level where managers protect workers against speed-up.

5  The Soviet system is not uniformly bureaucratic. There are many avenues of public participation at the grassroots level and while many of these are supervised by local government departments (and are therefore partly bureaucratic) not all are. This applies also within the factories where a great deal of the supervisory function of local trade union committees is done entirely by unpaid officers, by ordinary workers. This aspect of the Soviet system will be discussed at greater length in a later chapter. It is sufficient to say here that it tends to be excluded in Trotskyist analyses because of their preoccupation with condemning Soviet bureaucracy.

Unlike Mandel, Ticktin is a specialist on Soviet economics and politics and has spent several years in the Soviet Union. His work is therefore characterized by a great knowledge of the details of recent Soviet history and his analysis is wholly focused on the post-Stalin period. Ticktin's analysis is still grounded on Trotsky's thesis about the Soviet Union being transitional between capitalism and socialism. He rejects much of Trotsky's (and Mandel's) argument about the bureaucracy and prefers to talk about the ruling elite, by which he means the upper echelons of the bureaucracy. The lower bureaucracy tends to merge with the intelligentsia and the workers. He does not believe that the Soviet Union has a planned economy. It is not planned because its central principle is waste and because the 'plans' which the elite administer are not democratically formulated or operated. He seems to take it for granted that a genuine socialist plan will be fully democratic and efficient. The ruling elite cannot contain the contradictions of Soviet society, which is inherently contradictory because it is not a 'social formation'. The elite tries to balance the interests of the intelligentsia with the pressure from the working class below. This has resulted in the convergence of salaries and wages since 1957, a movement which leaves the intelligentsia unsatisfied. As for the workers, their improved conditions are not likely to last so that sooner or later they will realize that 'their only solution is socialism, the revolutionary overthrow of the ruling elite in Russia'.[23]

Since the early sixties two schools of critics have argued that the USSR is a state capitalist society. These are the International Socialists* whose chief spokesman is the British writer Tony Cliff, and the self-styled Marxist-Leninists, with Bettelheim, Sweezy, Nicolaus and a number of other Western writers besides Chinese writers taking this position. These writers differ in the details of their analysis but are united in their theoretical perspective. Unlike the orthodox Trotskyists they consider that the Soviet bureaucracy constitutes a new ruling class, that of state monopoly capitalists. They differ only in when they believe this class came to power; for Cliff it was early in the First Five Year Plan, 1929–31; for the Chinese theorists and for most of their followers it was in 1953 with the death of Stalin.[24] The two approaches share most basic assumptions as to what features constitute the restoration of capitalism although these are differently ordered. They share the view that the chief reason for the bureaucracy exercising control over the process of capital accumulation is to guarantee its continued preference in the distribution of consumer

---

* Later called the Socialist Workers Party in England.

goods. The Chinese school is more heavily ideological and often includes in its analysis the ultimate Chinese condemnation of the Soviet Union as 'social imperialist'.[25] With the exception of Cliff and Bettelheim, very few of the writers in either school are experts on the Soviet system. The worst example of ignorance and misunderstanding of the Soviet Union is afforded by Martin Nicolaus.

Tony Cliff's analysis is applied to the contemporary Soviet Union although most of the research in the book relates to the Stalinist period. The book was in fact written in the late 1940s, although not published until 1964. In its underlying assumptions the analysis is Trotskyist; its starting point is the belief that socialism was impossible in a backward and isolated country, that socialism is of necessity internationalist. The accumulated capital, which ought to have been there before the revolution took place, had to be created in a post-revolutionary society by the bureaucracy forcing the workers and peasants to produce surplus value for social investment:

> Thus industrialisation and technical revolution in agriculture ('collectivisation') in a backward country under conditions of siege transformed the bureaucracy from a layer which is under the direct and indirect pressure of the proletariat, into a ruling class, into a manager of 'the general business of society: the direction of labour, affairs of state, justice, science, art and so forth'.
>
> Dialectical historical development, full of contradictions and surprises, brought it about that the first step the bureaucracy took with the subjective intention of hastening the building of 'socialism in one country' became the foundation of the building of state capitalism.

Cliff is firm in his assertion that the Soviet bureaucracy is a ruling class:

> It would be wrong to call the Stalinist bureaucracy a caste for the following reasons: while a class is a group of people who have a definite place in the process of production, a caste is a judicial-political group; the members of a caste can be members of different classes, or in one class there can be members of different castes; a caste is the outcome of the relative immobility of the economy – a rigid division of labour and immobility of the productive forces – whereas the Stalinist bureaucracy was transformed into a ruling class on the crest of the *dynamism* of the economy.
>
> We can therefore say that the *Russian bureaucracy*, owning as it does the state and controlling the process of accumulation, *is*

*the personification of capital in its purest form.*

To say that a bureaucratic class rules in Russia and stop at that, is to circumvent the cardinal issue – the capitalist relations of production prevailing in Russia. To say that Russia is state capitalist is strictly correct, but not sufficient; it is also necessary to point out the differences in the juridical relations between the ruling class in Russia and that in a state capitalism which evolved gradually from monopoly capitalism. The most precise name for the Russian society is therefore Bureaucratic State Capitalism.[26]

Martin Nicolaus in *Restoration of Capitalism in the USSR* (1976) argues that the USSR has become capitalist since the death of Stalin. This followed the official Chinese line at the time which had never incorporated the criticisms of Stalin made at the Twentieth Congress of the CPSU in February 1956. To support his claim that the USSR is now a capitalist society Nicolaus advances the following arguments.

1  Commodity production (including labour power as a commodity) has been restored in the USSR.
2  The Soviet workers have been separated from the means of production.
3  A capitalist ruling class has been restored in the USSR.
4  The Soviet working class has experienced a worsening of living standards and growing inequality of income, especially since the death of Stalin.
5  Centralized economic planning has been abandoned and there has been a return to the anarchy of capitalist production.
6  Proletarian internationalism has been replaced by social imperialism.[27]

Some of these propositions are completely untrue, others are less than half-truths. In so far as they are true they have been characteristic of the Soviet Union since the early years and are not the product of the post-Stalin years. At the back of these misunderstandings lies not only a particular ideological stance but a confusion over the use of basic Marxist terms which stems from the same source as it does with Trotskyist critics, namely, the compacting of historical epochs.

Before making a more detailed analysis of Nicolaus's argument I will give my definitions of the basic terms capitalism, socialism and communism.

By *capitalism* I mean a form of production relations characterized by the division of society into two basic classes: the owners of the means of production (the capitalists) and the sellers of their labour power (the workers), in which generalized commodity production occurs and capital reproduction takes place through the transfer of some of the surplus value exploited from the working class. The basic economic law under capitalism is that of profit maximization in order to replace, extend and continually to revolutionize the instruments of production.

By *socialism* I mean a form of production relations characterized by public (state or collective) ownership of the principal means of production and where there is a beginning of the process of reducing inequalities of opportunity and income and of the importance of commodity production. A socialist economy is characterized by the operation of a general economic plan which has as its purpose the movement of society slowly in the direction of communism. (That is to say, under socialism, unequal incomes, the sale of commodities – including labour power – value, surplus-value, class and status divisions in society, division of labour and role specialization, must continue.)

By *communism* I mean a form of society characterized by the abolition of classes, the distinction between town and country and between physical and mental labour; by a high level of material production so that the rule, 'From each according to his ability, to each according to his need' operates, and in which the state and all forms of oppression and exploitation have ended.

Theorists of state capitalism blur the distinction between socialism and communism. It is not surprising that the sharp-eyed English economist, Alec Nove, concludes his short review of the theories of state capitalism with this observation:

> Underlying this critique, there is a vision of a classless, moneyless, socialist society, corresponding to what the Soviet theorists call 'full communism'. Abundance, unselfishness, interchangeability of jobs, equality, peace, and all this worldwide, would characterize such a society. There would be no bureaucracy, no markets, there would be harmony.[28]

There are capitalist elements in Soviet society but are they obviously increasing? I think not, or if some of these elements do appear to be increasing others seem to be diminishing. Who controls the means of production? Is it a new state bourgeoisie? The answer is surely that the Soviet state owns and controls the main means of production and minor means of production are owned co-operatively or individually. Politicians, administrators and managers (if you like, the bureaucrats) exercise most important control functions but they do not exercise exclusive control. Nor can they as individuals or as a group dispose of the means of production. It is not obvious that they use this control primarily to further their own material wealth. Nor can they transmit that control to their heirs. What we have in the USSR would seem to be not state capitalism but state socialism.

Are Soviet workers exploited? Do Soviet managers have control over labour power? Is the condition of the workers worsening? If by exploitation is meant the production of surplus-value then Soviet workers are clearly exploited for they do not receive in wages the full value of what they produce. This surplus-value provides the basis of the profits of the socialist industries, the turnover tax and other government revenues. The bulk of this is used for capital investment, social services, science and defence, education, income subsidies, subsidies to housing and transport, and not to boost the wealth of the bureaucracy. Direct and indirect payments to the bureaucracy probably amount to between 3 and 4 per cent of the national budget. Soviet managers do not control more than a small percentage of total investment and they have limited control over labour. Nicolaus's claims here are based on a misunderstanding of the importance of the Shchekino experiment introduced in 1966. This experiment began in the chemical industry and after more than a decade had spread to plants employing fewer than 60,000 workers. Dismissals were possible to improve productivity but managers were still obliged to find positions for retrenched workers elsewhere. Wholesale dismissals are illegal and individual dismissals are closely controlled by the trade unions.[29] Are manual workers exploited for the benefit of the elite and the intelligentsia in general? In 1973, out of a total workforce (including collective farmers) of 113.6 million, 68.8 million were manual workers, 28.7 million were mental workers. An absolute majority of all Soviet workers, 48.2 million, were unskilled workers. In most cases their monthly wages came to less than 100 roubles. Many of them were very poor, even by Soviet standards. But white-collar workers and many specialists received salaries not much above 100 roubles a month and lower than the average wage. Since 1955 wages of 'employees' and technicians have declined relative to wages of manual workers. Salaries of officials, including higher paid officials have also been reduced. The main beneficiaries of the shift in incomes over recent years have been the collective farmers, and the skilled and semi-skilled (numbering 25.4 million in 1973) workers. Clearly the low level of most Soviet incomes is a reflection of the level of development of the economy and of the workforce; also of the relative inefficiency of many sectors of the economy and the high costs of defence spending. But average wages of Soviet workers have risen by more than 2 per cent per annum for more than twenty years and collective farmers' incomes have risen more rapidly. Over the past decade this rate of increase has barely kept up with hidden inflation. On the other hand the government has managed to maintain and even increase the weight of the 'social income' and this has some redistributive effect as even if payments have no means test they are probably used more extensively by the very poor.* [30] Thus the average amount paid out of 'social funds' represented 33.9 per cent of the average money wage in 1965 but 36.8 per cent in 1978. In the latter year the average monthly money wage was 160 roubles while the average payment from 'social funds' was 59 roubles.[31]

Has central economic planning been abandoned? Those who argue that it has been abandoned because of increases to managers' powers over recent years are mistaken. The powers of the individual manager have been increased several times since 1958 and managers have gained greater legal powers over investment. By 1973 there were 740 wholesale stores selling producer goods which managers could purchase without any allocation certificate. But managers have limited funds to purchase such equipment and although sales at these stores amounted to nearly four billion roubles in 1973 this was only 3 per cent of capital investment in that year. In other words, 97 per cent of capital investment still came by means of central allocation through *Gossnab* (State Committee on Material-Technical Supplies).[32]

Can Soviet managers control wages? Is there an open market in labour? The answer is clearly in the negative. Wages are centrally determined with regional variations also centrally determined. Only 2.5 per cent of the factory 'incentive fund' can be used for bonus payments and distribution of these funds requires the approval of the trade union committee in the factory. Such payments amount to only a small proportion of total wages. Clearly, whatever the inefficiency of central economic planning in the Soviet Union it has not been abandoned.

Finally, has international socialism been abandoned? Has it been replaced by 'social imperialism'? International socialism is still part of the official ideology and it is an element of Soviet policy. But it has never been the overriding factor in Soviet foreign policy and it was diluted by Lenin and Stalin as well as by more recent leaders. The concept 'social imperialism' was an ideological one invented by the Chinese leaders in the early 1960s when the Sino-Soviet conflict was at its peak. Since the Soviet Union had already been classified as 'state capitalist' the Soviet Union was clearly, in Leninist terms,

---

* The above sparse comments should not be taken as a full analysis of the complex problem of income redistribution in the Soviet Union.

imperialist. Since it claimed to be socialist it must be somewhat different to normal capitalist imperialism. Therefore it must be social imperialist. The term was never precisely defined and has largely been abandoned. The Chinese now prefer to talk about 'great power hegemony' and especially 'Soviet hegemonism'. But since all large powers, irrespective of their social structure or politics, tend to be hegemonic this tells us nothing in particular about the Soviet Union.

Is the USSR socialist? I believe that it is, even if it falls short of its own ideals as well as those of many socialists elsewhere. It is not useful to describe it as 'advanced socialism' as this term suggests a society on the verge of becoming communist. The spartan quality of much of Soviet life, the continued restrictions to democratic self-government and individual liberty suggest an underdeveloped (or unevenly developed) socialism. I would call it *bureaucratic state socialism*.

Political power is very unevenly distributed in the Soviet Union but no sections of society (other than the insane) are totally excluded from the political process. The nature and limits of this popular political participation will be discussed in later chapters.

The upper layers of the bureaucracy constitute an elite but not a ruling class. Nor are they in any normal sense of the term a caste. The nature of this elite and its relation to other elites will be discussed in Chapter 3.

Finally I would argue (and will argue in Chapters 6 and 7) that the Soviet Union is more than an immense bureaucracy and that therefore an exclusively bureaucratic model is inadequate for the analysis of Soviet politics.

# 2 THE SOCIAL STRUCTURE OF THE SOVIET UNION

The concept of 'social structure', as it is currently understood by Soviet sociologists, includes more than class structure. It is normally said to include at least four sets of social relationships: those between social classes, intra-class and status relationships, relations between urban and rural populations and cultures, and relationships between mental and manual labour.[1] Writers such as Yu.V. Arutyunyan go beyond this and include nationality and religious differences.[2] But despite these recent extensions to the concept 'social structure', class and class relations remain at the basis of Soviet analysis. At the same time the concept 'class' is applied less rigidly than it was in the Stalin era.

Stalin defined classes in terms of their relations to the means of production, property relations. Thus by 1936 it was held that there were only two basic classes in Soviet society, the working class and the collective farm peasantry. These were two distinct classes because while the workers were dependent on the sale of their labour-power and did not as individuals own the means of production, the collective farmers held their property collectively and still operated small individual plots from which they received a substantial proportion of their income. The working class was divided into two segments, manual workers and mental workers, according to the nature of their work. Those engaged in mental labour were known as *sluzhashchie* (employees or white-collar workers). The better qualified members of the employees were referred to as the intelligentsia. The intelligentsia was not considered to be a class as it had no special relation to the means of production. It was consequently described as a *sloi* (a layer or a stratum). In the Stalin period the intelligentsia was generally treated as a composite but fairly homogeneous group, but nowadays Soviet sociologists vie with one another in subdividing the group. Seven or eight sub-groups are now often recognized.[3] Besides the working class, collective farm peasantry and intelligentsia, Stalin recognized that there were also still in existence small numbers of petty-bourgeoisie, individual farmers, hunters and trappers, artisans and craftsmen. No property-based ruling class was recognized in such a picture.

Contemporary Soviet sociologists apply a more flexible and more complex concept of class to the analysis of social structure. Thus F. Burlatsky and A. Galkin use no less than four criteria for determining class position. These are:

1 Property relationships.
2 Place in the social division (or role in the social organization) of labour.
3 The method used in achieving a share in social wealth.
4 The size of the acquired share of social wealth.[4]

1 determines 2 and 2 determines 4. 1 is also a determinant of 3 and 4, as 3 is of 4. Other Soviet sociologists formally accept the convention-al Soviet 'two classes, one stratum' model of Soviet society but place their main emphasis on distinguishing divisions within these three primary groups. Thus manual workers are usually divided into three or four functional sub-groups, collective farmers into three to six groups,[5] and intelligentsia into three to seven sub-groups. However Soviet writers do not attempt a global class picture of Soviet society as do some Western sociologists.[6] While there is sometimes a blurring of the distinction between broader functional groups and occupational groups these sub-groups are always contained within the 'two classes, one stratum' formula.

How then do I propose to analyse the Soviet social structure? I will begin by accepting the Soviet two-class model of Soviet society and analyse the composition of these two classes, the relations between them and relations within the classes. I will then explore the relations between manual workers and mental workers and those between town and country. This will be a shorter version of the analyses provided by Mervyn Matthews and David Lane.[7] But my criticism of the Soviet approach will be rather different. I will not suggest modifications to Soviet use of basic concepts such as 'working class' or innumerable empirical criticisms. Rather I will be concerned with pointing out more general deficiencies in the Soviet approach, while suggesting additional structural elements, and finally with assessing current trends in structural change.

## The basic class structure

As we have already seen, classes in the Soviet Union are defined largely in terms of relations to the means of production. This is a definition of class in terms of the working population. Many Soviet statistics relating to class relate to the working population only. Sometimes children and other non-working members of families are added to those in employment making classes cover the entire population. There is a certain statistical arbitrariness about this method. For a start the workforce today represents not much more than half of the total population. Thus in 1979 only 51.5 per cent consisted of the state and collective farm workforce while 30.6 per cent were dependants, housewives or self-employed. There were over 40 million pensioners, 15.3 per cent of the total population. There were also 6.6 million students on state stipends, 2.5 per cent of the population.[8] Furthermore, are the class categories logically determined? Are the children of a skilled factory worker classified as working class when the mother is employed as a specialist? Are factory workers receiving an old age pension classified as pensioners or manual workers when they continue to work in the factory, as very many do? Is a retired unskilled worker classified still as a worker if he now spends his time producing vegetables on his private plot for sale in the open market?

A further problem concerns the disappearance of the petty-bourgeoisie from Soviet class statistics. They are supposed to have been absorbed into the two basic classes, the working class and the collective farmers. In the 1959 census individual peasant farmers still gained statistical recognition, 0.3 per cent of the population. By 1970 this percentage had sunk to 0.01 and they were unnoticed in the 1979 census. According to the census data the urban petty-bourgeoisie had ceased to exist by 1939. Yet these claims are clearly inaccurate. By the end of the 1970s there were millions of Matryonas in the villages, nominally collective farmers but doing little or no work in the collective and operating as traditional small peasants. Nor are these small peasants exclusively women. The same phenomenon is to be found in the state farms. It is also present in the cities and provincial towns. It was estimated that there were 300,000 private plots being operated by Leningraders in 1980 while there were 100,000 in Tomsk, a city of a little over half a million, in 1979. In the Kemerevo province almost half of the urban population possessed private plots in 1979.[9] Then there is the problem of workers operating after hours (and sometimes inside working hours) in the 'second economy'. Construction workers who form themselves into partnerships or teams (*shabashniki*) to work as 'finishers' to flats they have constructed as state employees are classified in Soviet statistics simply as workers and not as tradesmen. It is assumed that all doctors and teachers work in the state service as salaried professionals. But a small number operate as 'independent professionals' and far more run private practices or conduct coaching as sidelines. Again, these irregularities are not noticed by the Central Statistical Administration. The problem is not only statistical but conceptual. It seems to be assumed in the Soviet Union that everyone belongs to one class only. A person may change class in the course of a lifetime. Thus a peasant may become a collective farmer and a collective farmer may become an industrial worker or an urban specialist. But in real life the boundaries between classes are blurred and many people fall into two classes simultaneously. Thus in a capitalist society small farmers or peasant farmers may be petty-bourgeois and working class. Their basic class is petty-bourgeois but when they work as wage labourers for richer land-owners or in a nearby factory they are simultaneously working class. If they themselves employ labour at particular times in the agricultural year they become capitalists.[10] If this more realistic approach were applied in the Soviet Union it would clearly be necessary to resurrect the class of the petty-bourgeoisie. Much but not all of this petty-bourgeois activity is legal, some of it is not. Now any revival of a bourgeoisie is illegal as well as ideologically unsound. But private employment for profit clearly does operate in the Soviet Union. This is mostly on a very small scale and it operates in areas such as repair work, contract work in outlying areas and in illegal transport. On rare occasions it reaches the level of *kustar* industry where entrepreneurs set up underground factories, sometimes employing more than fifty workers. Such factories sometimes operate for years before they are suppressed and their owners arrested.

The most general trends in the transformation of Soviet society, the reconstitution of the peasantry as a collective farm workforce and the elimination of the last remnants of urban and rural bourgeoisie as well as the rapid growth of the manual working class, are clearly indicated in Table 2.1. Poor and middle peasant households comprised 74.9 per cent of the Soviet population in 1928, 2.6 per cent in 1939 and only 0.3 per cent in 1959. The urban and rural bourgeoisie fell from 4.6 per cent of the population to nil in 1939. On the other hand collectivized peasant households, which represented 2.9 per cent of the population in 1928 formed 47.2 per cent in 1939. At the latter date manual workers constituted 33.5 per cent of the population. By 1979 manual workers represented 60 per cent while collective farmers had fallen to 14.9 per cent. But the 77 million manual workers in 1979 included 11.5 million state farm (*sovkhoz*) workers who in many ways have more in common with the modern collective farmers (*kolkhozniki*). Over the period 1928 to 1979 the white-collar section of the working class (the 'employees' including the specialists) rose from 5.2 per cent to 25.1 per cent of the population.

TABLE 2.1 Class composition of the Soviet population (in percentages)

|  | 1928 | 1939 | 1959 | 1970 | 1979 | 1985 |
|---|---|---|---|---|---|---|
| Workers and employees | 17.6 | 50.2 | 68.3 | 79.5 | 85.1 | 87.6 |
| (a) Manual workers | 12.4 | 33.5 | 49.5 | 56.8 | 60.0 | 61.6 |
| (b) Employees | 5.2 | 16.7 | 18.8 | 22.7 | 25.1 | 26.0 |
| Collective farmers | 2.9 | 47.2 | 31.4 | 20.5 | 14.9 | 12.4 |
| Peasantry | 74.9 | 2.6 | 0.3 | — | — | — |
| Bourgeoisie and kulaks | 4.6 | — | — | — | — | — |

SOURCES: *Nar. khoz. SSSR v 1979g.*, pp. 8–9, and 1979 Census data.
*Nar. khoz. SSSR v 1984g.*, p. 7.

The Central Statistical Administration does not issue figures showing the distribution of the Soviet workforce between primary, secondary and tertiary sectors. Nevertheless it is possible to re-work Soviet statistics to produce a table which is roughly comparable. This has been attempted in Table 2.2. Between 1940 and 1979 the agricultural and forestry sector of the Soviet workforce fell from 54 per cent to 21 per cent. Over the same period secondary industry (including construction, transport and communications) rose from 28 per cent to 48 per cent, while tertiary (services) industry rose from 18 per cent to 31 per cent.

TABLE 2.2 Distribution of the workforce according to sectors (in percentages)

|  | 1940 | 1965 | 1970 | 1979 | 1984 |
|---|---|---|---|---|---|
| Agriculture and forestry | 54 | 31 | 25 | 21 | 20 |
| Secondary industry (*including construction, transport and communications*) | 28 | 44 | 46 | 48 | 47 |
| Tertiary (*including trade, finance, health, education, science, administration, etc.*) | 18 | 25 | 29 | 31 | 33 |
|  | 100 | 100 | 100 | 100 | 100 |

SOURCES: *Nar. khoz. SSSR v 1979g.*, p. 385 (rearranged).
*Nar. khoz. SSSR v 1984g.*, p. 407.

The distinction between collective farmers and state farm workers is much less today than it was in earlier years. While collective farm property is formally owned by the collective farmers of each individual farm they are not able to dispose of their property any more than are the state farm workers able to dispose of the assets of their farms. Collective farms are permitted to sell agricultural surpluses on the collective farm market while state farms must sell all their production to the state. Collective farmers still receive a part of their income in produce but the bulk of it comes from the collective farm management in the form of monthly money payments. Both collective and state farmers have private plots although it is easier for collective farmers to market any surplus production from these plots. Collective farmers have been included in comprehensive pension payments since 1964 although the amounts paid are generally lower than those paid to state farmers. Since 1958 (when the Machine Tractor Stations were abolished) collective farms have owned and operated their own machinery pool, thus making them more comparable – while not identical – to the state farms. Since the early 1960s inter-farm economic enterprises, often involving both kinds of farms, have steadily increased. By 1979 there were 9,289 farm-based inter-farm enterprises with 146,729 people working in them. Most of these were collective farmers but there were nearly 24,000 state farm workers involved.[11] There was a time when state farms were much larger than collective farms, when they had far more capital equipment and more specialist and skilled workers, when they were more efficient and when incomes were far higher than in collective farms. These differences still remain but they are of declining importance.

Over the past thirty years the number of collective farms has steadily declined so that by 1979 only 26,000 remained. On the other hand the number of state farms has continued to increase so that there were 20,767 in 1979. By 1979 the average collective farm included 526 households while the average state farm had 553 workers. The average collective farm had 21.4 leaders and specialists as against 28.7 per state farm. The average collective farm had 86.5 mechanizers (tractor drivers, combine harvester operators, other drivers and mechanics), while the average state farm had 101.4. About four-fifths of collective farmers remained as unskilled labourers in the collective farm peasantry. On the state farms slightly more than three-quarters of all workers were unskilled. The average income for a state farm worker was 146.4 roubles a month, while the average income per collective farm household was about 84 per cent of this.*[12] While the earnings from private plots continue to be more

---

* Soviet statistics do not publish average wages for individual collective farmers.

important to collective farmers than they are to state farm workers they are clearly declining in importance. In 1977 collective farm families obtained 72 per cent of their meat, 76 per cent of their milk and most of their potatoes from their private plots.[13] Whereas in 1965 collective farmers still derived more than a third of their income from their private agriculture, by 1978 the proportion had fallen to a quarter.[14]

## The manual working class

Lane and O'Dell in their book *The Soviet Industrial Worker* (1978) have made a number of generalizations about the nature of the industrial proletariat in the Soviet Union that are worth noting.[15] In explaining the specific features of the Soviet worker in comparison with his Western capitalist counterpart they emphasize differences in the political contexts in which they operate. Soviet workers belong to a different class structure and they operate in a different political culture. That political culture has a revolutionary tradition and a proletarian basis. Even if the USSR is not a 'workers' state' in the fullest sense of the term, workers have always played a significant role in the Communist Party and in its leadership. Communist Party ideology emphasizes the social and political role of the working class in a way that is unusual in Western political cultures.

Secondly, Soviet trade unions play a different role from their Western counterparts. Their main social role is to integrate Soviet workers into industrial society. Thirdly, the Soviet working class is essentially a new working class. It is not a working class with long traditions going back to an earlier capitalist era but one that has been established in the process of Soviet industrialization since 1928. The experiences and traditions it has developed since then differ widely from those acquired under capitalist industrialization. Fourthly, the Soviet working class is wholly employed in state enterprises and it operates in an economy which has not been subjected to market conditions for over fifty years. The absence of market conditions and of long-term unemployment has produced less sectional bargaining by particular groups of Soviet workers and the Soviet working class remains less differentiated than the working classes of advanced capitalist societies. Furthermore, Soviet factory managers are largely recruited from the ranks of the skilled workers and are not seen by the workers as belonging to a separate social class: 'The Soviet working class has a greater unity between manual and non-manual, between managers and workers, between union and Party, than is the case under capitalism.'

Later in their book Lane and O'Dell discuss working-class discontent and dissatisfaction but argue that it is something less than 'alienation' in the Marxist sense.[16] I have seen the same argument about the absence of alienation in Soviet sources but not found it at all convincing.[17] Sociological study of this problem in the Soviet Union has shown a wide range of factors producing worker dissatisfaction, some of which could be analysed in terms of Marx's theory of alienation as set out in the *Economic and Philosophical Notebooks* of 1844. Beyond this, Marx's theory of alienation is clearly in need of revision.

The above caveat apart I am in general agreement with Lane and O'Dell. The contemporary working class is less differentiated both in their work positions and in their unions. All workers are organized into large industrial unions. There are no craft unions and all workers in a particular plant belong to the same union. This includes managers, engineers, technicians and office and cleaning staff. Most manual workers are unskilled and many of them are new recruits drawn from both urban and rural areas. Skilled work is usually divided into five to seven grades and promotion through these grades depends on training, skill and experience. Wage differentials relating to these various skill grades have been much reduced in recent decades and the wages of unskilled workers have been substantially improved. While Soviet trade unions have no real institutional independence from the Party or state they do act to promote the interests of their members and they do involve ordinary workers in their various activities. Between 30 and 40 per cent of Soviet workers are regularly engaged in trade union activity. Despite the suggestion of many Western writers that Soviet workers are 'atomized' I do not believe that this is so. Soviet workers are very conscious of the fact that they work as members of a 'collective' and they regret the loss of this feeling of belonging to a collective if they retire or emigrate to Israel or America.[18] But there is a danger in overemphasizing the unity of the Soviet working class. There is evidence that even the present level of wage equality is resented as insufficient. There is evidence that many manual workers resent the higher earnings and other privileges of engineers, technicians and other specialists. There is even more evidence that many better-educated younger workers feel resentful because their promotion is blocked. Beyond all this very many workers are dissatisfied with their pay and work conditions. The lack of unemployment gives opportunities to dissatisfied workers to change jobs in the hope of finding something better. Labour turnover is greater in the Soviet Union than it is in most capitalist countries.[19] The extent of involvement of millions of Soviet workers in the 'second economy' is further indication of the inadequacy of average rates of pay for work done for the socialist economy.

## White-collar workers

This is a declining sector of the Soviet workforce since most 'employees' are now specialists with tertiary or secondary specialist education. The others normally have complete secondary education. They are the office workers, secretaries, typists and clerical workers. In 1979 they represented only 5.9 per cent of the Soviet workforce, 7.4 million people. At that time there were already more than 26 million specialists in the workforce. The specialists (intelligentsia and intellectual workers) include some of the most highly paid persons in Soviet society who sometimes earn as much as four or five times the average wage. Nevertheless the majority of intellectual workers earn salaries which are comparable with those paid to

TABLE 2.3  Class and sub-class divisions in the Soviet workforce, 1973

*Total workforce*: 113.6 million (Figures in brackets are percentages of total workforce.)

| STATE ECONOMY | | COLLECTIVE FARM ECONOMY |
|---|---|---|
| **I** *Working class and employees* | | **II** *Collective farmers* |
| (1) *Mental workers* | (2) *Manual workers* | |
| A | A | A |
| Superior intelligentsia (*leading administrators and managers*) | Skilled and semi-skilled | Managers and specialists |
| 2 million (1.8) | c.20.6 million* (18.1) | 552,000 (0.5) |
| B | B | B |
| General intelligentsia | Unskilled | Skilled and semi-skilled (*mechanizers*) |
| 16.2 million (14.3) | c.48.2 million* (42.4) | 2,148,000 (1.9) |
| C | | C |
| White-collar workers | | Unskilled (*Kolkhozniki*) |
| 10.5 million (9.2) | | 13.4 million (11.8) |
| *Total*: 28.7 million (25.3) | 68.8 million (60.5) | 16.1 million (14.2) |

SOURCE: *Nar. khoz. SSSR v 1973g.*, pp. 386–7 (rearranged).
* Calculated on a Soviet estimate that 30 per cent of all manual workers in 1973 were skilled and semi-skilled.

TABLE 2.4  Class and sub-class divisions in the Soviet workforce, 1979

*Total workforce*: 124.3 million (Figures in brackets are percentages of total workforce.)

| STATE ECONOMY | | COLLECTIVE FARM ECONOMY |
|---|---|---|
| I *Working class and employees* | | II *Collective farmers* |
| (1) *Mental workers* | (2) *Manual workers* | |
| A<br>Superior intelligentsia<br>(*leading administrators and managers*)<br>2,411,000 (1.9) | A<br>Skilled and semi-skilled<br><br>c.24.1 million*<br>(19.4) | A<br>Managers and specialists<br><br>557,000 (0.4) |
| B<br>General intelligentsia<br><br>24 million (19.3) | B<br>Unskilled<br><br>c.52.9 million*<br>(42.5) | B<br>Skilled and semi-skilled (*mechanizers*)<br>2,261,000 (1.8) |
| C<br>White-collar workers<br><br>7.4 million (5.9) | | C<br>Unskilled<br>(*Kolkhozniki*)<br>10,882,000 (8.8) |
| *Total*: 33.8 million<br>(27.1) | 77 million **(61.9) | 13.7 million (11.0) |

SOURCE:  Calculated from *Nar. khoz. SSSR v 1979g.*
  * Calculated on a personal estimate of 32 per cent of manual workers.
** The figure is obviously a projection from the earlier 1978 figure. However the 1979 Census showed only 60.0 per cent manual workers.

highly skilled manual workers. The trend in earnings over recent decades is shown by the fact that the 1940 ratio of wages paid in industry was 100 : 220 :110 as between manual workers, engineers and technicians, and white-collar workers, whereas by 1970 the ratio was 100 : 140 : 77. It was only in the early years of the Soviet regime that white-collar workers enjoyed an obvious advantage in income over manual workers. They earlier enjoyed higher prestige but this also was lost during the years of accelerated industrial growth after 1928. Nowadays white-collar jobs carry low prestige and they are predominantly held by women. Nothing will be said here about the position and composition of the intelligentsia. This will be the theme for Chapter 4.

TABLE 2.5 Average monthly income of different categories of workers in the state economy (in roubles)

|  | 1965 | 1970 | 1975 | 1979 | 1984 |
|---|---|---|---|---|---|
| All workers | 96.5 | 122.0 | 145.8 | 163.3 | 184.8 |
| *Engineers, technicians and other specialists* | | | | | |
| ● In industry | 148.4 | 178.0 | 199.2 | 208.9 | 228.1 |
| ● In agriculture | 138.4 | 164.3 | 179.4 | 186.7 | 235.0 |
| ● In construction | 160.7 | 200.0 | 207.0 | 211.1 | 233.5 |
| *Manual workers* | | | | | |
| ● In industry | 101.7 | 130.6 | 160.9 | 180.3 | 205.5 |
| ● In agriculture | 72.4 | 98.5 | 124.7 | 144.9 | 174.4 |
| ● In construction | 108.4 | 148.5 | 180.3 | 202.5 | 237.7 |
| *White-collar workers* | | | | | |
| ● In industry | 85.8 | 111.6 | 131.3 | 142.9 | 159.0 |
| ● In agriculture | 82.3 | 95.6 | 114.0 | 123.0 | 171.2 |
| ● In construction | 102.4 | 136.8 | 145.8 | 147.2 | 183.1 |

SOURCES: *Nar. khoz. SSSR v 1979g.*, pp. 394–5.
*Nar. khoz. SSSR v 1984g.*, pp. 417–18.

## Town and country

Russian Marxism, like early Marxism, was urban-based. Unlike the earlier Russian revolutionaries the Russian Marxists in the late nineteenth and early twentieth centuries played down the revolutionary role of the peasantry and emphasized that of the urban working class. On the eve of the November Revolution the Bolsheviks enjoyed massive support in the larger cities but only meagre support in the countryside. In the years after the revolution a major priority in their policy was to maintain the hegemony of the proletariat over the peasantry, of the town over the country. The poor and very poor peasants were seen as the main allies of the proletariat. The Bolshevik Party both before and after the revolution was in membership primarily a working class party and even today about three-quarters of Communist Party Members are urban. The merging of town and country which the Bolsheviks have long predicted has been largely a process of reducing the peasantry and transferring them to the cities where they are transformed into industrial or other workers.

In 1926 only 18 per cent of the Soviet population was urban but by 1959 the proportion was 48 per cent and by 1980 it was 63 per cent. In the RSFSR and Estonia it had reached 70 per cent by 1980. This urbanization trend is general throughout the USSR although it is not

TABLE 2.6 Distribution of the Soviet workforce (state sector) 1979: Moscow and the USSR

|  | No. in 1000s | USSR Percentages | MOSCOW Percentages |
|---|---|---|---|
| Industry | 36,496 | 33.0 | 26.5 |
| Agriculture | 11,381 | 10.3 | — |
| Construction | 11,156 | 10.1 | 7.3 |
| Transport | 10,110 | 9.1 | 8.1 |
| Trade and public catering | 9,526 | 8.6 | 7.9 |
| Education* | 8,893 | 8.0 | 5.5 |
| Health, physical education, social security | 6,197 | 5.6 | 5.2 |
| Public housing and municipal services | 4,354 | 3.9 | 4.7 |
| Science and science services | 4,264 | 3.9 | 19.4 |
| Administration | 2,411 | 2.2 | 4.9 |
| Communications | 1,613 | 1.5 | 1.5 |
| Culture | 1,235 | 1.1 | 1.0 |
| Credit and state insurance | 632 | 0.6 | 0.5 |
| Forestry | 458 | 0.4 | — |
| Art | 456 | 0.4 | 0.6 |
| Miscellaneous | 1,410 | 1.3 | 6.9 |
| Totals | 110,592 | 100.0 | 100.0 |

NOTE: Tertiary teachers are included under Science and science services.
SOURCES: *Nar. khoz. SSSR v 1979g.*, pp. 387–8.
    *Moskva v tsifrakh 1980*, p. 95.
    (I have reworked the percentages in certain cases.)

proceeding at a uniform rate. Only in Central Asia, where the rate of natural increase in the rural areas remained as high as 3 per cent during the 1970s has this outflow of rural population been checked or even reversed (see Table 2.8).[20] The urban growth has occurred not only in the older cities but through the development of new cities and industrial settlements in what were formerly rural areas. Since the early 1960s the emphasis has been on upgrading the rural areas in terms of facilities, housing, educational, cultural and health services. By the early 1980s most rural children were getting a full secondary education, something the urban children had secured in the early 1970s. Educational levels are rising in the rural areas but they remain low as a high proportion of those with full secondary or higher education migrate to the cities. Until there is a greater range of professional jobs available in the countryside the imbalance is likely to continue. Only in limited areas, chiefly on the outskirts of large cities such as Moscow and Tashkent, are educational levels more evenly spread. Thus in Moscow oblast 6.8 per cent of the urban population and 4.2 per cent of the rural population had tertiary education in 1970 while in Tashkent oblast 3.6 per cent of the urban population and 2.3 per cent of the rural population had tertiary qualifications. By way of contrast in Smolensk oblast in 1970 only 1.2 per cent of the rural population and 4.6 per cent of the urban population had tertiary education. In Ryazan oblast 5.2 per cent of the urban population but only 0.8 per cent of the rural population had tertiary education.[21]

As early as 1965 workers and employees in the rural areas represented 46.8 per cent of the population and they were an absolute majority from the early 1970s. But these figures tend to distort the decline in the farming population as they exclude workers on state farms from the peasantry. Despite the steady increase in the number of specialists and skilled workers on the farms in recent years the farm workforce remains less qualified and less differentiated than the urban workforce. Thus in 1979 managers and specialists comprised only 4.1 per cent of the collective farm workforce and 5.3 per cent of the state farm workforce. Skilled workers comprised 16.3 per cent and 18.3 per cent of the farm workforces. The range of both skilled manual jobs and professional employment remains much lower in the rural community generally. Despite the reduced economic growth in the 1970s the rate of urbanization has scarcely slackened. Thus while the rural population in the USSR declined by almost seven million between the censuses of 1970 and 1979 the urban population increased by 27.6 million, an increase greatly helped by the movement of 15.6 million villagers to the towns.[22]

The migrants from the villages come from all age groups but they come disproportionately from the young adults. School graduates move to the cities to undertake courses at technical colleges and at VUZy. Skilled workers transfer to the cities to gain higher wages and to improve their chances for promotion. Unskilled workers move to the cities to become industrial or construction workers. There are variations in the patterns of this migration as between collective farmers and state farm workers. The former tend to move first to the large villages or small country towns and only later to the large cities. The latter are far more likely to move direct to the bigger cities. The problem of uprooted villagers being absorbed into the cities has not been closely studied by Soviet sociologists. They do not seem to form local groups or *zemlyachestva* as they did in Tsarist Russia. The problem of adjustment is undoubtedly greater for the old and the less educated than it is for the young and higher educated. Soviet research has shown that religious belief is stronger in the country than it is in the city and that new arrivals in the city, especially if of low education, are much more likely to remain religious and to continue as active churchgoers. Not only do they sustain the congregations of the Orthodox churches but they flock in their thousands into sects such as the Baptists. Clearly the churches offer comfort to the newly urbanized villagers.[23] It is probable that the majority of the ten million urban private plot farmers reported in 1977 were recent migrants from the countryside. If so, the country is invading the city and not merely the city the country.

## Manual and mental labour

The differences between physical and intellectual labour are generally considered to be declining in the Soviet Union. Certainly the income differences between manual workers and employees* are much less today than they were thirty years ago and are not comparable with what they were in pre-revolutionary Russia. Housing is more comparable although intellectual workers do seem to secure slightly larger apartments than manual workers. On the other hand manual workers have the same access to education, health, pensions and other services as intellectual workers. In some ways they are better off as factory canteens are often better than those operating in institutes, offices and hospitals where the workforce is mainly white-collar or specialist. Factory workers also have more sanatoria and health resorts at their disposal than many ordinary intellectuals.

Despite all that has been said above there is evidence that traditional resentments still prevail. Manual workers in industry are sometimes highly critical of engineers and technicians, especially those remote from the production line. This is partly a consequence of the sheer size of this section of the workforce in the Soviet Union. There are so many ITRs and yet the results of their labours are often mediocre. While Soviet factory workers and intellectuals are not so separated in their housing as is the case in most Western cities and while they share common services they tend to lead rather different lives. This helps to keep them socially apart. Even their participation in voluntary public activity tends to still keep them apart as much of this activity is based on work collectives so that teachers, doctors and

* Perhaps not synonymous with the category 'primarily engaged in mental labour'.

research scientists are rarely working side by side with factory workers. The Soviets and their Standing Commissions are an exception to this for they bring together citizens from all walks of life.

## Inequalities between sexes in the workforce

Women moved into the Soviet workforce in increasing numbers after the revolution. They constituted 39 per cent of the total workforce in 1940 and 51 per cent during the 1970s.[24] This is sometimes said to demonstrate the liberation of women. But though women enjoy equal access to employment and receive equal rates of pay and conditions of work they are not fully equal economically. Women have not yet escaped the double burden of domestic labour and public employment. Because of domestic duties and child bearing and child care women generally have lower qualifications than men whatever field they work in. They usually dominate the lower and intermediate grades in a profession and are under-represented at the senior levels. They dominate the lower paid professions and industries. Thus in 1970 women constituted 99 per cent of all typists, 98 per cent of kindergarten teachers, 95 per cent of secretaries and office workers, 89 per cent of medical workers (including 74 per cent of doctors and 77 per cent of dentists), 72 per cent of teachers and 65 per cent of postal workers, 85 per cent of textile workers and 91 per cent of those employed in cultural services. They constituted 84 per cent of those employed in trade and public catering. In contrast in 1970 only 16 per cent of the workers in machine building and metallurgy were women. At the time women represented only 16 per cent of the heads of economic enterprises, 25 per cent of school principals, 43 per cent of tertiary teachers and 53 per cent of chief doctors and heads of medical establishments.[25] The situation is even worse in agriculture. In the early 1970s, when women constituted more than half the total workforce in Soviet agriculture, only 1.5 per cent of chairmen of collective farms and directors of state farms were women. At the same time women constituted about a third of all agricultural specialists.[26]

The inevitable consequence of the under-representation of women at the higher levels of the workforce is that women's average earnings are lower than men's earnings. There are no Soviet statistics for average earnings as between sexes but Western writers have estimated that Soviet women in the 1970s earned on average only 65 to 70 per cent of male earnings.[27] It is obvious that Soviet women have not yet gained full equality with men in public employment or in political and social participation. A Soviet sociologist Z.A. Yankova, concludes her 'social portrait' of the Soviet woman by outlining four basic types:

1 Those who are active participants in professional work, in social and political work, and in the family and in the education of their children.
2 Those who formally fulfil all three roles but who tend to put most effort into maintaining the family.
3 Those who isolate themselves from the work collective and from friends and even family and pursue a single-minded devotion to maximizing economic gain (the 'atomized' workers).
4 Those who concentrate all their energy and time on caring for the family.

This last group is drawn chiefly from the older women and it represents a declining proportion of working women.[28]

### Nationality and regional differences

Soviet writers usually emphasize the declining importance of differences in the social structure between nations and regions. However a survey of the available statistics as well as critical observation of different regions suggests that these differences continue to be important. Thus in 1970 when 56 per cent of the USSR population was urban there were still seven out of fifteen Union Republics with rural majorities. In 1980 when 63 per cent of Soviet people were urban there were still five Union Republics with rural majorities (Table 2.8). While the rural population of the USSR declined between 1959 and 1970 by more than three million the rural population of the four central Asian Republics rose by 37.6 per cent. While the rural population of the USSR fell by 6,879,000 between 1970 and 1979, that of the four central Asian Republics rose by 2,847,000.[29] This reversal of rural population decline is most obvious in the case of Tadjikistan which reached 38 per cent urbanization by 1959 but recorded only 35 per cent twenty years later.

The same variations are found in the representation of different classes and social groups in the population. Thus while manual workers comprised 60.0 per cent of the population of the USSR in 1979 they formed 68.0 per cent in Kazakhstan* but only 44.2 per cent in Turkmenia. Collective farmers comprised 14.9 per cent of the population of the USSR in 1979 but only 6.5 per cent in Kazakhstan and 33.4 per cent in Turkmenia (Table 2.7). Women also participate unevenly in the workforces of republics and regions.[30] Thus women constituted 51 per cent of the USSR workforce in 1981 but 39 per

---

\* Kazakhstan has more state farms and fewer collective farms than other Union Republics.

TABLE 2.7   Variations in the social structure as between different Union
Republics, January 1979

|  | (Percentages) | | |
|  | Workers | Employees | Collective farmers |
|---|---|---|---|
| USSR | 60.0 | 25.1 | 14.9 |
| RSFSR | 63.0 | 26.9 | 10.0 |
| Ukraine | 54.8 | 22.2 | 23.0 |
| Belorussia | 55.8 | 22.8 | 21.3 |
| Uzbekistan | 52.9 | 22.3 | 24.7 |
| Kazakhstan | 68.0* | 25.5 | 6.5 |
| Georgia | 55.6 | 26.5 | 17.8 |
| Azerbaidjan | 59.6 | 23.6 | 16.7 |
| Lithuania | 56.8 | 23.1 | 20.0 |
| Moldavia | 52.6 | 17.5 | 29.8 |
| Latvia | 58.6 | 27.8 | 13.5 |
| Kirgizia | 57.8 | 21.9 | 20.3 |
| Tadjikistan | 53.0 | 20.6 | 26.3 |
| Armenia | 64.2 | 26.1 | 9.7 |
| Turkmenia | 44.2 | 22.2 | 33.4 |
| Estonia | 60.9 | 29.8 | 10.2 |

Total population USSR
262,084,654                157,122,843    65,666,500    39,144,472

* Most farming in Kazakhstan is state farming, hence the high figure for workers.
SOURCE: 1979 Census figures. Vestnik statistiki, No. 1, 1981, p. 66.

cent of the Tadjikistan workforce and 41 per cent of the Turkmenian
workforce. On the other hand they represented 54 per cent of the
Latvian workforce. In Central Asia the women of the indigenous
nationalities are still less involved in public economic activity than
are their sisters in European Russia.[31] In such areas the women are
still the guardians of traditional values about women's role in
society. These traditional attitudes are particularly strong in rural
areas, not only in Central Asia but in Azerbaidjan. The workforce of
Siberia is very much affected by the isolation of the region and the
severity of its climate. Young males predominate and there is a high
turnover of labour as few can stand the rigours of the climate and
work. The young are attracted by high wage rates as well as by the
challenge of pioneering and the appeals of Party and Komsomol
leaders. Hundreds of thousands moved into Northern Kazakhstan
and Southern Siberia in the late 1950s during the Virgin Lands
Campaign and have gone since to construct such massive works as
Bratsk and the BAM railway in Eastern Siberia. Much of the manual

TABLE 2.8  Percentage of total population living in urban areas

|  | 1926 | 1939 | 1959 | 1970 | 1980 |
|---|---|---|---|---|---|
| USSR | 18 | 32 | 48 | 56 | 63 |
| RSFSR | 18 | 33 | 52 | 62 | 70 |
| Ukraine | 19 | 34 | 46 | 55 | 62 |
| Belorussia | 17 | 25 | 31 | 43 | 56 |
| Uzbekistan | 22 | 23 | 31 | 36 | 41 |
| Kazakhstan | 9 | 28 | 44 | 51 | 54 |
| Georgia | 22 | 30 | 42 | 48 | 52 |
| Azerbaidjan | 28 | 36 | 48 | 50 | 53 |
| Lithuania | — | 23 | 39 | 54* | 62 |
| Moldavia | — | 13 | 22 | 32 | 40 |
| Latvia | — | 35 | 56 | 62 | 69 |
| Kirgizia | 12 | 19 | 34 | 37 | 39 |
| Tadjikistan | 10 | 17 | 38 | 37 | 35 |
| Armenia | 19 | 29 | 50 | 59 | 66 |
| Turkmenia | 14 | 33 | 46 | 48 | 48 |
| Estonia | — | 34 | 56 | 65 | 70 |

* I have recalculated the 50 per cent given in Arutyunyan.
SOURCES: Yu.V. Arutyunyan (1971), p. 82.
    1980 figures are from *Nar. khoz. SSSR v 1979g.*, pp. 12–17.

work is done by groups of contract labourers organized into small teams. The high earnings attract even city intellectuals. In 1982 I heard of a Moscow scientific worker who had worked for three long spells in Siberia as a *shabashnik* in an effort to raise sufficient funds to acquire a larger apartment through a housing cooperative. There are also many thousands of intellectuals who have been excluded from the large cities of European Russia and are now enduring a Siberian exile. There is even a special name for such displaced intellectuals. They are called *bich* (from *byvshii intelligentnyi chelovek*), a former member of the intelligentsia.

## Future trends

Over recent decades the Russian proportion of the USSR population has been steadily declining. It was 54.8 per cent of the total in 1959, 53.4 per cent in 1970 and 52.4 per cent in 1979. Between 1959 and 1979 the proportion of Ukrainians in the total population declined from 17.7 to 16.2 per cent while that of Belorussians fell from 3.7 to 3.6 per cent. Over the same period the proportion of Uzbeks in the population increased from 2.8 to 4.7 per cent, while that of Kazakhs rose from 1.7 to 2.5 per cent. Should present trends continue the central Asian nations will constitute over 15 per cent of the population by 2000 while the Russians will be a minority. The proportions of central Asians entering the Soviet workforce will be even higher, as much as 20 per cent of the total. It is not clear whether any attempts will be made to transfer any of this abundant labour to areas of labour shortage such as European Russia or Siberia. What is more likely is further transfers of light industry and of scientific research to Central Asia.

Ever since the adoption of the 1961 Party Program Soviet writers have been saddled with the obligation to identify signs of rapprochement between different elements of their social system. The word *sblizhenie** is liberally sprinkled through the pages of sociological articles and books and it even appears at the head of statistical tables.[32] It is sometimes translated in English as 'convergence' but its Russian meaning is less precise, meaning 'rapprochement' or 'moving together'. 'Convergence' (or 'merging') is normally translated in Russian as *sliyanie*. According to Soviet theory as their society moves closer to communism the existing differences between classes and sub-classes, town and country, manual and mental labour, between republics, nations and regions will diminish. But is this really happening? There is certainly considerable evidence to support the claim that country and urban life is becoming more similar in terms of income levels, education, health and other social services. But it remains very different in terms of housing, culture and in beliefs. The smaller and more remote the village, the stronger traditional and religious beliefs, and the lower the frequency of newspapers, journals and books.[33] State farms apart, modern housing is still very scarce in the villages and smaller country towns. Individual houses (often built of wood) prevail. Though they are sometimes more spacious than urban apartments they often lack urban comforts of heating, running water and radio and television. Not only are farmers' incomes lower than city workers' incomes but rural incomes generally are well below urban incomes. There is more evidence to support the contention that living standards between intellectual workers, white-collar workers and manual workers are becoming more even. But the differences in working conditions and work satisfaction between manual and non-manual workers continue and are likely to remain, notwithstanding the rapid improvement in the educational standard of industrial workers over recent years. More manual workers are also studying in secondary specialist and tertiary educational institutes but this brings such workers into the ranks of the

---

* The term does not appear in the new Party Program adopted in March 1986.

intelligentsia not closer to them. As far as the levelling of standards between Russian and other nationalities is concerned, it is certainly happening. This is most obvious in the rapid increase in native intelligentsia. Yet the differences here continue to be almost as important as the similarities, a point I will develop further in Chapter 4. The inequalities in various republican workforces between men and women are changing very slowly.

I conclude this chapter by suggesting that the coming together of different sections of the Soviet workforce is much less a reality than a hope that springs from the underlying ideology. It is one of those things that must happen before communism can be achieved.

# 3 RULING CLASS OR POWER ELITE?

The concept of the ruling class is not exclusively a Marxist one. It has been argued by various schools of political theory and often by those who present alternative theories to those of Marx. What distinguishes the Marxist theory of the ruling class from other theories is its identification of the dominant economic class as the ruling class. In ancient society this was the class of slave owners, in feudal society it was the feudal lords and in capitalist society the class of capitalists: the manufacturers, mine owners, land owners, merchants and bankers. Marx saw the ruling economic class as dominating all social relationships, including the ideological and the political. The state was seen as the executive committee of the ruling class, as an apparatus for generalizing the interests of the ruling class. Thus every state represented the hegemony or dictatorship of one class over other classes. The feudal state represented the dictatorship of the feudal landlords over other classes, the capitalist state represented the dictatorship of the capitalist class over the workers, peasants and other petty-bourgeois elements.

In the late nineteenth century the Russian Marxists sought to apply classical Marxism to the peculiarities of the Russian social structure. The ruling class was identified as a loose coalition of landed aristocracy and urban bourgeoisie. The industrial proletariat was seen as the leading revolutionary class in the struggle to overthrow the old order but its small size and late development was an obvious problem. The mainstream of Russian Marxism consequently did not expect an early socialist revolution in Russia. Between 1894 and 1917 Lenin made a progressive reassessment of the social scene. He maximized the size of the proletariat by the addition of numerous semi-proletarian elements (landless peasants, domestic servants, etc.) and revised the theory on the revolutionary role of the peasantry, especially the poor peasantry. Long before 1917 he saw the revolutionary forces as an alliance of industrial workers, revolutionary intellectuals and peasants (the vast majority of the population) mobilized against the Tsarist autocracy, the aristocracy and the bourgeoisie (a very small minority).

The Russian Revolution of 1917 overthrew the old ruling class but it did not totally destroy it. The revolutionary scythe cut unevenly. The landed aristocracy (including the royal family and the church) had lost their estates by February 1918. The urban bourgeoisie survived in a depleted and circumscribed form for a few years and even revived somewhat under the NEP. The traditional theory had no difficulty in adjusting to these changes. The Bolshevik Revolution was seen to have brought the working class to power – the landlord-capitalist dictatorship had been replaced by the proletarian dictatorship. The aim of this dictatorship was to defend the gains of the revolution against attempts at counter-revolution, to strengthen and extend socialist property relations and eventually to achieve complete socialism. By the end of the Second Five Year Plan in 1937 the bulk of the peasantry had been collectivized while the urban bourgeoisie and petty-bourgeoisie had virtually ceased to exist. This simplified class structure was presented as an alliance of two basic classes, the working class and the collective farm peasantry, with the intelligentsia constituting a rapidly expanding stratum. Relations between these two classes were said to be non-antagonistic and basically friendly. This socialist order was described as a proletarian dictatorship, although Stalin sometimes conceded that this was in essence the dictatorship of the Party.

The concept of the dictatorship of the proletariat remained dominant in the Soviet Union until 1961 and was not fully displaced even after the adoption of the concept of 'the state of the whole people'. The proletariat remains the leading class even if no longer the ruling class. This adjustment to the Soviet theory of the state caused obvious strains in the overall Leninist theory which Chinese and other doctrinaire Marxists were quick to exploit. Be that as it may, for the Soviet leaders there is no longer a ruling class in the USSR.

## The search for the ruling class

Most Western specialists on the Soviet Union are historians, economists or political scientists and they are not much concerned with the existence or non-existence of a Soviet ruling class. Marxist critics on the other hand are preoccupied with this question. Often the ambiguities of the Marxist conception of social class are manipulated to match a hunch or a prior ideological position. Thus if one believes that a premature revolution in a backward society cannot produce socialism then the post-revolutionary society must be characterized by class conflict, must contain exploiting and exploited classes. If private ownership of the means of production has been replaced by socialist property relations it must be argued that those who hold political power 'control' the means of production even if they do not legally own them. Hence the bureaucracy (or some sections of it) must constitute the ruling class or at least the ruling caste. From another angle, if the communist party has confiscated power from the working class the communist party (or its apparatus) must constitute the new ruling class. Marxists with more flexible definitions (and Weberian overtones) of class will perhaps go further and argue that the concept of 'relation to the means of production' is a complex one which includes position in the production process, level of skill and qualification, type of work performed, level of responsibility, and so on. Unequal distribution of power, prestige and income produces different classes. The ruling class consequently consists of those who possess high intellectual skills, the intelligentsia.[1]

The identification of the intelligentsia as the Soviet ruling class is clearly misplaced. The intelligentsia is far too large and diverse a group to constitute a class. It is larger than the collective farm peasantry and the white-collar workforce and is smaller only than the manual workforce. In comparison with manual workers intellectual workers enjoy only marginal privileges in working conditions, housing and social prestige and political power. Less than 10 per cent of the intelligentsia hold administrative posts and an even smaller number enjoy high incomes. While the children of intelligentsia families enjoy some advantages over others in gaining entry into the intelligentsia, membership of the intelligentsia is not based on inheritance – recruitment to the intelligentsia is competitive and is based on the gaining of formal professional qualifications.

Does the communist party constitute a ruling class? It is even more difficult to argue this than it is to argue that the intelligentsia is the ruling class. By 1986 the CPSU numbered more than nineteen million, about 10 per cent of the adult population. More than 40 per cent were manual workers and over 10 per cent collective farmers. It represents all sections of Soviet society and all national groups and regions, although the representation is somewhat uneven. Thus intellectual workers are over-represented while manual workers and collective farmers are under-represented. Russians, Jews and Georgians are over-represented while some national groups are clearly under-represented. This distortion results both from historical tradition as well as from biases in Party recruitment, caused by the desire to have more party members in certain key areas such as the aviation industry, transport, education and science, defence and public administration. But while the likelihood of a Communist being an administrator is more than four times as great as it is for others the overwhelming majority of Communists work as active supporters of Party policy in their ordinary occupations. The educational level of party members is much higher than that of the general population, but education is not a clear indicator of power or wealth in the Soviet Union.

The CPSU is a large and complex organization but it is not a social class. Its basic organizational principle is that of 'democratic centralism' which means the maximum centralization of authority in the higher organs of the Party and the subordination of lower organs to the central organs. An organization of such size and complexity requires tens of thousands of paid officials, the Party functionaries. The Party officials have much in common (and are often interchangeable) with Soviet officials, trade union and Komsomol officials and with the officials of other social organizations. These officials (or *apparatchiki* as they are termed in Soviet oppositionist and Western writing) are sometimes identified as the Soviet ruling class. While some officials exercise small power it is clearly the general body of officials which is identified in Soviet writing as the *nachalstvo*, the command or the authorities. Beyond the *nachalstvo* lies the *aktiv*, the activists, officials and others, Party members and non-Party persons, who provide the core around which others are mobilized for the implementation of specific Party objectives.

### The *nomenklatura* as the ruling class

In 1975 Alec Nove suggested the *nomenklatura* as the key to identifying the Soviet ruling class.[2] Since then others have followed suit, most notably the emigré Soviet historian, Michael Voslensky.[3]

The *nomenklatura* is a list of official positions and of persons eligible to fill them. Communist party organs, from the Central Committee of the CPSU down to city and district committees have their own *nomenklatury*, as do Soviet organs, ministries, trade unions and other social organizations. If a position in the State structure is on a Party *nomenklatura* the Party organ does not formally appoint to that position but merely 'confirms' the appointment or dismissal. This power of *utverzhdenie* or confirmation is exercised throughout the Party hierarchy. Besides the *nomenklatura* proper there is also the *uchetnaya nomenklatura* which is a kind of additional list which also operates as a reserve list. Positions on this second list do not require the confirmation of the appropriate Party organ but the Party organ must be informed of any personnel changes on this list. These lists are not entirely separate but rather tend to overlap as between different hierarchical levels. Thus the same person might be on a District Committee's *nomenklatura* but also on the Regional Committee's *uchetnaya nomenklatura*.[4] Because many nomenklatured positions are not all that important most writers who take this approach limit the ruling class to those persons holding positions on the *nomenklatura* of the Central Committee of the CPSU or on those of the Central Committees of the Union Republics. This identification of the ruling class in terms of those holding important office is excused by Nove on the grounds that 'there are circumstances in which power determines the relations of production rather than vice versa'.[5]

The recent book by Michael Voslensky, *La Nomenklatura: Les Privilégiés en URSS* (Paris, 1980) is the fullest presentation of the thesis under review. For that reason, as well as for its interest and residual Marxism (if only in definitions) I will discuss it at some length. Voslensky left the Soviet Union in the early 1970s after holding nomenklatured positions over many years including a spell as a sectional departmental head within the Central Committee apparatus, which makes his book of special interest.

Voslensky applies Lenin's definition of the state: 'The state is the product of the irreconcilability of class contradictions.' Therefore the administrators of the Soviet Union constitute the ruling class.[6] The Bolshevik Revolution was not a working class revolution but a revolution planned and directed by professional revolutionaries. These professional revolutionaries became the directors of the new Soviet state. Under Stalin the old revolutionaries were swamped and eventually eliminated by the apparatchiks, the nomenklaturists.[7] He regards the *nomenklatura* as a kind of bastard feudalism in which instead of feudal fiefs nomenklaturists are given grants of power to exploit all persons within a given territory or particular sector of an enterprise.[8]

Unlike some other writers Voslensky gives a fairly exact estimate of the size of the *nomenklatura*. Taking 1970 as his reference year he estimates about 750,000 nomenklaturists. If their families were added in, this would represent three million people, or 1.5 per cent of the total population.[9] There are some problems with this estimate. It clearly does not include all nomenklatured positions but presumably only those at central and Union Republican levels. The distinction between the upper and lower level nomenklaturists is not made fully clear. He gives minimum and maximum estimates for both levels and the distinction here would seem to be between the Party *nomenklatura* and that of the Party and State *nomenklatury*. Even so there seems to be some double counting in his total estimate of 750,000.

A great deal of Voslensky's book is taken up with detailing the privileges of the nomenklaturists. He calculates that the nomenklaturist receives an income five to eight times that of the average worker, that he enjoys enormous privileges in his access to goods and services, in his right to travel (especially overseas travel) and in securing the best education for his children and their accession to the *nomenklatura* class. He argues, somewhat unconvincingly, that the privileges of elites in Western societies are much less than those of the Soviet Union and that an abyss separates the *nomenklatura* from the rest of the population.[10]

Voslensky puts Lenin's question of 1918, 'What is Soviet Power?' but he provides a different answer: 'Soviet power is the dictatorship of the *nomenklatura*.'[11] This dictatorship has regained control over and extended the Tsarist Empire. It has gained complete control over several countries of Eastern Europe. It finances and guides communist Parties in most parts of the world and struggles relentlessly against those parties which do not submit to it. It seeks to destabilize the situations of countries under American influence and to extend its influence and control in all parts of the globe. The *nomenklatura* aims at world hegemony.[12] The final chapter seeks to argue that the *nomenklatura* is a parasitic class. The argument here seems to be that the nomenklaturists serve no useful purpose, live lives of pretence, have others to work for them and generally are redundant. Thus we are told that the President of the USSR has sixteen aides, the Chairman of the Council of Ministers twelve and the Foreign Affairs Minister ten. The Director of an Academy of Science Institute will have several assistants but only one if it is a small and unimportant institute.[13] But this is understaffing by Western standards. And no one can accept his portrait of the Oblomov-like workday of his typical departmental section head as anything but a caricature.

Can we then regard the *nomenklatura* as the Soviet ruling class? I do not think so, although the recognition of the *nomenklatura* is crucial for understanding the Soviet elite. The *nomenklatura* does not constitute a social class any more than the bureaucracy as a whole. Even in terms of Mosca or Pareto it would be difficult to establish the *nomenklatura* as the ruling class (or ruling elite) because it does not exercise a monopoly of political power.[14] In Marxist terms a collection of high office holders cannot be held to constitute a ruling class since they do not own the means of production nor pass them on to their children. They merely manage them on behalf of society and they do not control them.

Secondly, there is the difficulty of identifying the *nomenklatura* within the general body of the bureaucracy. Voslensky's estimate of 750,000 for the year 1970 is one of the largest suggested yet there were in that year 1,838,000 heads of government and Party organizations and departments, of economic organizations and their structural divisions, and of cooperative enterprises and various social organizations. Most of these would be within some *nomenklatura*. There are also some nomenklatured positions which are not essentially administrative. Many of these positions are of relatively small power or privilege. For example, the academic secretary of an Academy of Science Institute is usually on a District Committee *nomenklatura* but he does not exercise much power. His salary is in accordance with his academic level. His privileges are small, perhaps a small room to himself, access to theatre tickets or some preference in the purchase of a private car. He will find it easier to travel abroad but will enjoy no special privileges in his access to materials for research or in housing. The secretary of a Society for Friendship and Cultural Relations with Foreign Countries is normally on the *nomenklatura* of a Central Committee but the office carries heavy responsibilities and quite arduous duties. It has some prestige but few privileges. It does not provide an official car, although that of the chairman is sometimes available for the use of the secretary. The director of a medium-sized industrial plant is not likely to be on the *nomenklatura* of the Central Committee of the CPSU but only on the republican or regional *nomenklatura*. But who can deny that he wields great power in his local community?

Thirdly, it needs to be asked whether the people of the Soviet Union regard the *nomenklatura* as a ruling class. I do not think that they do. The highest leaders (Politburo members, members of the Secretariat and the Council of Ministers of the USSR) are certainly considered to be remote and apart from ordinary people as indeed they are. Lower officials in the Central Party or state apparatus often share this remoteness but not always. It depends largely on the nature of their special work. Local officials and even republican officials are likely to be more accessible. The distinction between 'we' and 'they' is not usually drawn along the line which divides the workforce into normal and nomenklatured positions. Amongst the intelligentsia one sometimes encounters criticisms of the *nomenklatura* system on the grounds of its exclusiveness, secrecy and inefficiency but these mild complaints are comparable with the criticisms of university appointment procedures in Western countries. And such criticisms have been lessened over recent years through the steady 'de-classification' of formerly nomenklatured positions.

Fourthly, there is a confusion in the argument on the question of social privilege. One cannot prove the existence of a ruling class by establishing that privilege exists. Nor is privilege as great as Voslensky argues. It is certainly a lesser problem in the Soviet Union than it is in the USA or most capitalist countries. Huge incomes coming from inherited wealth and private investment do not exist in the Soviet Union. The salary range is also less, especially if the private sector is taken into account. In 1970 the lowest monthly wage in the Soviet Union was 70 roubles a month while the average wage was 165.5 roubles. The highest paid Party official, L.I. Brezhnev received a salary of 900 roubles a month. These disparities, while still great, are much less than they were in the Stalin years. Mervyn Matthews is nearer the mark on this matter. He finds that the American elite threshold income is about twelve times the average income, while in the USSR elite incomes (including extras) are five to eight times the average income.[15] However, Matthews like Voslensky, tends to discuss privilege and income differences against an abstract ethical ideal of equality.[16] But neither Marx nor Soviet leaders have advocated wage equality either under socialism or under communism. And wage differentials based on the value of the work performed are widely accepted in the Soviet Union. On the other hand there is considerable evidence that many Soviet workers would prefer a more equal distribution than that which operates at present.[17]

There is undoubtedly a residue of truth in the theories I have been criticizing. Privilege and power are not only unequally distributed in the Soviet Union but they are closely related to administrative structures. High privilege does not always coincide with great administrative power but it often does. Structural inequalities in power relate to the scope and complexity of bureaucratic hierarchies and not to the marketplace. Strategic positions in this mechanism (such as General Secretary of the Party, Chairmen of Councils of Ministers, members of the Secretariat of the Central Committee, regional Party secretaries, USSR Ministers, etc.) exercise enormous power because of the positions they hold. They also receive high salaries, bonus payments, privileged access to quality consumer goods, cars, apartments and holiday accommodation. Their children often receive special access to higher education and to positions. They accumulate sizeable personal property (including bank balances) which they pass on to their children. There is thus a tendency towards the inheritance of wealth, privilege and position even though it has not yet produced a new ruling class in the Marxist sense of the term. It is perhaps not even appropriate to analyse these phenomena in class terms.

## Elite theory and Soviet society

Elite theory developed in Western Europe in the late nineteenth and early twentieth centuries in opposition to Marxist class theory. This was also true for the two widely read American books published in the 1950s and 1960s, C. Wright Mills' *The Power Elite* (1957) and Suzanne Keller's *Beyond the Ruling Class* (1963). In a revealing footnote to *The Power Elite* Mills states that: ' "Class" is an economic term; "rule" a political one. The phrase "ruling class", thus contains the theory that an economic class rules politically.' [18]

Such a formulation reflects the author's preference for Weber rather than Marx. For Marx drew no clear distinction between economic and political orders as did Weber and 'class' for Marx was not purely an economic term. For Marx a 'ruling class' was the dominant class economically, socially, politically and ideologically.

*The Power Elite* is an analysis of American politics, not of Soviet politics. Mills argues that there are three spheres in which national decisions are taken: the economic, the military and the political. Three elites, numbering only a few thousand individuals, operate, one in each sphere. These are distinct but interlocking elites which collectively constitute a 'power elite'. The theoretical sources for the argument are not purely Weberian and much of the empirical evidence produced to sustain the thesis could well support a Marxist interpretation.

Mills did not immediately apply his thesis to the Soviet Union. In *The Causes of World War Three* (published a few years after he wrote *The Power Elite*) Mills suggested that the driving force for war both in America and the Soviet Union was the power elites in both countries.[19] But there is nowhere in Mills' works any detailed discussion of the Soviet Union. He was only beginning to research the Soviet system at the time of his death in the early 1960s.

Suzanne Keller's *Beyond the Ruling Class* is at once a reaction to Marx and to Mills. She argued that Mills' concept of 'the power elite' contained most of the defects that he found in Marx. For Keller, modern industrial societies were characterized by a large number of elites: industrial, scientific, educational, administrative, military, cultural, and so on. These elites were not integrated although there was some overlapping. Nor were all elites equally important, some had strategic advantages over others. These 'strategic elites' (which included the three identified by Mills) were the dominant groups in American politics. While the argument is mainly about America, Keller sought to argue that it applied also to Western Europe and to the Soviet Union. However the few pages which discuss the Soviet Union are very general and show no close knowledge of the social or political system of that country.

How useful then is elite theory for the interpretation of Soviet politics and society? Fairly obviously something could be made out of applying Mills' thesis to the Soviet Union. But of the three elites identified by Mills the political elite is obviously dominant and the 'business elite' is much weaker and has no separate representation in the Politburo, although it is well represented in the Central

Committee of the CPSU and in the USSR Council of Ministers. The exclusion of obviously important elites such as the police and security elites, the scientific, educational, cultural and ideological elites, would suggest that more mileage could be found in Keller's concept of 'strategic elites'. Unfortunately this concept has built into it certain assumptions about the plurality of society and elites which do not correspond to the reality of Soviet life. While some Western political scientists have tried to use pluralist theory to analyse Soviet politics they have not had much success.[20] Recent writers who have used the term 'institutional pluralism' have used it with discretion.[21]

In general I find elite theory of small value in explaining the Soviet or any other political system. By recognizing that political power is very unevenly distributed the theory draws attention to an important fact but then fails to do more than suggest a pattern to the distribution. I fully agree with the complaint by T.B. Bottomore that:

> The concept of a governing elite avoids, in particular, the difficulty of showing that a particular class defined in terms of its economic position, does in fact dominate all the spheres of social life; but it does so only at the cost of abandoning any attempt to explain the phenomena to which it refers.[22]

Murray Yanowitch, in his essays on *Social and Economic Inequality in the Soviet Union* (1977) makes a complaint about the inadequacies of Soviet sociology:

> Until Soviet sociologists are able to confront the issue of power — power over both the production and distribution process — and the whole mechanism of political stratification, their reliance on the 'social division of labour' to explain social and economic inequality will conceal at least as much as it reveals.[23]

But this, and other similar advice, is not applied in his own analysis so that the reader is left wondering exactly what is meant by the phrase 'the whole mechanism of political stratification'.

I will conclude this chapter by seeking to apply Burlatsky and Galkin's definition of class to the Soviet bureaucracy. In terms of their first criterion for establishing class location, property relationships, the bureaucracy is not distinguished from the rest of the intelligentsia or, for that matter, from the manual workers. Their second criterion, 'place in the social division (or role in the social organization) of labour' is regarded as a secondary determinant of class. The bureaucrats clearly have a particular place in the division of labour. They do not own the means of production but are concerned, directly or indirectly, with their management. This marks them off from other intellectual workers but does not make them a separate class. The third criterion used by Burlatsky and Galkin to establish class position – 'the method of achieving a share in social wealth' – does not mark the bureaucracy off from the rest of the workforce in the state sector. Like other workers they receive a salary (or wages) paid by the state for work performed. The fourth criterion, 'the size of the acquired share of social wealth', would seem to mark at least the upper echelons of the bureaucracy off from the rest of the intelligentsia and from manual workers. But this distinction is not clear-cut. Many members of the creative and scientific intelligentsia receive incomes comparable to those of higher Party and state officials while the most highly paid manual workers receive wages that are equal to or better than the salaries of middle-level officials. In any case income differences cannot, in themselves, establish separate classes.

If the bureaucracy does not constitute a class then how should we regard it? It can be regarded either as a social layer (stratum) or as a sub-class. It is a sub-class within the working class but situated within the intelligentsia. Almost everyone in the Soviet bureaucracy has tertiary or secondary specialist qualifications. Bureaucrats are distinguished from the rest of the intelligentsia not so much by the scale of their incomes or by the degree of prestige and privilege they possess, but by the fact that they hold administrative office which gives them special power over others. At the higher and intermediate levels of the bureaucracy most officials are on the *nomenklatura* but this is not so at the lower levels. Throughout this book I use the concept 'superior intelligentsia' * as a synonym for the term 'bureaucracy'. I have not sought to make an independent estimate of the number of people involved but have accepted the Soviet figure for the number of persons holding leading administrative and managerial positions. This was 2,411,000 in 1979, considerably more than Voslensky's 750,000 and even more so than Mervyn Matthews' estimate of the size of the Soviet elite in the late 1970s (those on incomes of 450 roubles or more a month) as about 250,000.[24] Clearly, on grounds of income alone my figure is too large. Income is not the main determinant of belonging to the superior intelligentsia, but position and power are. Further aspects of the position of this group will be discussed in later chapters, especially Chapter 7. My next chapter will deal with the intelligentsia as a whole.

---

* I have borrowed this term from Alex Inkeles (1950, 1969) although I use it differently. As I use it, it applies to the administrative-managerial intelligentsia and not merely to the intermediate ranks of the bureaucracy.

# 4 THE INTELLIGENTSIA REVISITED

Fourteen years ago I was writing a general analysis of the Soviet intelligentsia. Since *The Soviet Intelligentsia* was published in 1973 I have continued to do research in this area but my research has been more specialized. I have been concerned almost exclusively with the position of the intelligentsia within Soviet society; with the level of professional training of the intelligentsia, with differences between national intelligentsias and with differences between female and male intelligentsia. The results of these investigations were presented at various conferences held in Sydney, Adelaide and Canberra between 1976 and 1981. The last of these papers, presented originally at an Australian National University seminar on the intelligentsia in July 1981 and in a somewhat revised form to postgraduate seminars at Essex and Birmingham Universities in February 1982, provides the basis for this chapter.

Throughout this intermittent research I have been plagued by the unavailability of recent statistical material. When I was writing *The Soviet Intelligentsia* only a small amount of material from the 1970 census had been published. More than seven years have passed since the last (January 1979) Soviet census but we are still awaiting the publication of the full census data. Hence the statistical material contained in this chapter is not as recent as I would have wished. Where possible I have used the 1979 census material or later data from yearbooks. At times I have had to fall back on 1970 census material.

## Who are the intelligentsia?

It is not possible to give a standard definition of the term 'intelligentsia' which will be accepted by everyone. This is partly because the term has not been used consistently since its invention in Russia in the 1860s. Beyond that there is considerable confusion over the use of the two terms 'intellectual' and 'intelligentsia'. Neither in Russian nor in English is this distinction clear or consistent.[1]

In my earlier book I defined the intelligentsia as 'persons with a tertiary education (whether employed or not), tertiary students, and persons lacking formal tertiary qualification but who are professionally employed in jobs which normally require a tertiary qualification'.[2] My definition therefore included gainfully employed professionals with tertiary qualifications, unemployed and retired persons with tertiary qualifications, tertiary students and military intelligentsia with higher qualifications. Whatever its shortcomings, the definition enabled me to identify fairly easily the number of people to be included in the terms 'intelligentsia'. But the definition was harshly dealt with by reviewers both in the West and in the Soviet Union.[3] Whereas the former criticized it for its objectivity and its scope, the latter criticized it for its exclusion of persons with secondary specialist qualifications and for its inclusion of tertiary students. To some extent Soviet criticisms of my definition are justified. It is not easy to disregard professionals with secondary specialist qualifications and I no longer attempt to do this. As Rutkevich has pointed out, part-time students have already been counted in the workforce (as workers or collective farmers) and therefore should not be double-counted by including them in the intelligentsia. But full-time students are excluded by Soviet writers simply because they are not in the workforce, just as retired professionals are excluded from the intelligentsia. These exclusions are necessary because of the restraints imposed by the standard contemporary Soviet definition of the intelligentsia. Thus M.N. Rutkevich uses the following definition:

> a large social group of working people professionally engaged in mental labour requiring high qualifications, normally requiring tertiary or secondary specialist qualifications.[4]

Soviet writers do not have a consistent definition of the intelligentsia. While most sociologists use a limited definition similar to the one quoted in the preceding paragraph, others (especially historians) still use a broader definition which includes not merely unqualified professionals but many others who are employed mainly in mental labour.[5] Even the narrower definition produces a sizeable social group. Thus there were 26.4 million specialists (including 11.1 million with tertiary qualifications and 15.3 million with secondary specialist qualifications) in the Soviet workforce at the beginning of 1979, 21.2 per cent of the total workforce. In the Soviet population at that time there were 38.3 million people with completed tertiary or secondary specialist qualifications. In other words only 69 per cent of fully qualified specialists were in the workforce at that time.

The vast majority of the missing 11.9 million were retired or were temporarily out of the workforce through illness or other causes.

## Historical development of the intelligentsia

My earlier work on the Soviet intelligentsia has been criticized as ahistorical and therefore misleading by Soviet critics.[6] This is because I was concerned with the intelligentsia in a single decade, that of the 1960s, and not with the history of the intelligentsia since 1917. It is of course necessary to understand the historical evolution of the Soviet intelligentsia, if only to better understand their present position. This I will attempt to outline as briefly as possible.

The contrast between the pre-1917 Russian intelligentsia and the modern Soviet intelligentsia is startling. Despite the great interest of Russians and of foreigners in the Russian intelligentsia of the late nineteenth and early twentieth centuries it was a very small segment of the society. It numbered approximately 190,000 in 1913, a very small elite of educated people. Today the Soviet intelligentsia is an enormous segment of society and is more numerous than the collective farm peasantry or the normal white-collar workers. The intelligentsia of Tsarist Russia mainly consisted of traditional intellectuals, in the Gramscian sense,[7] and consisted mainly of teachers, professors, lawyers, doctors, artists, writers, priests and higher civil servants and military officers. There were some elements of an 'organic' intelligentsia, persons more directly related to the economic structure of capitalist society such as industrial managers, architects, engineers and technicians. Specialists with tertiary training predominated – 72 per cent of employed specialists in 1913 had tertiary qualifications.

In his essay on 'The Formation of Intellectuals' Gramsci argues that every social class coming into existence creates its own intellectuals as well as absorbing elements of the existing traditional intelligentsia.[8] This dual process was certainly operating in Russia after the October Revolution. From the beginning of 1918 Lenin, Trotsky and other Bolshevik leaders emphasized that a precondition for the building of socialism was the recruitment of 'bourgeois specialists' into the service of the revolution. Lenin even went so far as to say that socialism could not be built without the aid of specialists. So specialists were recruited into the army, the police and every branch of public administration, especially into economic management. At the same time new elements, drawn largely from the industrial workers and the peasants, were being recruited into the intelligentsia. At first these recruits came mainly from the ranks of the Red Army or from the Party. From the early 1920s they were graduates from the expanding network of tertiary and secondary specialist educational institutions and above all from *rabfaks*, the Workers' Faculties. The majority of these new specialists received only secondary specialist education and often this was of a diluted kind. But standards apart, the intelligentsia grew rapidly and it numbered 521,000 by 1928. Only 45 per cent of these had tertiary qualifications. Just as the capitalist entrepreneur was the key figure in the development of the capitalist order, so the worker-technician became the most representative figure in the new proletarian intelligentsia. Along with the technicians came engineers, industrial managers, economists, designers, agricultural scientists and other elements of a new organic intelligentsia. The expansion of public administration gave rise to an enlarged, more broadly recruited intelligentsia, to act as officials in the superstructure: as civil servants, Party workers, educationalists, journalists and propaganda workers, legal workers, theatre managers, etc. This transformation was controlled and directed by the political leadership but it was not fully controlled in these early years.

The early Five Year Plans accelerated this transformation of the Soviet intelligentsia. Bourgeois specialists – those who survived the trials and purges of 1928–39 – were finally swamped by the newly recruited specialists. With accelerated economic growth and industrialization more and more specialists were required to take positions in production as well as in construction, transport and communications. The engineers and technical workers (ITRs) became even more decisive in the ranks of the intelligentsia. But because the economy was diversifying as well as expanding more and more specialized educational establishments were required to produce more and more specialists: engineers, technicians, draftsmen, architects, geologists, agronomists, economists, doctors, teachers, lawyers, writers, librarians, cultural workers, etc. By the eve of the War in 1941 there were almost two and a half million specialists in the Soviet workforce, 37 per cent of whom had tertiary qualifications (Table 4.1).

The War checked but did not halt this expansion of the intelligentsia. It increased the number of women specialists and gave them a significant place in some hitherto mainly male preserves. It also increased the proportion of specialists with tertiary qualifications. By 1950 almost one and a half million, 44 per cent of the total, had tertiary qualifications. The total number of specialists was 3,254,000 in 1950. The size of the intelligentsia more than doubled during the 1950s to reach 8,184,000 by 1960, of whom 43 per cent had tertiary qualifications. The intelligentsia more than doubled over the 1960s to reach 16,841,000 by the beginning of 1970 with

TABLE 4.1  Number of specialists with tertiary and secondary specialist education in the workforce (figures in 1000s)

| Year | All employed specialists | Including: | |
|---|---|---|---|
| | | Specialists with tertiary qualifications | Specialists with secondary specialist qualifications |
| 1913 | 190 | 136 | 54 |
| 1928 | 521 | 233 | 288 |
| 1941 | 2,401 | 909 | 1,492 |
| 1950 | 3,254 | 1,443 | 1,811 |
| 1955 | 5,133 | 2,184 | 2,949 |
| 1960 | 8,784 | 3,545 | 5,239 |
| 1965 | 12,066 | 4,891 | 7,175 |
| 1970 | 16,841 | 6,853 | 9,988 |
| 1975 | 22,796 | 9,477 | 13,319 |
| 1977 | 25,178 | 10,537 | 14,641 |
| 1979 | 26,400 | 11,100 | 15,300 |
| 1983 | 31,628 | 13,487 | 18,141 |

SOURCES: *Nar. khoz. SSSR v 1979g.*, p. 377.
*Nar. khoz. SSSR v 1984g.*, p. 420.

almost 41 per cent having tertiary qualifications. This was the decade which saw the beginning of what Soviet scholars (and eventually the political leadership) came to call the scientific and technological revolution. It saw the development of electronic and computer technology and the rapid expansion of scientific research. New disciplines and new specialities were created so that by 1970 tertiary and secondary specialist establishments were training professionals for several hundred specializations.[9] The slower rate of economic expansion in the 1970s no doubt accounted for the slower growth of the intelligentsia. But it was still growing and by 1979 it reached 26.4 million of whom 42 per cent had tertiary qualifications. And while the composition of the intelligentsia has become much more complex than it was in 1928, engineers and technicians are still the main group and today constitute more than a third of the intelligentsia. Almost half of all specialists are directly employed in production if agriculture and transport are added to industry and construction.

Although Soviet writers maintain that Gramsci's analysis of intellectuals has no relevance to the Soviet intelligentsia I do not think that this is correct.[10] There is a close relationship between the Soviet intelligentsia and the Soviet economy and between the regime and the intelligentsia, both organic and traditional. There are virtually no independent professionals in the Soviet Union. Most Soviet specialists are state employees and are trained to serve the communist regime and to further its economic, political and cultural objectives. Like the manual working class the Soviet intelligentsia is largely the creation of the regime. Its rate of development, its size and composition runs according to a plan. While there is competition between enterprises and other agencies over the recruitment of graduates there is an unusual degree of direction by the planning agencies. This direction covers the first three years (or two years in the case of those who have done their military service) of employment. Beyond that Party members are subjected to continued close supervision in their places of employment and may not change their job without Party approval. Their employment is only slightly less controlled than that of *nomenklaturists*. Thus more than most modern intelligentsias the Soviet intelligentsia are 'officials' of the ruling elite in Soviet society; serving directly in the economy, in the political apparatus or in other spheres of the superstructure.

## The structure of the Soviet intelligentsia

Throughout this chapter I will be using the general contemporary Soviet definition of the Soviet intelligentsia, i.e., employed specialists normally possessing tertiary or secondary specialist qualifications. The level of qualification reflected in this definition enables us to divide the intelligentsia into three large groups according to those possessing tertiary, secondary specialist qualifications, or neither. The distinction between these three groups in terms of position and salary is somewhat blurred. In general, however, those with tertiary qualifications have higher prestige, gain higher positions and enjoy higher salaries than the other two groups in the same sector of employment. They also exercise marginally more power.

Functional divisions within the Soviet intelligentsia are of greater importance. Soviet writers normally recognize between four and seven functional groupings within the intelligentsia. Thus M.N. Rutkevich in his 1977 book, *Intelligentsia v razvitom sotsialisticheskom obshchestve*, recognizes seven functional groups.[11] Using the 1970 census figures (which gave a total intelligentsia as 16,840,700) he divides the intelligentsia in this way:

| | | |
|---|---|---|
| (a) | Production intelligentsia | 46.5% |
| (b) | Educational-cultural intelligentsia | 23.3% |
| (c) | Medical intelligentsia | 14.6% |
| (d) | Administrative intelligentsia | (8.6%) |

| (e) | Scientific intelligentsia | (5.0%) |
| (f) | Artistic intelligentsia | (1.1%) |
| (g) | Military intelligentsia | (0.9%) |

(Figures in brackets are my own calculation.)

In Gramscian terms the first group is almost entirely an 'organic' intelligentsia. Groups (d) and (g) are also primarily organic while the other groups all have a mixture of traditional and organic elements. Academics have been included in group (e) as is customary in the Soviet Union. This of course inflates the size of the scientific workers and reduces the size of the educational-cultural intelligentsia. The size of group (c) is impressive but it needs to be recognized that it includes not only doctors but dentists, medical assistants, nurses, sport and physical culturists. The estimate for the military intelligentsia is probably understated (160,000) as army doctors are possibly not included and some military specialists would be working in defence industry or research and are perhaps included elsewhere.

## The specialist qualification ratio

By this I mean the ratio between specialists in the workforce with tertiary qualifications and those with secondary specialist qualifications. This has varied over time. Thus in 1913 it was 72 : 28. In the Soviet period the ratio was 45 : 55 in 1928, 37 : 63 in 1941, 41 : 59 in 1970 and 42 : 58 in 1979. But this ratio differs as between the sexes and as between different nationalities. The ratios here tell us rather more than the percentages of all specialists. Thus women comprised 29 per cent of all employed specialists in 1928, 36 per cent in 1941, and 59 per cent in 1960, 1970 and 1979. In 1928 the specialist qualification ratio (sqr) for women specialists was 43 : 57 while it was 45 : 55 for men. In 1941 it was 36 : 64 for women but 39 : 61 for men. In 1960 the sqr for women specialists was 34 : 66 but it was 47 : 53 for men. In 1970 the sqr for women was 36 : 64 but 48 : 52 for men. In 1979 the sqr was 37 : 63 for women but 49 : 51 for men.[12] The uneven sharing of professional training and positions between women and men is also reflected in the figures in Tables 4.8 and 4.9 (see pp.71–2). The proportion of women students has not much improved over the past forty years. Most of the improvement in recent years has been recovery from the slump in 1960–61 when women comprised 43 per cent of tertiary students and 47 per cent of secondary specialist students.[13] Between 1950 and 1980 women reached approximate equality with men amongst junior scientific workers but their representation in more senior positions remained very unequal. Women still form a minority in more prestigious professions such as physics, mathematics and engineering and even in professions which they dominate (medicine, education, economics, law, etc.) they are unequally represented in the higher positions. Thus women formed 71 per cent of all teachers in 1980–81 but only 34 per cent of the directors of secondary schools.[14]

If the specialist qualification ratio is different as between women and men it is even more so as between nationalities. Thus in 1970 the ratio was 36 : 64 for Russians, 35 : 65 for Ukrainians, 34 : 66 for Belorussians and 32 : 68 for Latvians. But the ratio was 52 : 48 for Uzbeks and Turkmen, 51 : 49 for Kirgiz and Tadjiks, and 54 : 46 for Georgians and Armenians. For Jews (in the RSFSR) it was 73 : 27. If only the urban intelligentsias are considered then the contrast between the European and the other national groups is even more startling. Thus for urban Russians and urban Ukrainians in 1970 the sqr was 38 : 62 while for urban Belorussians it was 36 : 64. For urban Uzbeks and Tadjiks it was 59 : 41 and for urban Kazakhs it was 55 : 45. The sqr for urban Georgians was 63 : 37 while for urban Armenians and Kirgiz it was 62 : 38. Amongst urban Jews in the RSFSR the sqr was 87 : 13!

TABLE 4.2  Educational level of occupied persons by nationality, USSR, 1970

| Nationality | %age with full tertiary | | | Nationality | %age with secondary specialist | | |
|---|---|---|---|---|---|---|---|
| | All | Urban | Rural | | All | Urban | Rural |
| Russians | 6.9 | 8.6 | 2.6 | Russians | 12.0 | 13.7 | 7.6 |
| Ukrainians | 5.3 | 8.3 | 2.0 | Ukrainians | 9.7 | 13.3 | 5.7 |
| Belorussians | 4.6 | 7.1 | 1.9 | Belorussians | 9.0 | 12.5 | 5.4 |
| Uzbeks | 4.8 | 10.1 | 3.2 | Uzbeks | 4.4 | 6.9 | 3.7 |
| Kazakhs | 6.0 | 11.4 | 4.0 | Kazakhs | 6.9 | 9.2 | 6.0 |
| Georgians | 13.3 | 23.8 | 4.8 | Georgians | 11.4 | 13.9 | 9.4 |
| Azerbaidjanis | 7.3 | 13.5 | 2.8 | Azerbaidjanis | 8.4 | 11.1 | 6.5 |
| Lithuanians | 5.2 | 8.8 | 1.5 | Lithuanians | 8.6 | 11.6 | 5.5 |
| Moldavians | 2.2 | 5.9 | 1.4 | Moldavians | 3.8 | 7.4 | 3.0 |
| Latvians | 5.8 | 8.2 | 2.7 | Latvians | 12.3 | 14.5 | 9.3 |
| Kirgiz | 5.3 | 14.8 | 3.7 | Kirgiz | 5.2 | 8.9 | 4.7 |
| Tadjiks | 4.3 | 9.0 | 2.8 | Tadjiks | 4.1 | 6.3 | 3.4 |
| Armenians | 9.6 | 12.8 | 3.0 | Armenians | 8.1 | 9.5 | 5.5 |
| Turkmen | 4.9 | 9.4 | 3.2 | Turkmen | 4.6 | 7.3 | 3.5 |
| Estonians | 7.0 | 9.5 | 3.0 | Estonians | 11.6 | 13.1 | 9.3 |

SOURCE: *Itogi vsesoyuznoi perepisi naselenia 1970 goda*, T.IV, Table 57, pp. 601f.

TABLE 4.3 Educational level of certain national groups in the RSFSR, 1970

| Nationality | %age with full tertiary | | | %age with secondary specialist | | |
|---|---|---|---|---|---|---|
| | All | Urban | Rural | All | Urban | Rural |
| Russians | 6.5 | 8.2 | 2.4 | 11.5 | 13.3 | 7.4 |
| Ukrainians | 9.4 | 11.4 | 3.8 | 13.5 | 15.1 | 9.0 |
| Belorussians | 6.9 | 8.1 | 3.1 | 11.6 | 12.7 | 8.0 |
| Balkars | 5.9 | 10.4 | 3.8 | 6.6 | 9.3 | 5.4 |
| Bashkirs | 2.8 | 5.5 | 1.7 | 5.4 | 7.8 | 4.3 |
| Buryats | 9.1 | 18.5 | 5.7 | 5.2 | 12.5 | 8.0 |
| Kumyks | 4.1 | 5.9 | 2.7 | 8.0 | 9.5 | 6.8 |
| Ingushis | 3.1 | 6.6 | 1.4 | 3.8 | 6.4 | 2.6 |
| Kalmyks | 3.8 | 7.2 | 1.5 | 6.6 | 9.6 | 4.6 |
| Karelians | 2.1 | 3.4 | 1.0 | 7.8 | 10.0 | 5.9 |
| Komi | 3.6 | 6.3 | 1.8 | 11.8 | 14.7 | 10.0 |
| Mari | 2.0 | 4.1 | 1.5 | 4.6 | 7.3 | 3.8 |
| Mordvians | 1.9 | 3.0 | 1.2 | 4.9 | 6.3 | 4.0 |
| Ossetians | 9.2 | 12.5 | 5.0 | 12.9 | 15.9 | 9.0 |
| Tatars | 3.7 | 4.9 | 2.0 | 6.5 | 7.8 | 4.8 |
| Tuvinians | 3.3 | 8.1 | 2.3 | 5.6 | 7.2 | 5.3 |
| Udmurts | 2.4 | 3.5 | 1.8 | 6.0 | 7.0 | 5.4 |
| Chechens | 1.5 | 3.3 | 1.1 | 2.7 | 4.0 | 2.4 |
| Chuvashis | 2.7 | 4.6 | 1.8 | 6.1 | 9.1 | 4.6 |
| Yakuts | 6.1 | 13.5 | 4.0 | 10.6 | 13.4 | 9.9 |
| Jews | 46.8 | 47.1 | 36.2 | 17.3 | 17.3 | 18.5 |

SOURCE: *Itogi vsesoyuznoi perepisi naselenia 1970 goda*, T.IV, Table 58, pp. 606f.

The differences between European and Asian and Trans-Caucasian national intelligentsias in terms of the level of qualifications reflect a continued preponderance of the traditional intelligentsia among the latter. The Slavic and Baltic nationalities' intelligentsias have been more 'modernized' with an increase in the organic elements and a relative weakening of the traditional elements. This reflects uneven rates of industrialization (especially in producer goods industry) and urbanization. There are proportionately more engineers and technicians but fewer teachers and cultural workers in European Russia than there are amongst central Asian and Trans-Caucasian nations (see Table 4.7). The expansion of tertiary education and the establishment of Academies of Science in the Central Asian republics (both of which were accelerated in the late 1950s) have provided new opportunities for the national intelligentsias. Thus the Uzbek proportion of academics and scientific workers in Uzbekistan increased from 34.4 per cent in 1960 to 48.1

TABLE 4.4 The ethnic composition of scientific workers, 1950 and 1960: USSR

| | 1950 | | | 1960 | |
| Nationality | Number | %age | Nationality | Number | %age |
| --- | --- | --- | --- | --- | --- |
| Total including: | 162,508 | 100 | Total | 354,158 | 100 |
| Russians | 98,948 | 60.9 | Russians | 229,547 | 64.8 |
| Jews | 25,125 | 15.4 | Ukrainians | 35,426 | 10.0 |
| Ukrainians | 14,692 | 9.0 | Jews | 33,529 | 9.5 |
| Georgians | 4,263 | 2.6 | Georgians | 8,306 | 2.3 |
| Armenians | 3,864 | 2.4 | Armenians | 8,001 | 2.3 |
| Belorussians | 2,713 | 1.7 | Belorussians | 6,358 | 1.9 |
| Azerbaidjanis | 1,932 | 1.2 | Azerbaidjanis | 4,972 | 1.4 |
| Latvians | 1,468 | 0.9 | Uzbeks | 3,748 | 1.1 |
| Tatars | 1,297 | 0.8 | Tatars | 3,691 | 1.0 |
| Estonians | 1,235 | 0.8 | Lithuanians | 2,959 | 0.8 |
| Lithuanians | 1,213 | 0.7 | Latvians | 2,662 | 0.8 |
| Uzbeks | 845 | 0.5 | Kazakhs | 2,290 | 0.6 |
| Kazakhs | 739 | 0.5 | Estonians | 2,048 | 0.6 |
| Chuvashis | 301 | 0.2 | Tadjiks | 866 | 0.2 |
| Ossetians | 300 | 0.2 | Turkmen | 707 | 0.2 |
| Tadjiks | 168 | 0.1 | Chuvashis | 606 | 0.2 |
| Bashkirs | 146 | 0.1 | Ossetians | 592 | 0.17 |
| Turkmen | 128 | 0.08 | Moldavians | 590 | 0.17 |
| Moldavians | 126 | 0.08 | Kirgiz | 586 | 0.17 |
| Kirgiz | 94 | 0.06 | Bashkirs | 391 | 0.11 |

NOTE: Minor ethnic groups are not included.
SOURCE: *Nar. khoz. SSSR 1922–1972*, p. 105.

per cent in 1975, while the proportion of Russians declined from 38.4 to 27.9 per cent. By 1975 the Uzbeks were the most highly qualified group amongst academics and scientific workers in Uzbekistan (Table 4.6).

## Differences in qualifications as between professions

Since the intelligentsia represent the most highly qualified mental workers in the general workforce it is useful to consider what proportion they are of various professional groups. It will be found that the highest proportions with tertiary qualifications are located in the traditional intelligentsia. Thus in 1970 amongst medical doctors 90.1 per cent had tertiary qualifications, compared with 85.5 per cent of research scientists and academics, 70.3 per cent of jurists, 54.7 per cent of workers in literature and journalism and 53

TABLE 4.5 The ethnic composition of scientific workers 1970 and 1975: USSR

| | 1970 | | | 1975 | |
|---|---|---|---|---|---|
| Nationality | Number | %age | Nationality | Number | %age |
| Total including: | 927,709 | 100 | Total | 1,223,438 | 100 |
| Russians | 611,883 | 66.0 | Russians | 818,246 | 66.7 |
| Ukrainians | 100,215 | 10.9 | Ukrainians | 134,243 | 10.9 |
| Jews | 64,392 | 7.0 | Jews | 69,374 | 5.7 |
| Armenians | 20,194 | 2.2 | Armenians | 26,777 | 2.2 |
| Belorussians | 18,968 | 2.0 | Belorussians | 26,501 | 2.2 |
| Georgians | 18,433 | 2.0 | Georgians | 22,673 | 1.8 |
| Azerbaidjanis | 13,017 | 1.4 | Azerbaidjanis | 16,826 | 1.4 |
| Uzbeks | 12,140 | 1.3 | Uzbeks | 16,062 | 1.3 |
| Tatars | 11,617 | 1.2 | Tatars | 15,920 | 1.3 |
| Lithuanians | 8,168 | 0.9 | Kazakhs | 11,463 | 0.9 |
| Kazakhs | 7,905 | 0.85 | Lithuanians | 11,230 | 0.9 |
| Latvians | 5,953 | 0.64 | Latvians | 7,469 | 0.6 |
| Estonians | 4,693 | 0.51 | Estonians | 5,829 | 0.48 |
| Moldavians | 2,485 | 0.27 | Moldavians | 3,560 | 0.29 |
| Tadjiks | 2,358 | 0.26 | Tadjiks | 3,235 | 0.26 |
| Kirgiz | 1,902 | 0.2 | Kirgiz | 2,708 | 0.22 |
| Turkmen | 1,825 | 0.2 | Turkmen | 2,504 | 0.21 |
| Chuvashis | 1,786 | 0.19 | Chuvashis | 2,469 | 0.20 |
| Osetians | 1,579 | 0.17 | Osetians | 2,265 | 0.18 |
| Bashkirs | 1,420 | 0.15 | Bashkirs | 1,962 | 0.16 |

NOTE: Minor ethnic groups are not included.
SOURCES: *Nar. khoz. SSSR 1922–1972*, p. 105.
*Nar. khoz. SSSR za 60 let*, p. 142.

per cent of engineers. On the other hand only 37 per cent of heads of Party and other public organizations and 35.4 per cent of heads of state departments and divisions had tertiary qualifications. Only 24.7 per cent of engineering-technical workers (ITRs) and 22.2 per cent of medical workers had tertiary qualifications. Only 12.8 per cent of workers in cultural-enlightenment, 8.0 per cent of workers in planning and accounting agencies and 5.8 per cent of workers in municipal services had tertiary qualifications. The proportion of professional workers without formal tertiary or secondary specialist qualifications ranged from 1.7 per cent amongst medical workers to 91.6 amongst typists and stenographers. It was 31.6 per cent of engineering-technical workers, 41.2 per cent amongst heads of state

TABLE 4.6   National composition of scientific workers in Uzbekistan 1960, and 1975

| | Nationality | | No. with degree of Dr. Sci or Cand. Sc. | |
|---|---|---|---|---|
| | *1960* | *1975* | *1960* | *1975* |
| Total including: | 10,329 | 30,835 | | |
| Uzbeks | 3,552 | 14,821 | 899 | 6,365 |
| | (34.4%) | (48.1%) | (25.3%) | (42.9%) |
| Russians | 3,971 | 8,623 | 995 | 2,334 |
| | (38.4%) | (27.9%) | (25.1%) | (28.2%) |
| Jews | 857 | 1,840 | 307 | 732 |
| | (8.3%) | (5.9%) | (36.6%) | (39.2%) |
| Tatars | 566 | 1,588 | 123 | 484 |
| | (5.5%) | (5.2%) | (21.7%) | (30.5%) |
| Ukrainians | 321 | 837 | 80 | 184 |
| | (3.3%) | (2.7%) | (24.7%) | (23.2%) |

NOTE:  Minor ethnic groups are not included.

(Adapted from table in *Sovetskaya intelligentsia Uzbekistana*, T.II, I.M. Muminov et al., Tashkent, 1979, p. 258.)

departments and their divisions and 28.9 per cent of economic managers (Table 4.10).

I have sought in this short chapter on the Soviet intelligentsia to show that it can be understood in terms of Gramsci's distinction between 'traditional' and 'organic' intellectuals. As Gramsci stated:

> One of the most important characteristics of every class which develops towards power is its struggle to assimilate and conquer 'ideologically' the traditional intellectuals. Assimilations and conquests are the more rapid and effective the more the given social class puts forward simultaneously its own organic intellectuals.[15]

This was particularly true of the development of the Soviet intelligentsia in the first decade after the October Revolution. In the years after 1928 autonomous 'civil society' was largely eliminated. The progressive transformation of the structure of the intelligentsia was no longer a relatively autonomous process but was controlled by the political leadership and the economic planners. The Party established a rigid control over the ideological and political training of

TABLE 4.7  Percentage of Asian nationals in particular professions (expressed as percentage of total number employed mainly in mental labour)

| | 1970 Census | | | | | |
| | USSR | Uzbek | Kazakh | Kirghis | Tadjik | Turkmen |
|---|---|---|---|---|---|---|
| Engineers and technicians | 26.9 | 13 | 12 | 10 | 11 | 13 |
| Teachers, academics, scientific workers | 15.7 | 32 | 25 | 33 | 34 | 30 |
| Doctors and medical workers | 8.7 | 10 | 7 | 8 | 7 | 10 |
| Cultural workers | 2.6 | 3 | 4 | 4 | 4 | 4 |
| Agronomists, zootechnicians, veterinarians, forestry specialists | 2.0 | 3 | 6 | 5 | 3 | 3 |

SOURCES: USSR Census and T.S. Labutova, 'The Occupations of the Population of the USSR', in G.M. Maksimov, *Vsesoyuznaya perepis naselenia 1970 goda*, Moscow, 1976.

Soviet specialists. Long before the outbreak of war in June 1941 the two most representative figures in the new Soviet intelligentsia were the engineer-technician and the 'official' of the superstructure – Party officials, state officials and educational-cultural workers.

Despite the tendency towards uniformity in the structure of the intelligentsia there are still important differences between rural and urban intelligentsia, between men and women specialists and between individual republics and nationalities. Differences between national intelligentsias reflect uneven rates of economic development but they also reflect traditional cultural preferences and prejudices. Thus not only are the 'traditional' intelligentsia stronger amongst Central Asian nationalities but the proportion of women students and professionals is much below that of European Russia.

Although women comprise the bulk of all professionals (59 per cent) they provide only 52 per cent of specialists with tertiary qualifications but 63 per cent of secondary specialists. If a distinction is to be made between the intelligentsia proper and the 'semi-intelligentsia' then women are more characteristic of this 'intellec-

TABLE 4.8 Women in the scientific workforce 1950–1980
Numbers in 1000s at the end of the year. Figures in brackets are
percentages of the total number of scientific workers in each
category.

|  | 1950 | 1960 | 1970 | 1980 |
|---|---|---|---|---|
| All scientific workers* | 162.5 | 354.2 | 927.7 | 1,373.3 |
| All women scientific workers | 59.0 | 128.7 | 359.9 | 548.1 |
|  | (36.3) | (36.3) | (38.8) | (39.9) |
| Number with higher degrees |  |  |  |  |
| ● Doctor of Science | 0.6 | 1.1 | 3.1 | 5.2 |
|  | (7.2) | (10.1) | (13.1) | (13.8) |
| ● Candidate of Science | 11.4 | 28.8 | 60.7 | 111.2 |
|  | (25.1) | (29.3) | (27.0) | (28.1) |
| Academicians, corresponding members professors | 0.5 | 0.7 | 1.8 | 3.0 |
|  | (5.6) | (7.1) | (9.9) | (10.9) |
| Readers | 3.2 | 6.2 | 14.4 | 26.3 |
|  | (14.7) | (17.1) | (21.0) | (23.8) |
| Senior research fellows | 3.5 | 5.8 | 9.8 | 14.9 |
|  | (30.7) | (28.6) | (25.1) | (22.6) |
| Junior research fellows | 9.4 | 13.6 | 24.3 | 19.1 |
|  | (47.9) | (50.9) | (49.8) | (46.5) |

* Including academics.
SOURCES: *Zhenshchiny v SSSR* (1982), p. 15.
*Nar. khoz. SSSR v 1980g.*, p. 95.
In 1983 40 per cent of all scientific workers were women. Of 577,300 women
scientific workers, 5,600 had the degree of Dr. Science and 123,200 that of Cand. Sc.

tual proletariat'. I would not force this distinction too far as most of
the modern Soviet intelligentsia, like most modern intelligentsias,
consist of narrow specialists. Whether they have tertiary or secondary specialist qualifications makes little difference. They are merely
intellectual workers. 'Intellectuals', in the narrower sense of the
term, are only a small segment of the Soviet intelligentsia, perhaps no
more than one or two million. These are more numerous amongst
the 'traditional' intelligentsia but they are to be found across the
entire stratum of the intelligentsia and semi-intelligentsia, and indeed, throughout the entire society.[16]

TABLE 4.9 Percentage of women students in tertiary and secondary
specialist establishments
(at the beginning of the academic year)

|  | 1940/1 | 1950/1 | 1960/1 | 1970/1 | 1980/1 |
|---|---|---|---|---|---|
| *Tertiary students* | | | | | |
| Percentage of women in total number of students | 58 | 53 | 43 | 49 | 52 |
| *Percentage in:* | | | | | |
| ● Construction, Transport, Communications | 40 | 30 | 30 | 38 | 42 |
| ● Agriculture | 46 | 39 | 27 | 30 | 34 |
| ● Economics and Law | 64 | 57 | 49 | 60 | 67 |
| ● Health, Physical Culture and Sport | 74 | 65 | 56 | 50 | 58 |
| ● Education, Art and Cinematography | 66 | 71 | 63 | 60 | 69 |
| *Secondary specialist students* | | | | | |
| Percentage of women in total number of students | 55 | 64 | 47 | 54 | 56 |
| *Percentage in:* | | | | | |
| ● Construction, etc. | 32 | 35 | 33 | 40 | 43 |
| ● Agriculture | 37 | 41 | 38 | 37 | 37 |
| ● Economics and Law | 60 | 73 | 75 | 83 | 85 |
| ● Health, etc. | 83 | 85 | 84 | 87 | 90 |
| ● Education, Art and Cinematography | 60 | 77 | 76 | 81 | 85 |

SOURCE: *Zhenshchiny v SSSR* (1982), p. 13.

TABLE 4.10 Educational level of persons employed mainly in mental labour 1970 (Figures are in percentages.)

|  | Tertiary | Secondary specialists | Other |
|---|---|---|---|
| Leaders of state depts and their divisions | 35.4 | 24.4 | 41.2 |
| Leaders of Party and other public organizations | 37.0 | 31.7 | 31.3 |
| Economic managers | 34.1 | 37.0 | 28.9 |
| Medical workers | 22.2 | 58.5 | 19.3 |
| ● incl. doctors | 90.1 | 8.2 | 1.7 |
| Scientific workers, academics and teachers | 49.4 | 35.1 | 15.5 |
| ● incl. scientific workers and academics | 85.5 | 9.5 | 5.0 |
| Engineering–technical workers | 24.7 | 43.7 | 31.6 |
| ● incl. engineers | 53.0 | 37.4 | 9.6 |
| ● incl. technicians | 2.3 | 59.0 | 38.7 |
| Agric. scientists and vets. | 30.6 | 50.3 | 19.1 |
| Workers in literature and the press | 54.9 | 19.1 | 26.0 |
| Cultural–enlightenment workers | 12.8 | 27.5 | 59.7 |
| Workers in art | 20.2 | 31.2 | 48.6 |
| Jurists | 70.3 | 15.8 | 13.9 |
| Workers in trade, catering and supply agencies | 8.1 | 28.5 | 63.4 |
| Workers in planning and account. | 8.0 | 27.3 | 64.7 |
| Workers in municipal services | 5.8 | 18.3 | 75.9 |
| Typists and stenographers | 0.8 | 7.6 | 91.6 |
| Secretaries | 2.2 | 12.3 | 85.5 |
| Agents and filing clerks | 2.1 | 14.1 | 83.8 |
| All categories | 23.5 | 35.4 | 41.1 |

SOURCE: *Itogi vsesoyuznoi perepisi naselenia 1970 goda*, T.VI, p. 628f.

# 5 Social Mobility in the Soviet Union

Social mobility is a feature of all modern societies. In the course of a single generation many people change their class and status position. They move into a different social class as they change their relations to production. Industrial workers become capitalists, owners of the means of production, although less frequently than they did in the past. Small farmers and peasants move to the cities and become urban small businessmen or industrial workers. The first example is one of upward social mobility as between classes, the second example is one of horizontal (from rural petty-bourgeoisie to urban petty-bourgeoisie) or downward mobility (from independent farmer to industrial worker). Vertical social mobility, both upwards and downwards, is more characteristic of societies undergoing rapid capitalist development, as in Britain and the United States in the late eighteenth and nineteenth centuries. Horizontal social mobility becomes more noticeable in mature capitalism where educational standards are rising rapidly and where the intensification of the division of labour and professional specialization gives rise to many new occupations. Under these conditions many people move out of manual into white-collar jobs. They move their social status and often their sub-class position but not always their class position.

Social status is a complex problem in any modern industrial society. This is not only because of the diversification of occupations but because the social prestige that is linked to a particular occupation or profession does not correspond all that closely to income or to material life-styles. Furthermore the social prestige which attaches to a profession changes over time. Thus farmers, country storekeepers, butchers, bakers, clergymen, doctors, engine-drivers and carpenters all enjoyed higher prestige seventy years ago than they do today. This makes it difficult to plot the patterns of social mobility as between generations. Thus a senior Australian academic has not necessarily improved his position if his father was a country parson and his grandfather a schoolteacher or a small farmer. A woman academic or doctor has more clearly gained in social esteem (at least amongst her contemporaries) as against her mother and grand-mothers who were but housewives.

I would suggest the following propositions about social mobility.

1  Social mobility, especially vertical social mobility, is characteristic of a society undergoing rapid economic development, indus-trialization and urbanization.
2  Countries undergoing controlled modernization by means of a social revolution often experience higher rates of social mobility than others. This is due to the need to replace the social wastage of war and civil war, to the consequences of class struggle and policies designed to accelerate the mobility of particular classes or social groups, and purges. (All were characteristic of the Soviet Union during the first forty years of its existence.)
3  The amount of social mobility does not necessarily decrease as economic growth slackens but it becomes more complex. The amount of horizontal social mobility may even increase and assume new forms.
4  Education, always important in the process of social mobility, becomes the main highway to social advancement under condi-tions of mature socialism. It follows from this that any restrictions on access to higher education will be unpopular since they limit the chances of social advancement.

## The Soviet record to 1970

The first decade of Soviet power saw little new economic growth although the economy experienced a rapid recovery after 1921 so that pre-War agricultural and industrial output was reached by 1927. There was urban recovery after 1922 but it was slow and the population was even more rural in 1927 than it was in 1917. Yet there was considerable social class mobility in these years. The former ruling and administrative class was displaced. Many were killed in the War and Civil War, others went into exile or were de-classed. Their places were taken by men who came up through the Red Army or the Party apparatus. The expansion in education (especially secondary specialist courses) produced a large number of places for specialists, who were recruited often from the ranks of the workers and the peasantry. If the early years favoured those with working-class or peasant background this was changed in 1926 with the adoption of competitive examinations as the main method of entrance to tertiary institutes. Even so about half of Soviet tertiary students in 1927 had working-class or peasant backgrounds.[1] The adoption of the First Five Year Plan in October 1928 intensified the industrialization drive and also urbanization. Collectivization displaced many millions of peasants most of whom became industrial workers. Industrial expansion required an increased number of skilled workers, technicians and engineers, making it possible for hundreds of thousands and eventually for millions to change their social status. Whereas only 16 per cent of the population was urban in 1922, by 1940 is was 33 per cent.[2] Between 1928 and 1941 the number of employed specialists with tertiary and secondary specialist education rose from 521,000 to 2,400,000, an almost five-fold increase. By 1941 engineers, technicians and agricultural scientists (production specialists) formed 32.3 per cent of all employed specialists and represented the second largest group (second to education and culture) in the intelligentsia.[3] The new specialists were drawn unevenly from various social groups. One Soviet estimate on the social origins of tertiary students throughout the 1930s gives 42.2 per cent of students coming from non-manual workers when this section represented 17.5 per cent of the population. On the other hand 33.9 per cent of students came from the homes of manual workers (32.3 per cent of the population and only 21.7 per cent came from the peasantry (46.4 per cent of the population).[4]

It must not be imagined that the accelerated social mobility of the 1930s was a peaceful process. Millions of peasants, and not merely *kulaks*, were uprooted during the collectivization drive of 1929–33. The purges of 1936–8 removed several million people either to their execution or to enforced dispersal in the Gulag archipelago. More than half a million Party members were purged. Since the purge was directed primarily at upper and intermediate levels of the Party and state apparatus and at the intelligentsia many vacancies occurred in these structures which had to be filled by new recruits. Future leaders such as Khruschchev, Brezhnev, Kosygin and Podgorny benefited and gained accelerated promotion. Hundreds of thousands did likewise. No wonder it was a decade which saw a rapid increase in social mobility.

In many ways the years of the Great Patriotic War (1941–5) saw a repetition of what had occurred during the Civil War. The Army again became the major road for promotion, at least for those who survived. Recruitment to the Party from both working class and peasantry was increased. Rank and file soldiers won promotion on battle fields and moved into Officers' Training Schools. At the end of the War ex-servicemen enjoyed preference in admission to both tertiary secondary specialist institutes. More than twenty million Soviet citizens lost their lives in the War. Since the largest number were young men between the ages of eighteen and thirty-five years, there were great gaps left in the civilian workforce. The War therefore saw a rapid acceleration in the movement of women into the workforce generally and into the professional workforce in particular. Women became a majority of the workforce during the War years while they increased their percentage of the specialists in the workforce from 36 in 1941 to 61 in 1955.[5] The evacuation of many large industries, educational and scientific institutes from European Russia and the Ukraine to Central Asia during the War years provided a stimulus to the economic and social development of that region. It also accelerated the educational development and the social promotion of the indigenous peoples.

Between 1950 and 1975 the urban proportion of the Soviet population increased from 39 to 60 per cent. The social consequences of this increase will be better realized if I cite the actual numbers. Over these twenty-five years the urban population more than doubled and it increased by 82.5 million.[6] Over the same period the rural population fell by 7.7 million people.* Urbanization at such a rate required great social mobility. Rural migrants as well as urban-born workers benefited by the vast increase in the range and number of jobs offering. In the countryside increased capitalization of agriculture and higher educational standards of the population meant more opportunities for skilled workers and specialists. More and more specialists were working directly in production. In 1975 production specialists (engineers, technicians and agricultural specialists) comprised 48.5 per cent of the specialist workforce. On the other hand some main groups of the traditional intelligentsia were in relative decline – educational and cultural specialists had fallen to 20.9 per cent and medical specialists to 13.3 per cent of the total.[7] The Soviet intelligentsia was increasing by leaps and bounds in these years and on into the early 1970s. Between 1950 and 1975 the number of qualified specialists in the workforce rose from 3,254,000 to 22,796,000, a seven-fold increase. This expansion of the intelligentsia was not confined to the European parts of the Soviet Union but occurred in other areas. Thus in Uzbekistan the number of tertiary educational establishments rose from 30 to 42 between 1960 and 1975 and the number of tertiary students rose from 25,016 to 49,011. Over the same period the number of secondary specialist institutes rose from 76 to 187 and the number of students rose from 20,573 to 67,321. There were 35,107 graduates from tertiary institutes but 51,007 from secondary specialist institutes in 1975. In

---

* The decline in rural population would have been greater had not the rural birthrate continued to be high, especially in Central Asia.

1975 secondary specialists outnumbered tertiary specialists in the Uzbekistan workforce, thus bringing the republic more into line with the USSR as a whole.[8]

## How equal are educational opportunities?

While formal education is not the sole avenue for upward social mobility it has long been the main avenue for those seeking entry into the intelligentsia. It is therefore of primary importance that open access to higher and secondary specialist education is maintained. Universal secondary education has long been the objective of the Soviet government and was to be universal in rural as well as urban areas by 1980. It was claimed that 96 per cent of children were completing full (10 or 11 year) schooling by 1978. Yet there are still drop-outs, especially in some autonomous republics and in some Siberian cities.[9] This arises because some children leave school after completing the 8th grade and although they are supposed to complete the last two years at night school it is difficult to enforce this requirement. But even so only a small proportion of school graduates (about one-eighth in 1979) could proceed immediately to full-time tertiary education. But this fact does not block entry at a later date or by means of evening and correspondence courses. Besides that there are additional places offered in secondary specialist educational establishments. In the 1979–80 academic year there were 5,185,900 tertiary students, 4,646,500 students at secondary specialist institutes and 4,026,000 students attending secondary professional-technical schools.[10] By 1979 there were approximately 600,000 VUZ entrants but over one and a half million applicants. This figure was less than 30 per cent of school graduates which confirmed sociological investigations during the late 1970s that had shown a declining enthusiasm (or greater realism) on the part of school leavers for VUZ education.[11] Sociological investigations in the 1960s had shown a much stronger demand for VUZ positions amongst school leavers.

The discussion in the preceding paragraph has shown that there is strong competition to secure tertiary education in the Soviet Union. How equal is the access to higher education? During the 1970s special efforts were made by the government to recruit as many students as possible from the ranks of working-class and rural youth. Most tertiary institutes reserve a certain proportion of places (usually between 20 and 30 per cent) for such applicants. In addition working-class and peasant youth compete with other groups for the open places. Because of the recognized social disadvantages of working-class and peasant youth compete with other groups for the most VUZy run a preliminary year-long course to bring them up to the necessary standard. These measures have certainly increased the proportion of working-class and peasant youth undergoing higher education. But (as the figures in Table 5.1 show) workers and peasant children are still proportionally less than the children of white-collar workers and specialists. This results largely from the fact that proportionally more of the latter have an uninterrupted and family-encouraged secondary education and therefore win more of the available open places at VUZy.

TABLE 5.1   Social composition of students entering VUZy 1969–75 (in percentages)

| Region | Social group* | Academic year | | | |
|---|---|---|---|---|---|
| | | 1969–70 | 1970/1 | 1973/4 | 1975/6 |
| Moscow | MW | 27.4 | 32.0 | 38.1 | 40.4 |
| | CF | 5.9 | 4.6 | 3.6 | 5.1 |
| | E | 66.7 | 63.4 | 58.3 | 54.3 |
| Novosibirsk | MW | 43.5 | 36.3 | 48.7 | 48.0 |
| | CF | 7.6 | 12.0 | 5.4 | 5.8 |
| | E | 48.9 | 51.7 | 45.9 | 46.2 |
| Sverdlovsk | MW | 42.5 | 47.7 | 49.7 | 49.1 |
| | CF | 3.2 | 3.6 | 2.4 | 2.1 |
| | E | 54.3 | 54.0 | 47.9 | 48.8 |
| Odessa | MW | 43.2 | 44.5 | 44.9 | 46.4 |
| | CF | 22.4 | 22.0 | 19.8 | 22.0 |
| | E | 34.4 | 33.5 | 35.3 | 31.6 |
| Estonia | MW | 40.5 | 39.9 | 47.0 | 51.1 |
| | CF | 10.0 | 9.8 | 6.8 | 6.2 |
| | E | 49.5 | 47.4 | 46.1 | 42.7 |

* Includes children of these social groups.
  MW = Manual Worker, CF = Collective Farmer, E = Employee.
SOURCE: M.N. Rutkevich and F.R. Filippov, (eds)., (1978). Adapted from Table 48, p. 141.

## Patterns of social mobility

I have already referred in the preceding section to various patterns of social mobility as between women and men, Russians and non-Russians, manual workers and white-collar workers and intelligentsia. In this section I will examine these differences more closely.

Quite a lot can be gained from Soviet statistics as well as from sociological research about the social mobility of Soviet women. Statistics show that women are more dependent on formal educational qualifications than are men. We also know that women – for whatever reasons – are much more heavily concentrated in the lower-grade professions. Thus in 1975 women comprised 52.4 per cent of specialists with tertiary qualifications but 63.4 per cent of specialists with secondary specialist qualifications. Women tertiary students are far from evenly spread between different VUZy and disciplines. Thus in the 1975–6 academic year women constituted 50.9 per cent of university students but only 41.5 per cent in technology and energetics. They formed 45.3 per cent of students in agriculture, 80.1 per cent of student teachers and 64.3 per cent of medical students.[12] Behind these differences lie different preferences for professional careers as between girls and boys, a subject much studied by Soviet sociologists during the 1960s and 1970s. Women seem to have lower expectations in choosing a professional career. They are willing to accept the less prestigious and less remunerative branches of teaching and medicine, to become primary or secondary teachers while the men seek jobs in educational research or as academics. Likewise women rate general medical practice highly whereas men value surgery and medical research work. The same preferences are found in women's choices within lower grade professions. Their greater strength in secondary specialist institutes seems mainly due to their preference for a shorter course of professional training. This choice is often linked to family responsibilities.

Marriage is not favourably regarded as a career in itself, except perhaps in the countryside of Central Asia. The extent to which this happens has not, to my knowledge, been closely examined by Soviet sociologists. But the practice is often noted in Soviet novels and films and no doubt is fairly common in real life. The female student who marries her professor on the eve of graduation or the secretary who marries the chief engineer are both experiencing upward social mobility, whether deliberate or not. (In like manner young ambitious males often experience accelerated academic or political promotion if they happen to marry the daughter of a Party boss.) Women professionals often marry skilled manual workers but this does not represent downward social mobility, at least not in the Soviet Union.

Political careers are more limited for women than they are for men. The percentage of women Party members is increasing; they formed 26.5 per cent of the membership in January 1981 but only 22.2 per cent ten years earlier. They are already becoming common as secretaries and committee members at district, city and area levels.* They are even more numerous in the lower levels of Soviets and trade unions. Thus in 1976 women constituted 34.6 per cent of central trade union officials, 44.2 per cent of republican officials and more than half of lower level union officials.

While formal education has been relatively more important to Soviet women than to men as a means of social mobility, many Soviet women in the manual workforce have gained promotion by acquiring skills through job training. This is particularly true of the urban workforce where as early as 1970 women comprised 54 per cent of the drivers of underground trains and trolleybuses, 16 per cent of workers in machine building, including one-quarter of lathe operators. Women provide most of the skilled workers in textile manufacture and a considerable number of those in construction. In agriculture women provide the bulk of the unskilled workers and only a minority of the skilled manual workers. But they dominate branches such as dairying and poultry keeping and there have long been women tractor drivers and combine-harvester operators.

Social mobility amongst national minorities is a complex and uneven process. As with women, education provides the main avenue for the socially mobile non-Russians. In the early stages of this development it was mainly through tertiary education but secondary specialist training was extending rapidly in the Central Asian republics and in autonomous republics from the late 1960s onwards. The importance of education in the social mobility of Central Asian nationalities is shown by the fact that as early as 1970 the educational level of the urban workforce (measured as a proportion of the workforce with tertiary qualifications) of Kirgiz, Kazakh, Uzbek, Turkmen and Tadjik urban workers and employees was higher than that of urban Russians. It was far higher in Georgia and Armenia. Such emphasis on higher education by indigenous nationals undoubtedly facilitated their movement into local administration and into the Party. Long before 1960 most administrative posts in Central Asia were held by members of indigenous national groups. By the beginning of 1982 there were one and a third of a million Uzbeks, Tatars, Kazakhs, Kirgiz, Tadjiks and Turkmen in the ranks of the Communist Party, more than 7.4 per cent of the total membership.†[13]

Most national intelligentsia make their careers in their own republics but many do not. They are more highly mobile than their countrymen both because of their qualifications and their greater

---

* Very few women were first secretaries – none at all at republican or regional levels.

† This still left most Asian nationalities grossly underrepresented in the CPSU.

fluency in Russian. Those who study at VUZy in cities like Moscow, Leningrad or Kiev often take jobs out of their own republic on graduation. Thus a Dagestani engineering graduate from a Moscow VUZ might take a job in a Riga research institute, stay there and marry a Latvian architect. An Armenian woman philology student at Leningrad might become an interpreter in a mainly Russian city and marry a Russian engineer. An Armenian secondary teacher might attend a Party school in Kiev, marry a Ukrainian woman and return to a *nomenklatured* position in Erevan. Arutyunyan's researches into ethnicity in the 1960s and 1970s showed that people with higher education were more likely to welcome friendships and marriage with those of other nations.[14]

Cultural resistance, rural predominance as well as slow diversification of the economy in some areas retarded the mobility of members of national minorities. Thus Akhmuradov complained of the slow movement of indigenous nationals into the expanding working class of Turkmenia.[15] Arutyunyan found that only one-tenth of Russian and Tatar children in the rural areas of the Tatar ASSR entered tertiary institutes whereas it was one in five in urban areas.[16] However he noted that more than a quarter of Tatars (26 per cent) and Russians (31 per cent) had raised their social status in comparison with their parents and that the Tatars had started from lower positions and had travelled much further in social development than the Russians.[17]

Formal education for professional occupations has not been the main road to social promotion for the rural farming population. Up until the end of the 1970s most children aspiring to higher education succeeded only in entering the farm workforce as manual workers or became industrial or construction workers. Movement out of agriculture was easier for young men who often acquired rudimentary skills while doing their military service and found it easier than the young women to transfer to the urban workforce. Those who stayed on the farms often became skilled workers, mechanizers, gaining this promotion after short on-site training courses. Few stayed as tractor drivers or harvester operators for more than two or three years; they transferred their skills to construction sites or to jobs in urban areas. It was generally easier for rural youth to get into agricultural or primary teacher training schools than to get into VUZy. Those who did manage to enter VUZy came disproportionately from the homes of rural specialists and white-collar workers.[18] Whether from tertiary or secondary specialist institutes, few of the students came from the countryside and then returned to the farms and country towns to take up the steadily expanding number of specialist positions.*

---

* Migration (and upward mobility) of rural youth is further restricted through the differential operation of the internal passport system. See, Victor Zaslavsky (1982).

Industrial workers enjoy greater opportunities for social mobility than do agricultural workers or collective farmers. The children of urban industrial workers are now mostly receiving a complete secondary schooling in the general school system. The minority finish secondary school at evening classes. Thus more working class youth are eligible to proceed immediately to higher or secondary specialist education and increasing numbers are doing so. Others become specialists by degrees. They enter the industrial workforce and qualify fairly quickly as skilled workers. In 1979–80 almost forty-one million workers and employees were undertaking various types of job training, upgrading and political study.[19] Some idea of the impact of this system on the workforce of an individual plant is revealed in a Soviet survey of 1000 workers in a Moscow electrical engineering plant taken in the mid-1960s. It showed that 680 who began as semi-skilled operators rose to skilled workers and 295 rose to engineer or technician over a ten-year period.[20] As people already in employment most of these upwardly mobile workers do their tertiary courses as evening students. In most VUZy workers form an absolute majority of evening students. In addition, many workers who do not secure formal professional qualifications nevertheless become specialists, through a combination of low-grade qualifications and practical experience.

The Communist Party has always been an important avenue for social and political promotion. The percentage of manual workers in new recruits has been rising since the end of the 1950s. So too has the percentage of manual workers in the party membership: from 34.5 per cent in 1960 to 45.0 per cent in 1986.* That this increase has not been more rapid is due to the fact that it is mainly skilled and leading workers who are recruited into the Party. They tend to move upwards more rapidly after joining the Party, gain higher education and cease to be manual workers. Some become administrators or trade union officials or are recruited to the Party apparatus. Some become managers – surveys in the Urals region in the late 1960s showed that up to 90 per cent of managers came from the ranks of the manual working class. Those who move up into leading administrative positions in Party and state apparatuses will most likely go through a regional Party-Soviet or a Republican Party School at some stage in their career.

The children who come from the urban specialist and white-collar workforce usually make their social advancement through means of acquiring higher or secondary specialist education. Not only do they complete their secondary education in the minimum time but they often receive private coaching to help them prepare for the VUZ

---

* Figures relate to social position at time of membership census.

entrance exam. They choose their VUZ because of interest in its courses, because of the reputation of its teaching and research staff or because they have friends there.[21] Children of white-collar workers are not quite so advantaged as those of specialists. Both groups have a preference for correspondence courses if they happen to miss out on full-time tertiary education.[22]

Since education is so highly valued as a criterion for admission to the Party, specialists are much more likely to be in the Party than are non-specialists. In January 1986, 31.8 per cent of Party members had a complete tertiary education while a further 2.1 per cent had unfinished tertiary qualifications. About 70 per cent of those with the degree of Doctor of Science were Party members and over half of the Candidates of Science.[23] A small proportion of these will have joined the Party while still students and begun their careers as Party functionaries by holding a position as Secretary of the Institute Komsomol. Such people move very quickly into senior *nomenklatura* positions. The majority however will join the Party after several years of professional work, usually in their thirties. Some prominent scientists join even later.

Within the intelligentsia there is a considerable amount of horizontal as well as upward movement between various professions. Some Soviet sociologists have detected different patterns as between male and female children of prominent intellectuals. There is very little downward mobility at this level and where it does occur it seems to be mainly into the skilled manual workers.[24]

The Soviet Union was often praised in the past as a remarkably 'open' society, more similar to the United States than it was to Western European countries.[25] In more recent times some Western writers have suggested that social mobility is lessening in the Soviet Union as privilege persists and the economy stagnates.[26] There is some evidence to support this view but the evidence is not conclusive. There has certainly been a slowing-down in the expansion of the intelligentsia since 1975 but the expansion has not ceased. In any case social mobility is not solely dependent on the gaining of professional education and other avenues of advancement continue. Urban growth has slowed down in the European part of the Soviet Union but it is accelerating in other regions, especially in Eastern Siberia. Both job placement and re-training of workers have improved considerably over the past fifteen years which will help to maintain social mobility. The countryside is becoming less dependent on agriculture and there is a slow but steady diversification of jobs.

There are limits to social mobility at present. These include restrictions on access to higher education, a lessening of the rate of economic development, continued domestic and social restrictions on the social mobility of women, and continued cultural restrictions operating against girls and women in some rural areas, especially in Central Asia.

Is there a contradiction between the ideal of social equality and the ideal of careers according to talent and social need? Some Western writers suggest that there is but I rather doubt this. The Soviet socialist ideal is for greater equality but not for absolute equality or uniformity even under Communism.

PART

**2** POLITICAL ESSAYS

# 6 TOWARDS AN ANALYSIS OF SOVIET POLITICS

There has been more written about the Russian Revolution than about any other revolution in history. Most of this writing has been partisan to a greater or lesser degree. This is natural enough when it is remembered that the leaders of the revolution sought the entire reconstruction of the existing social and political order. So participants, witnesses and distant observers were hopelessly divided in their assessment of the revolutionary events. While there were survivors of the revolution, these arguments were continued, for little was forgotten or forgiven. The intense political and military rivalry that has characterized relations between the United States of America and Western Europe on the one hand and the Soviet Union on the other has deepened this partisanship. Academic writing has not escaped these divisions of opinion; indeed it has often intensified them. This was particularly so with the writings of American political theorists, sociologists and political scientists in the 1950s and 1960s.

After the journalists, the historians were the first Westerners to attempt to come to grips with the Bolshevik Revolution. Beginning with historians such as W.H. Chamberlin, Michael T. Florinsky, Bernard Pares and John Maynard in the 1930s the task has continued unabated ever since. All of these works – including the greatest, the fourteen-volume history by E.H. Carr – are to some extent partisan accounts. But they are generally empirical, based on a close attention to historical evidence and seeking to interpret the history of revolutionary Russia against the special circumstances of the Russian past. And in recent years at least much of the bias of historians was not so much outright political partisanship as preference for a particular line of historical interpretation, whether to emphasize the role of individual leaders, competing parties, or of broader social forces.[1]

Political scientists were slower than historians in their attempt to analyse revolutionary Russia. This was not because political science was a weaker discipline than that of history but simply because, much more than the historian, the political scientist was required to focus on the revolutionary present and not merely on the revolutionary past. Besides, it took somewhat longer to sort out the rapidly changing political institutions of Soviet Russia. It was almost twenty years after the Bolshevik Revolution before full length studies of the Soviet political system began to appear in English. Two books appeared in 1935, that by B.W. Maxwell and that by Sidney and Beatrice Webb. By far the more influential of these was the book by the Webbs. Despite its enormous length – the second edition ran into more than 1,200 pages – the book went into three editions in twelve years and sold by the ten thousand.

*Soviet Communism: A New Civilisation?* by Sidney and Beatrice Webb was published in London in 1935. It had an immense impact at the time although it is seldom consulted today. Few Western specialists under fifty would have read it and more conservative specialists openly condemn it. Thus it was described in 1962 as 'one of the most embarrassing performances ever perpetrated by foreign observers of the Russian scene.' [2]

This is somewhat unfair. The Webbs never felt embarrassed at their optimistic evaluation of the Soviet Union and indeed they removed the question mark from the title when they published the second edition in 1937. They were old when they made their visit to Russia in 1934, both nearing eighty. They knew no Russian and so were dependent on interpreters when they made their interviews and dependent on official translations of Soviet material. They were not political scientists by training nor were they experts on any aspect of Russian history. Yet they had the assistance of a Russian emigré historian Mr. S.P. Turin of the School of Slavonic and East European Studies and of the London School of Economics and of other experts.[3] As Fabian socialists they were impressed at the apparent successes of the Soviet regime in its drive to build a more equitable and humane society, at its achievements in the sphere of economic planning and the development of social services. They were gullible and lacking in judgement on many matters but they were not uncritical. They condemned barbarous actions and mistakes of Soviet leaders but they tried to understand why these actions and mistakes occurred. They grossly underestimated the personal power of Stalin and denied his dictatorship, even after the onset of the great purge. The book is sadly lacking in perspective on many things. In the postscript to the second edition the Stakhanovite movement gets almost as much coverage as the treason trials and the terror while 'the success of collective agriculture' gets more attention than either.

Yet *Soviet Communism: A New Civilisation* was not wholly misguided. Unlike the majority of the books published since 1950 the Webbs' book did focus on the democratic elements in Bolshevism. Their concept of 'multiform democracy', of man as citizen, producer and consumer, enabled them to take into their analysis Soviets, public administration, Party, trade unions, cooperatives and social organizations. Their analysis is not wholly focused on central decision-making agencies but also takes in lower levels such as republican and local government. And by more than forty years they anticipated Jerry Hough and Theodore Friedgut in their emphasis on the importance of public participation.[4] Nor was the Webbs' emphasis entirely misplaced as this trend toward mass participation was characteristic of Soviet politics in the years 1934–6 and was only curtailed in the height of the Yezhovshchina and during the War and early post-War years.

The Webbs' book influenced not merely general readers but students and established scholars. I read the book towards the end of 1938 during the second year of my undergraduate course. It had more impact on me than anything I read on Soviet politics in the pre-War years. When I began teaching Soviet politics at the University of Melbourne in early 1945 I found the Webbs an essential reference book. It remained so for several years. It influenced my later decision to concentrate my research into the investigation of local government, and especially into the changes that had occurred since the death of Stalin. I was one of the first Western writers to re-emphasize the importance of Soviet local government.[5]

The influence of the Webbs' book on contemporary writers may be illustrated by a brief reference to two books, one by an Englishman, the other by an American. Pat Sloan's 1937 book on *Soviet Democracy* reveals the strong influence of the Webbs and also of official Soviet material. The influence of the Webbs is even stronger in the case of Samuel N. Harper, whose book *The Government of the Soviet Union* was published in New York in 1937. Samuel N. Harper (1882–1943) was one of the pioneer American specialists in Russian and Soviet studies. He was in Russia during the Russian revolution of 1905. For a quarter of a century he taught Russian Language and Institutions at Chicago University. The book is unusual for books of the 1930s in that it contains an isolated reference to the term 'totalitarian': 'Under a revolutionary regime of constant and intense struggle, political control and manipulation have been extended to all fields. Thus the Soviet system represents a type of "totalitarian" state.'[6]

Despite this acknowledgment of a new concept it plays no role in his analysis. His central framework is derived from the earlier Webbs' book and mass participation is a main concept. The second edition of Harper's book, revised by his last research student Donald

Thompson and published in 1949, is vastly extended to take in the War and post-War years. It still uses the same framework and acknowledges its indebtedness to the Webbs. The concept 'totalitarian' has been dropped in favour of that of 'the Soviet Leviathan'.[7]

It has been argued that the concept 'totalitarian' was fully accepted as applicable to the Soviet Union before the Cold War developed in 1946–7.[8] The term had some acceptance among political theorists and historians but certainly not among political scientists. By and large political scientists of the 1930s and 1940s used a historical-institutional approach. This was true of the books already cited. It was also true of two other key books on Soviet politics published in these years. Michael T. Florinsky of Columbia University published his *Toward an Understanding of the USSR* in New York in 1939. As was to be expected the emphasis was heavily historical. It was also based largely on official Soviet sources and argued against a background of Soviet political theory. In this respect it was like the later books by Towster and myself. Apart from its emphasis on the state structure and Soviet public administration there were chapters on 'Economic Planning' and 'The State in Business'. Julian Towster's *Political Power in the USSR 1917–1947: The Theory and Structure of Government in the Soviet Union* came out in 1948. There are similarities with the earlier books by Harper and Florinsky but it is far more detailed and scholarly in its exposition of both the theory and the practice of Soviet government.

Why then were the books of the 1930s and 1940s so rigidly institutional? The answer is surely to be found in the state of the discipline of political science in these years. It was before the days of political culture, political socialization, developmental politics and model building. The historical emphasis was unquestioned since many of the authors were historians and since books often appeared at the time of important anniversaries such as the twentieth or thirtieth anniversaries of the Bolshevik Revolution. Books were often written as one of a series and were even written to a prescribed formula derived from the analysis of Western states. This was true, for example, of the books by Harper and Florinsky.

## Is the USSR totalitarian?

It is difficult to answer this question without first discussing the history of the term. The word was first used by the Italian philosopher Giovanni Gentile early in 1925. It was soon adopted by Mussolini and the Fascist movement generally. It was occasionally used in English from 1928 onwards to refer to Italian Fascism. The term was appropriated by Nazi German constitutional theorists such as Hans Keller and Carl Schmitt in 1933–4 and by Hitler and other Nazi leaders, although Hitler abandoned it after 1934. Nazi theorists applied the term more widely than did their Italian counterparts. They drew a distinction between German and Italian totalitarianism and also considered Stalinist Russia as totalitarian.[9] Some English theorists (notably G.H. Sabine) accepted this extension of the term as early as 1934 but this was not common. Some historians were using the term by 1936 but not usually in reference to the Soviet Union.[10] And as we have already seen, specialist political scientists did not use it at all. On the eve of the War some Marxist writers began to use the term to describe Stalinist Russia, or at least its economy. Thus Trotsky in 1938 referred to the USSR as being 'totalitarian-bureaucratic', while Hilferding in 1940 defined the Soviet economy as 'a totalitarian state economy'. During the years of the grand alliance 1941–5 the term 'totalitarian' was usually reserved for the enemy Fascist states, Nazi Germany, Fascist Italy, and (less properly) Imperial Japan. The term was not carefully defined and it was not usually applied to the Soviet Union which was an ally.

Early English definitions of totalitarianism stressed the mono-party system and the drive to concentrate all power into the hands of the central state. The historian C. Grant Robertson defined it in 1936 as follows:

A totalitarian state was one where:
(a) the individual exists only for the state;
(b) the function of the state is to concentrate into a collective unity all the power and activities of the life of the community; and,
(c) the supreme end of the state is power – physical power, material power, intellectual, moral and spiritual power, and the acceptance of the principle that 'the end justifies the means'.

The 1938 edition of the *Concise Oxford Dictionary* defined totalitarianism as 'relating to a polity that permits no rival loyalties or parties'. For a time at least post-War definitions remained similar. Thus Rudolf Schlesinger defined it in 1947 as, 'the restriction of the freedom of the individual citizens by a socio-political system dominating and regulating all aspects of their lives and regulating all their actions'.[11]

The conceptualizing of totalitarianism began only after the outbreak of the Cold War in March 1946. It was the work of political theorists and sociologists and to a degree, of constitutional historians, rather than of political scientists specializing in the Soviet system. There were some exceptions amongst sovietologists, in particular Merle Fainsod, McClosky and Turner, and for a time, Z.K. Brzezinski. In England the chief exception was Leonard Schapiro. The pioneer study was that by Hannah Arendt. *The Origins of Totalitarianism* was completed in 1949 although not published until 1951. It is a highly emotional book which is understandable from one who was a refugee from Nazi Germany and who believed that the failure to understand totalitarianism would precipitate World War Three.[12] Despite the title and the theme of the book it does not anywhere set out a careful or elaborate definition of totalitarianism. It is referred to as synonymous with 'total control' and as a novel form of government. Arendt finds the origins of totalitarianism in the atomization of individuals which occurs with the development of mass society: 'Totalitarian movements are mass organizations of atomized, isolated individuals.'[13] The atomization of society leaves the individual a prey to mass organizations, and under the totalitarian state, completely dominated by the leader. The book is mostly about the rise of Nazism and the Soviet Union is not mentioned until almost halfway through the book. Her sources on Soviet politics are meagre and her judgements are sometimes very dubious. Thus she attributes Stalin's success in the succession struggle after Lenin's death as chiefly due to the support he had from the secret police.[14] She also holds that Stalin completed the process of mass atomization of Soviet society through 'the skillful use of repeated purges', an inadequate explanation.[15] The argument that mass society produces atomization and threatens totalitarianism was developed by other American writers in the 1950s, especially by William Kornhauser in *The Politics of Mass Society*.

Since the early 1950s political scientists generally, and American political scientists in particular, have been concerned with the elaboration of models for the analysis of political systems. The totalitarian model was one of these but it was not the only one developed for the analysis of Soviet politics.[16] A model of a political system is an artificially constructed elaboration of the essential features of that system. It is an abstraction from reality designed to facilitate its theoretical analysis. Some writers distinguish between a 'model' and an 'ideal type' but the distinction is difficult to maintain: they are both abstractions from reality. Despite Weber's repeated warnings against the misuse of 'ideal types' many writers have ignored them in practice in their analysis of totalitarianism.[17] They have repeatedly confused the complex and contradictory reality with the purity of the ideal type. This has had disastrous consequences in the interpretation of Soviet politics. For example, very many writers have found it impossible to assess the reduction in the coercive police system in the USSR since 1954, because they held fast to the view that terror is a fundamental and unchanging element in a totalitarian system. Indeed, many models of totalitarianism have been too rigidly constructed to allow them to accommodate anything more than minor change.

Models of political systems are differently constructed. Some are relatively simple and adjustable. Some are relatively rigid while others are coupled to specific changes of historical development or to particular societies. All models of totalitarianism produce difficulties when applied to the Soviet Union, although the difficulties are not always the same.

Perhaps the most influential model of totalitarianism was that produced by Professor C.J. Friedrich of Harvard University. His two major studies (published in 1954 and 1956) involved the use of a relatively static model. This consisted of a six point syndrome of the essential elements of totalitarianism. These were:

- An official chiliastic ideology.
- A single mass party, led typically by one man, such a party being hierarchically, oligarchically organized and either superior to or completely intertwined with the bureaucratic governmental organization.
- A system of terroristic police control.
- A monopoly by the party of the means of control and communication.
- A near monopoly of control of the effective means of armed combat.
- Central control and direction of the entire economy through the bureaucratic coordination of its formerly independent corporate entities, including most associations and group activities.[18]

This model, while certainly not useless as a basis for the analysis of the Soviet Union (especially in the Stalin period), has some obvious deficiencies. Its basis is the identification of the USSR and Nazi Germany, which are regarded – without careful prior examination – as merely variants of a single system: 'Fascist and Communist totalitarian dictatorships are basically alike or at any rate, more nearly like each other than any other system of government, including earlier forms of autocracy.'[19]

This is a circular pattern of argument so it is not surprising that the conclusion merely restates the premise, that 'modern totalitarian regimes are basically alike'. To demonstrate this proposition all that is necessary is to construct a model so that it consists of similar or apparently similar characteristics of Nazi Germany and the Soviet Union. The distortion of Soviet reality is thus two-dimensional. First, major differences in social structure, class basis, party structure, policy, content of ideology, etc., are altogether excluded. They are either ignored or are not even noticed. Second, apparent similarities (as for example, those referred to in the sixth point in the syndrome) are seen as real and the equally important and perhaps more fundamental differences are not examined. Thus the analysis of the similar party-controlled economies ignores such obvious differences as the question of how this 'political penetration' of the economy affected the class relations in the two countries, property ownership, the status and economic role of industrial workers, the objectives and achievements of state planning, etc. Instead we are offered such useless generalizations as the following:

> the modern totalitarian regimes are basically alike in recognizing the vitality of the industrial process, and in considering it as the key to political success, domestic or external. As a result they have made the 'battle for production' a central theme of their action programs, and to achieve it they have penetrated and subordinated their industrial machine to the requirements of the regime.[20]

A second weakness of Friedrich's model is its content. Sympathetic critics have sought to add to its list of essential features or to remove some of its more awkward elements. Thus W. Ebenstein in his review of the 1956 book published in *World Affairs*, January 1958, suggested that two further points be added to Friedrich's syndrome, namely:

- The principle of the totality of goals and means.
- The principle of world domination.

Friedrich obligingly incorporated these two additional points into his syndrome during the 1960s.[21] John S. Reshetar Jr. in 1971 had extended the list to ten essential characteristics.[22] Many critics have pointed out that the fifth point in the original syndrome – a near-complete monopoly of the effective means of armed combat – is an essential characteristic of any modern state. Many have been worried at the rigidity of the model, at the difficulty of applying it to the post-Stalin era. Co-author Brzezinski soon detached himself from the syndrome and in an article 'Totalitarianism and Rationality', published originally in the *American Political Science Review* in September 1956, he not only reduced the number of elements in the system but by reversing the emphasis on terror and ideology made it inherently more flexible. His revised definition was stated thus:

Totalitarianism is a system in which technologically advanced instruments of political power are wielded without restraint, by centralized leadership of an elite movement, for the purpose of effecting a total revolution, including the conditions of man, on the basis of certain arbitrary ideological assumptions proclaimed by the leadership in an atmosphere of enforced unanimity of the entire population.[23]

In later writings Brzezinski argued that the USSR was 'an increasingly mature and voluntarist totalitarian system' (1961), that it was not a totalitarian but an 'ideological system' (1964), and then that it was undergoing degeneration rather than transformation and was best described as a 'bureaucratic Communist dictatorship'.[24] And this ultimate conclusion stemmed directly from his revised totalitarian model which, though more flexible than the original model, still could not accommodate the Brezhnev era.

One of the most persistent British advocates of a totalitarian model has been Leonard Schapiro. It is therefore worth looking at his 1972 book on *Totalitarianism*. Schapiro criticizes the Friedrich syndrome for failing to distinguish instruments from 'contours'.[25] To correct this failure he suggests dividing the 'contours' (the essential shapes) of totalitarianism from the 'pillars' (the instruments of power). Under the former classification he places the Leader, the subjugation of the legal order, control over private morality, and mobilization and mass legitimacy. Under the pillars he places ideology, the Party and the state. This distinction is meant to divide the general features from the particular instruments (varying from one totalitarian country to another) on which the Leader's power is based. There are problems in this distinction. The metaphor is tangled and moves from geography to architecture. Nor is the symmetry of the scheme (3 + 3) self-evident. And why should ideology be regarded as merely a pillar and not a contour? In short, I find this revised version needlessly confusing.

Leonard Schapiro is best known for his book *The Communist Party of the Soviet Union*. He did however publish a short book on the Soviet system generally. *The Government and Politics of the Soviet Union* was published in 1965. This is an admirably concise account of the Soviet system. It makes no use of totalitarianism as a concept or model. It is strictly in the earlier historical-institutional pattern. A single quotation will illustrate its basic approach:

The circumstances in which Lenin's party, the Bolsheviks, became the dominant party, have left their indelible mark. The nature of the revolutions of 1917 (there were two) shaped the

future of the Soviet state. The pattern of Stalin's 'third
revolution' – rapid industrialization, collectivization of
agriculture and total control over society – determines the shape
of government today. It is to history therefore that we turn at the
outset.* [26]

The only worthy textbook on Soviet politics which uses a totalitarian model is that by Merle Fainsod. *How Russia is Ruled* was
completed while Stalin was still living although it was not published
until after his death. The book is historical-institutional in its
approach but the analysis is vastly different to books which preceded
it. The central organizing concept of the book is that of power. The
four parts of the book deal with 'The Pursuit of Power', 'The Role of
the Party', 'Instruments of Rule', and 'Control and Tensions'. To a
much greater extent than in earlier books the focus is on the
Communist Party. It is probably the first textbook on Soviet politics
which makes 'totalitarian' a key concept. Fainsod's book preceded
Friedrich's formulation of his totalitarian syndrome although it
came out after the appearance of Hannah Arendt's *The Origins of
Totalitarianism*. He makes no use of her sociological concepts of
'atomization' and 'mass society'. He did not even bother to define
'totalitarianism' nor did he conceive of it as a movement to transform society totally. He used it only to describe the Leader's drive to
power and to maintain control when he was in power. Power,
control and terror are its essential ingredients.[27] The following
passages from the first edition of the book highlight Fainsod's use of
the term:

> One of the most striking characteristics of modern totalitarian
> dictatorship is its dependence on bureaucratic organization to
> make its control effective . . .

> One of the salient outgrowths of modern totalitarianism is the
> bureaucratization of the power structure. The leader who
> bestrides the peak of the totalitarian edifice is the victim of his
> own limitations. He cannot decide everything, and even when he
> exercises his power to decide he must depend on bureaucratic
> instruments to project his will . . .

> As Stalinism entered its mature phase of totalitarian
> development, its institutional characteristics tended to harden.
> The Party, police, military and administrative apparatuses took

---

* Schapiro's strength was not as a social scientist but as a historian of the theory and
practice of Bolshevism.

on the character of rigid bureaucratic hierarchies . . .

What distinguishes twentieth century totalitarianism from earlier patterns of more primitive dictatorship is not the use of terror and secret police as instruments of control but rather their high development as an organized system of power.[28]

Totalitarianism is still a key concept in the second edition of *How Russia is Ruled* (1963) but it has a lower profile. Whereas the preface to the first edition commenced with the bold statement that 'The aim of this book is to analyse the physiology as well as the anatomy of Soviet totalitarianism', the key concept is missing from the preface to the second (1963) edition. The preface states, more soberly, that: 'The aim of this book is to communicate a sense of the living political processes in which Soviet rulers and subjects are enmeshed.'[29]

There is no explanation of this change unless it is a consequence of the improvement in information about the Soviet system which had occurred over the ten years between the two editions. The term 'totalitarian' appears in the text even more frequently than in the first edition but the references are muted. Thus the opening sentence to Chapter 13 ('Terror as a System of Power') which was quoted earlier for the first edition becomes simply: 'Every totalitarian system makes some place for terror in its system of controls.' [30]

Yet Fainsod was reluctant to abandon the totalitarian framework of his book and this continued to influence his evaluation of the extent of change in the post-Stalin USSR. Thus, after noting the decline in police terror under Khrushchev, he remarks that:

Whether exercised on a massive scale by a Stalin or held in reserve by a Khrushchev, an awareness of its potentialities conditions the behaviour of the totalitarian subject.[31]

But the concluding emphasis is somewhat different:

The Khrushchevian drive for political homogeneity seeks to mobilize the forces and pressures of social coercion as a supplement to and substitute for police coercion.[32]

Chapter 17, the final chapter, had a ring of rigidity about it in the first edition, 'The Political Cohesion of the Soviet System'. But by 1963 prediction seemed less certain and the chapter becomes, 'The Soviet Political System – Problems and Prospects'. The one certainty is that the Soviet political system has changed: 'The Soviet regime today is different in many respects from the political order that took

shape in the first decades after the revolution.' [33]
The third edition of this book, revised and largely rewritten by
Jerry F. Hough came out in 1979. The title was changed to *How the
Soviet Union is Governed*. The 'totalitarian facade' has been abandoned and the emphasis shifted from power to the policy-process.
This change in focus prompts reflections such as the following: 'Yet,
one of the great paradoxes of the systems we have called "totalitarian" has been their strong emphasis upon mass participation as well
as upon tight central controls.' [34] Totalitarian has ceased to be useful
as a concept for the analysis of contemporary Soviet politics and it is
duly confined (as it is in most books published during the 1970s and
1980s) as an exhibit in a museum of historical models. [35]

Merle Fainsod apart, the only other major textbook on Soviet
politics published in English in the 1950s and 1960s to make
'totalitarianism' a key concept was McClosky and Turner, *The
Soviet Dictatorship*, published in 1960. The term gets only fleeting
reference in John N. Hazard's *The Soviet System of Government*
(1957), and it is not used in the books by Derek J.R. Scott of
Manchester (1958), Richard C. Gripp of San Diego (1963), Leonard
Schapiro of London (1965) or in my own 1968 book. McClosky and
Turner are not content with a 'totalitarian facade' as the concept is
part of the central architecture of the book. The term 'dictatorship'
or 'modern dictatorship' is used as a synonym for 'totalitarianism'.
The book is organized along similar lines to Fainsod's but it is less
perceptive and less scholarly. It is based entirely on translated
sources and shows scant familiarity with the problems of historical
interpretation that beset the student of Russian and Soviet history.
Consequently it is more than usually studded with loose generalizations. Thus 'Lenin was more Russian than Marxist' (p.57), the
Bolshevik Revolution was nothing but 'a *coup d'état* engineered by a
small band of hardened revolutionaries' (p.72), while the USSR
Supreme Soviet is a pretence designed to cloak the 'totalitarian
purposes' of the regime (p.349). The book also has more than its fair
share of factual errors. Mass participation is mentioned but it is only
to dismiss it as a myth for it cannot be a reality in a totalitarian
dictatorship. [36] In short, it is a book well forgotten.

If the totalitarian model had been largely abandoned by political
scientists specializing in Soviet politics by the mid-1960s it was still
being used by political theorists, including those specializing in
comparative politics. Thus Almond and Powell in *Comparative
Politics: A Developmental Approach* (1966), distinguished between
primitive and modern political systems and in the latter between
democratic and totalitarian systems. Totalitarian systems are divided into two types, conservative totalitarian systems (as in Nazi

Germany) and radical totalitarian systems (such as the USSR).[37] They do not use a model of totalitarianism and their own conceptual framework is fairly flexible. They are therefore able to achieve a degree of detachment in their comments on the USSR. Thus they observe that:

> The model of totalitarianism would suggest that there is little or no responsive capability in the Soviet system. In fact there is a flow of demands into the political system and a kind of bargaining process among unorganized interest groupings and factions.[38]

Yet while recognizing that political participation is a basic fact of the Soviet system they insist on putting it into a special box of its own; the Soviet Union has only a 'subject political culture' whereas Western democracies have 'participant political cultures'.[39] The theory underlying this book, and others in the same series (the Little, Brown series on comparative politics) derives from the earlier writings of two of its general editors, Gabriel A. Almond and Lucian W. Pye. The first book in the series was an abridged version of Almond and Verba, *The Civic Culture* (1963), a book which marked a major shift in American political science from institutional and group theory to political culture and political socialization.[40]

Frederick C. Barghoorn of Yale provided the volume on the Soviet Union for the series referred to above. The first edition of his *Politics in the USSR* came out in 1966 and immediately achieved distinction. The book provided the first approach to Soviet politics using political culture and political socialization as key concepts. More than half the book is taken up with an exploration of the Soviet system in terms of these concepts. Not only does Barghoorn discuss the dominant political culture but he also explores incipient political subcultures. Consider for example, the following passage:

> The political culture of the USSR, despite the extreme centralization of the Russian political system, is not completely uniform. There are even in this self-proclaimed 'monolithic' polity, pluralistic tendencies, nurtured both by the stubborn survivals of tradition and by the emergent differentiations of a developing industrial economy.

As a consequence of this emphasis on political culture and political socialization Barghoorn expresses no surprise when he acknowledges:

the development of at least a passive acceptance of the political system by a majority of the Soviet citizens and of the passionate conviction of some that they are indeed riding the wave of the future.[41]

All this is in the Almondian tradition. Not so his omission of 'totalitarian' as a useful concept for analysing Soviet politics. The book is notable also as one of the first to focus on 'oligarchy' as a key concept in Soviet politics: 'Post-Stalin Soviet politics has been primarily oligarchic. It is probably true that oligarchy prevailed under Stalin, at least up until 1936–38.[42]

The best proof of the validity of a model in political science is its utility for the analysis of a given field or problem. Judged by this criterion the totalitarian model soon proved unsuitable for the analysis of Soviet politics. The model was discarded by the specialists before it was discarded by the discipline generally. Some specialists, including T.H. Rigby and myself never used the model either in teaching or in research.

How then do I explain the resilience of the model? It is to be explained partly by its ideological content: when the Cold War intensifies it is always able to regain some popularity. It has remained popular with political scientists generally and with comparative politics teachers in particular because of its obvious heuristic qualities. It provides a useful framework around which to organize a comparative course which is theoretical and not merely institutional.[43] Besides that, the totalitarian model at least encouraged students and teachers to focus on the dynamic rather than on the formal institutional aspects of Soviet politics. And it never avoided Weber's admonition that power is the central concept in politics.

## A note on research institutes for the study of the USSR

A research institute for the study of the USSR existed in Berlin as early as 1931, and another at Prague from the early 1930s, but their development in America and Great Britain occurred only after World War Two. The first major centres were the Russian Institute at Columbia and the Russian Research Center at Harvard, both started in 1945. Many early staff members at both centres had worked as interpreters and translators for the OSS (Office of Strategic Services) and other federal government agencies during the War. Some had spent months or years in the Soviet Union during the War or in the immediate pre-War period. Thus Professor John N. Hazard, Professor of Public Law at Columbia, had spent three and a half years in Moscow as a postgraduate student in Law. These two pioneer research centres provided models for later US institutes established in many cities during the Cold War. They also provided the inspiration for the development of the Toronto Centre for Russian and East European Studies, established by H. Gordon Skilling in 1963.

The pioneers of the post-War development of Soviet Studies in Great Britain were often refugees from Soviet Russia or from Nazi Germany or Central Europe. Some had come from families which were strongly anti-Bolshevik; others had been communists or strong supporters of the Soviet Union in the War years or earlier; some were former members of the CPGB while some came from families with interests in tsarist Russia. Whatever their background they shared a common determination to make Soviet Studies an expanding area for teaching and research. Unlike the later generation of Soviet specialists (those who gained their academic positions in the 1970s or early 1980s), they were persons with strong political opinions about the Soviet Union.

The two pioneer British research centres for the study of the USSR were established at Glasgow and Birmingham. Shortly after the end of World War Two Glasgow University established a Department for the Study of the Social and Economic Institutions of the USSR. In July 1949 this department launched the journal *Soviet Studies*, with two of its staff, Rudolf Schlesinger and Jacob Miller, as editors. Almost immediately the journal established itself as the main scholarly journal in English dealing with the Soviet Union. Much of the early material printed consisted of articles, commentaries and translations contributed by the editors themselves. The editors were well-suited to the task. Dr Schlesinger was a Viennese, a graduate in Law of Vienna University. He became a communist while still a student and later settled in Moscow where he became a Comintern official and eventually the secretary of the German Section. He knew Stalin personally. During the purges he was expelled from the Party for being too soft towards Trotskyists. He left the Soviet Union before the War and fled from Poland to England after the Germans invaded Poland in September 1939. He settled in Kilmun on Holy Loch towards the end of the War. Jacob Miller was an economist who had worked in Moscow as an economic planner during the Second Five Year Plan. Together they had an unrivalled experience and understanding of the Soviet system. They remained joint editors for many years, Schlesinger until his retirement from the University in 1966. In mid-1963 the department was reorganized to become the Institute of Soviet and East European Studies. It contains a magnificent specialized library and offers an MA course in Soviet Studies.

Despite its diversification in the mid-1960s it is still primarily concerned with the analysis of Soviet economics and politics. Professor Alec Nove was its director for many years (from 1958). Its present director is Professor W.V. Wallace. Many senior British specialists have held positions at the Glasgow Institute, including Alastair and Mary McAuley, R.W. Davies, J. Newth, John Miller and Archie Brown.

If the early years of the Glasgow Institute owed much to Rudolf Schlesinger, the Birmingham Centre was the result of the efforts of a Russian emigré, Alexander Baykov. Baykov had lectured on Soviet Economics at Charles University in Prague from 1933 and had been a member of the Prokopovich Research Centre. He fled to England in March 1939. He was appointed to a lectureship at Birmingham University at the end of the War and he soon established the Department of Economics and Institutions of the USSR. A considerable research library was built up in what was popularly referred to as the Baykov centre. By the end of 1956 Baykov had been joined by a team of younger English scholars from London and Cambridge, including R.W. Davies, R. Smith and G. Barker.

The Hayter Report produced a qualitative change in the development of Soviet Studies in Great Britain. The report, which came out in 1961, recommended a ten-year programme of government funding to expand regional studies. The government accepted the report and the special funding began in 1962. Much of the funding went to the School of Slavonic and East European Studies in London and to other London colleges already specializing in regional studies. Glasgow received no additional funding but Birmingham was an immediate beneficiary. The existing department became a new inter-faculty Centre for Russian and East European Studies. The new Centre was opened on 1 October 1963 with Professor R.W. Davies as its first director. It was moved to a new octagonal building with ample space for its research staff and its steadily expanding Alexander Baykov Library. Its staff was more diverse than that of any other Soviet Studies centre in Britain. It included linguists, specialists in Soviet literature, economists and economic historians, historians and political scientists, sociologists, engineers and mining specialists. It soon became the most productive research centre in Britain operating in the area of Soviet and East European Studies. In addition to the generous exchange opportunities provided by the British Council, the Birmingham CREES developed its own exchange agreements with Soviet and other East European institutes. Birmingham engineering firms and other exporting firms were also involved in these exchanges.

Whether through the special funding provided under the Hayter report or through normal channels, there was a remarkable expansion of university teaching and research in Soviet Studies during the 1960s and early 1970s. New positions and departments were created at the LSE (ably directed by Professor Leonard Schapiro), Birkbeck, Sussex, Swansea, Leeds, Essex, Oxford (mainly at St Antony's College) and Cambridge. Of these, only the Swansea CREES (under Professor Roger Pethybridge) was a Hayter centre. The newly established University of Essex (at Colchester), with its initial emphasis on the social sciences, provided a unique opportunity for Soviet Studies to develop a new emphasis on the sociological as well as the political analysis of Soviet society. Leading younger specialists such as David Lane, Alastair and Mary McAuley, Geoffrey Hosking and Peter Frank were attracted to Essex and it soon began to rival other centres such as Glasgow, Oxford and Birmingham. The many graduates from its research schools included such outstanding younger specialists as Ronald Hill and Leslie Holmes.

Special funding under the Hayter grants ended in 1972–3, and since 1976 there has been virtually no expansion of Soviet Studies in Britain and a contraction of Russian language training since 1979. However, the larger centres seem to have been fairly successful in holding the ground gained in the 1960s and early 1970s. Another phase of expansion must await the reversal of the restrictive financial policy of the government and an increased public awareness that improved relations and expanded trade with the USSR require further investment in Russian and Soviet Studies.

# 7 Bureaucracy and Communist Politics

Soviet bureaucracy has excited comment and criticism from 1918 onwards. Max Weber and Karl Kautsky drew attention to it in 1918 to be quickly followed by successive left oppositional groups within the Communist Party itself. The culmination of this line of internal criticism was Trotsky's *The Revolution Betrayed*. Criticism of Soviet bureaucracy and bureaucratism has also been a persistent element in official Soviet comment on the Soviet political system at least since 1920.* None of these critics described the Soviet system as purely bureaucratic. This more comprehensive definition is to be found only in the writings of neo-Trotskyists and some Western political scientists. This chapter will be concerned both with modern attempts at analysing the Soviet system in terms of bureaucracy, and the limits of that approach, and with the phenomenon of Soviet bureaucracy. It will also include a discussion of some other post-totalitarian models for the analysis of Soviet politics.

Models of Soviet bureaucracy are almost as old as models of Soviet totalitarianism. In 1954 the Harvard political scientist Barrington Moore published his *Terror and Progress – USSR* which was perhaps the first conscious attempt at applying Max Weber's 'ideal type' for the analysis of the Soviet system. Just as Weber had constructed three ideal types of authority (traditional, charismatic and rational-legal) so Moore found three ideal types in which position and power are distributed in society. These he called traditional, rational-technical and political power (in which position and power are awarded according to loyalty to a political system or leader, party or regime). He found elements of all three types in the Soviet Union but felt that it conformed mainly to the rational-technical type. This type was essentially a bureaucratic type directed at maximizing industrial development. Writing about this model fifteen years later Professor Jerry F. Hough described it as 'by far the

---

* See the Note on the official Soviet approach to bureaucracy at the end of this chapter.

most successful model of its time in predicting the major developments of the post-Stalin political system'.[1] Nevertheless, Hough
made a number of salient criticisms of the model. He criticized it
because it did not recognize that certain Soviet administrative practices could not be summarized as ones of 'enforced conformity to
law'. Secondly, Hough pointed out that Moore was wrong in his
prediction that the Party would decline in influence along with the
police. Thirdly, he criticized Moore for ignoring the continuing role
of local Party organs in industrial administration.[2] Hough was not
rejecting a bureaucratic model but merely seeking one that would
allow for the analysis of the pecularities of the Soviet bureaucracy,
particularly the relations between Party and state agencies.

A decade after the publication of Barrington Moore's *Terror and
Progress – USSR* Professor T.H. Rigby of the Australian National
University, Canberra, published a long article entitled 'Traditional,
Market and Organizational Societies and the USSR', in *World
Politics*, July 1964. Like many other articles of the time this article
reflected the author's increasing discomfort with the totalitarian
model, especially in its mass society variant. It also reflected Rigby's
long-standing interest in Weberian theory. Like Moore's typology
Rigby's is deliberately borrowed from Weber, despite its ignoring of
the distinction between the economic order and the political order.
Rigby's three models are constructed as 'ideal types' which are not
meant to describe any society past or present. Authority in Rigby's
three types of society is based respectively on custom, contract and
command. He finds that the USSR contains elements of all three
types but that it is still predominantly an organizational society,
although less so than it was in the Stalin period. Western parliamentary (capitalist) societies are predominantly market societies,
although they also contain elements of the other two types of society.
Within these broad 'ideal types' Rigby is able to develop a fairly
flexible approach to the changing patterns of Soviet politics.

The organizational society is of course a bureaucratic society
although it is not wedded to Weber's theory of bureaucracy. Indeed
Rigby has been more successful than most writers in his research for
a broader, more relevant bureaucratic theory. He has drawn heavily
on the British theorists Burns and Stalker and tends to argue that
Soviet bureaucracy combines two types of bureaucratic organization: a mechanistic, hierarchical (Weberian) type found characteris-
tically in Soviet state administration, and a generalist or 'staff' type
found more in the Communist Party.[3] This theory of the Soviet
Union as a 'mono-organizational society' has become the dominant
line of interpretation and research at Canberra and is influential
elsewhere. It has been applied to the analysis of changes in the Soviet

system, to the explanation of patronage within the bureaucracy, to
the Soviet approach to research and development, and even to the
analysis of Party Primary Organizations.[4]

Not all those who have argued about Soviet politics in terms of its
essential bureaucracy have been as concerned to use 'ideal types' as
Barrington Moore and T.H. Rigby. This has sometimes been so even
when the writer has invoked Weber's name. Thus Allen Kassof in
1964 described the Soviet Union as an 'administered society'. He
described this as a Weberian 'ideal type' but he did not argue in
Weberian terms. The concept was defined in this way:

> The administered society can be defined as one in which the
> entrenched and extraordinarily powerful ruling group lays claim
> to ultimate and exclusive scientific knowledge of social and
> historical laws and is impelled by a belief not only in the practical
> desirability, but the moral necessity, of planning, direction, and
> coordination from above in the name of human welfare and
> progress.
>
> The administered society is thus a variety of modern
> totalitarianism with the important difference that it operates by
> and without the elements of gross irrationality . . . and terror.[5]

Kassof, like Brzezinski eight years earlier, sought to retain the
totalitarian model but to give it a different emphasis. In this he was
unlike writers such as Alfred G. Meyer and T.H. Rigby who sought
to replace the totalitarian model.

Professor Alfred G. Meyer of Michigan (formerly of Harvard)
developed his interpretation of Soviet politics as 'bureaucracy writ
large' during the early 1960s.[6] In his book *The Soviet Political
System* (1965) he states that 'the USSR can best be understood as
modern bureaucracy writ large' or as 'total bureaucratization'.[7] The
advantage of this approach, he claims, is that bureaucracy is a less
emotive term than totalitarianism and since it is a feature of American society, it enables American students to start examining the
Soviet system on the basis of known institutional and behavioural
patterns. However it is doubtful if either the American political
system or the Soviet political system is fully bureaucratic. To classify
the Soviet political system simply as a bureaucracy is to encourage
the student to ignore the non-bureaucratic aspects of the system and
to distort the evaluation of Soviet bureaucracy itself. Meyer's analysis does not bring out the special features of Soviet bureaucracy as
distinct from other bureaucracies. Thus features such as the extent of
the bureaucracy's direct control over society and the economy, the
extent to which the bureaucracy must function in atypical ways (e.g.,

the pursuit of value-oriented and long-range political and social objectives), the existence of parallel and overlapping Party and state bureaucracies, the extent of political patronage in appointments, the elements of insecurity in the Soviet bureaucratic structure, and the existence of special types of social or public control over bureaucracy which are not normally found in parliamentary systems, are ignored or overlooked.

On the other hand, the emphasis on the similarity of Soviet and American bureaucracy produces some exaggerated comparisons such as that between the role of the ordinary shareholder in an American corporation and the ordinary Party member in the CPSU.[8] But the Communist Party of the Soviet Union is a much larger and more complex organization than an American corporation. Nor is it wholly concerned – or even mainly concerned – with business administration. While rank and file Party members have limited powers and are largely the agents of the Party bureaucracy they do not behave like ordinary shareholders, and indeed, would not survive long in the Party if they did so behave. The best analogy with an American industrial corporation would surely be not the CPSU but an all-Union industrial ministry. Thus General Motors might usefully be compared with the USSR Ministry of Automobile Industry or International Harvester with the USSR Ministry of Tractor and Agricultural Machine Building, and so on.

Not all the interest in Soviet bureaucracy in the 1950s and 1960s went into the production of general models for the analysis of Soviet politics. There were at least as many books devoted to the analysis of particular bureaucratic levels or groups. All such books made use of bureaucratic theory to some degree. One has only to recall the books by John A. Armstrong (*The Soviet Bureaucratic Elite*, 1959), David Granick (*The Red Executive*, 1960), Jerry R. Azrael (*Managerial Power and Soviet Politics*, 1966), R. Kolkowicz (*The Soviet Military and the Communist Party*, 1967), and Jerry F. Hough (*The Soviet Prefects*, 1969) to recognize the truth of this observation. Perhaps because such writers were analysing particular problems in Soviet politics rather than the whole of Soviet politics they were generally attentive to the limits of Weberian theory. Thus Granick found that Soviet managers had so much freedom of management that they could not rightly be termed 'bureaucrats' in the Weberian sense. Jerry Hough repeatedly found the same problem in his study of regional Party secretaries. Thus he states:

> The Soviet leadership seems to believe quite deeply that a
> Weberian type of organizational structure with a clear line of
> command and clearly defined spheres of competence, is not, in

fact, the best form of organization for producing optimal
decisions from a rational-technical point of view.[9]

and again:

> It must be recognized that the more the office entails the
> performance of nonroutinized developmental responsibilities, the
> more the requirements of effective administration deviate from
> the Weberian ideal-type and the conventional monistic model.
> The model of effective development administration must include
> a number of these deviations among its most basic features.[10]

Hough then lists a number of peculiarities of the Soviet bureaucratic system including the selection of personnel not purely on grounds
of merit and technical knowledge and the system of incentive
payments to those bureaucrats operating in areas where the rules are
vague and the tasks far from routinized. However he stops on the
verge of setting out a fully comprehensive alternative model. Many
of the peculiarities he raises could be accommodated in the Rigby
model of a mono-organizational society referred to earlier.

## The limits to bureaucratic analysis

All modern industrial societies are bureaucratic but they are not
bureaucratic in the same way. It is therefore not very helpful to use a
single ideal type – Weberian or other – for the analysis of all
bureaucracies. A series of historical models as suggested by writers
such as Merle Fainsod and Carl J. Friedrich would be more useful.[11]
Whether such historical models based on the empirical evidence of
'recurrent patterns' would, as Friedrich argued, allow cross-country
comparisons and accurate measurement of 'more' or 'less'
bureaucracy I very much doubt. Few if any political systems are
wholly bureaucratic. Some writers who emphasize the bureaucratic
aspects of Soviet politics are able to realize this – it was not accidental
that the article which helped to recall the importance of public
participation in the Soviet political system was written by Jerry
Hough.[12] It remains true, however, that the preoccupation with
bureaucratic explanations of Soviet politics is partly responsible for
the neglect of what I have called the non-bureaucratic elements. If
these elements have been noticed, they tend to be explained in a
one-sided manner, as extensions of bureaucracy rather than as
something not wholly bureaucratic.

To illustrate the points made in the previous paragraph I will refer
to some of the publications of the past decade. William Taubman's

1973 monograph *Governing Soviet Cities* has the sub-title *Bureaucratic Politics and Urban Development in the USSR*. He makes his approach clear at the outset:

> The Soviet political system is a huge bureaucratic arena in which bureaus compete, bargain and negotiate to such a degree that although all are officially subordinate to one central leadership there is virtually no sphere of administration immune from bureaucratic politics. [13]

On the basis of bureaucratic conflicts in American urban politics as well as in Soviet politics, Taubman suggests six laws of bureaucratic behaviour. These are:

1 Division of bureaucratic labour produces competition.
2 Bureaucratic institutions act incrementally.
3 Bureaucratic competition and incrementalism complicate one another and inhibit change.
4 Scarcity at once increases the need for coordination and frustrates attempts to achieve it.
5 The centre's attempts to counteract 4 can often make matters worse.
6 When urgent tasks have to be accomplished the centre has to set up special agencies and launch special campaigns. [14]

The entire book is focused on the conflicts between competing industrial and city Soviet bureaucracies. As such it adds greatly to our knowledge of the problems of Soviet local government, especially in the small and medium-sized 'company' towns. Yet it is clearly an unbalanced book which has only passing reference to public participation, which is so important at this level of Soviet politics. Nor does it make any serious attempt at examining Soviet legal theory (in particular the concepts of 'democratic centralism' and 'dual subordination'). In this respect it is inferior to Hough's handling of Soviet regional administration.

In my opinion Professor Rigby's theoretical approach to Soviet bureaucracy is superior to most others. But it still tends to exclude from the picture some important dimensions of Soviet politics. To make this point I will need to give fairly lengthy quotations from his writing before developing my critique. I will take two quotations, both from works published in 1976. In a contribution to the ANU monograph *Political and Administrative Aspects of the Scientific and Technical Revolution in the USSR*, appears the following passage:

The present socialist system in the USSR, which has remained essentially unchanged since the early 1930s, is characterized not only by its comprehensive bureaucratic structure – all economic and other social activities being run by governmental or other official command hierarchies – but by the directing and coordinating role of the Communist Party. The Party is not content to exercise a policy-making and ideological monopoly, but plays a vital role in the *administration* of policy, through its hierarchy of offices parallel with and superordinate over the central, regional, city and district bodies of the state.[15]

That is a typical passage which elaborates the central concept of the 'mono-organizational society'. The second extract is taken from his short comment on Hough's article on public participation in the USSR, both printed in *Soviet Studies*:

In all industrialized countries much of the politics that counts is bureaucratic politics, but this is in my view overwhelmingly the case in the Soviet Union.

By the character of their reports and advice, by the twist they give to policies and decrees in putting them into practice, by their departmental style and 'culture', by their successes in struggles over jurisdiction and organization, by their use of personnel powers to reward friends and punish enemies, by the effectiveness of their informal communication and patronage links, by their access to top leadership, Soviet party and government officials participate crucially in the determination of political outcomes. It is not only the far wider scope of government that makes Soviet bureaucratic politics more important than its Western equivalent, but the limited character of the public political process, which means that the advancement and protection of sectional interests and commitments depends mainly on the behind the scenes efforts of sympathetic officials.[16]

The above quotation indicates one of the problems in using concepts such as 'mono-organizational'. If Soviet bureaucracy is all-pervasive then there can surely be nothing other than bureaucracy? Practices which at first sight are not obviously bureaucratic such as elections, self-help activities, citizen involvement and mass participation have to be explained as extensions of bureaucracy. And if such activity is at the lower or receiving end of the administrative structures it is surely of lesser importance than bureaucratic conflicts at higher levels? Yet, as I shall argue presently, the detection of strong bureaucratic elements in Soviet public participation does not mean that the process is entirely bureaucratic. It is only possible to argue this if one accepts the proposition that bureaucracy is the only thing that counts. Many of the practices referred to by Rigby in the above passage are not specifically Soviet or are not obviously bureaucratic. Lower officials in any administrative structure are apt to twist central policies in putting them into practice. Patronage, 'rewarding friends and punishing enemies', is a common practice in most political systems and is not peculiarly bureaucratic. Protection of sectional (and indeed of individual) interests often depends on 'behind the scenes efforts of sympathetic officials' in many Western countries. Perhaps Professor Rigby requires the open conflict of sectional interests as a precondition for genuine public participation? Or does it require the public to determine central policy?

## Public participation – a personal view

It is not only the advocates of a bureaucratic interpretation of Soviet politics who are likely to underestimate the importance of public participation. Other writers do it because they hold to a particular conception of 'participatory democracy' derived from Almond and Verba which does not seem to operate in the Soviet Union. Thus the keenest Western researcher on this problem, Theodore H. Friedgut, concludes his book on *Political Participation in the USSR* with the observation:

> In organizing public participation down to the grass-roots level, the Soviet government attempts to set up a series of screens which will turn all demands articulated at the local level into supportive and positive elements in the functioning of the system. Thus while the grass-roots community self-help organizations are outside of the state structure, they are practically an extension of the state's capacities.[17]

But from the Soviet point of view an extension of state (or Party) activity through mass participation is a proof of the success of Soviet democracy. It is yet another illustration of the correctness of the slogan, '*Vmeste s massami*' (Together with the masses).[18] While Soviet theory on the relations between Party, state and people has been adjusted several times since the death of Stalin, there is continuity in its basic propositions. Party, state and public participation are expected to grow together and not one at the expense of another.

How extensive is Soviet public participation? While Soviet figures are general and often inconsistent they do bring out its massive scale.

TABLE 7.1 Indices of public participation in local Soviets 1978–82

### 1 Base figures

| Year | No. of local Soviets | No. of deputies |
|------|---------------------|-----------------|
| 1978 | 50,815 | 2,230,384 |
| 1979 | 50,897 | 2,230,972 |
| 1980 | 51,124 | 2,272,731 |
| 1981 | 51,379 | 2,278,379 |
| 1982 | 51,565 | 2,285,941 |

### 2 Standing commissions

| Year | No. of commissions | No. of serving deputies | Percentage participating | No. of non-deputy members |
|------|-------------------|------------------------|-------------------------|--------------------------|
| 1978 | 331,437 | 1,805,191 | 80.9 | 2,700,000 |
| 1979 | 330,000+ | 1,805,378 | 80.9 | 2,727,000 |
| 1980 | 333,547 | 1,833,223 | 80.7 | 2,620,000 |
| 1981 | 335,066 | 1,837,910 | 80.7 | 2,682,000 |
| 1982 | 335,503 | 1,839,463 | 80.5 | 2,518,000 |

### 3 Questions considered at sessions of local Soviets

| Year | No. of questions | Percentage of deputies participating |
|------|------------------|-------------------------------------|
| 1978 | 782,000 | 65.3 |
| 1979 | 767,482 | 65.5 |
| 1980 | 832,508 | 63.3 |
| 1981 | 869,215 | 67.2 |
| 1982 | 879,000 | 65.7 |

### 4 Fulfilment of electors' mandates (Nakazy)

| Period | Mandates accepted | Mandates fulfilled | Percentage |
|--------|-------------------|-------------------|------------|
| June 1977 to Dec. 1979 | 776,014 | 708,253 | 91.3 |
| Feb. 1980 to June 1982 | 796,000 | 731,684 | *91.9 |

* Recalculated. The percentage shown in SND is 91.5.

TABLE 7.1 contd.

5 *Non-staff personnel working in local government departments*

| Year | No. of non-staff departments | No. working in non-staff departments | No. of non-staff instructors and inspectors working in other departments |
|------|------|------|------|
| 1978 | 9,976 | 83,532 | 435,000 |
| 1979 | 10,369 | 87,307 | 430,000 |
| 1980 | 10,679 | 89,309 | 424,000 |
| 1981 | 11,044 | 92,000 | 434,000 |
| 1982 | 10,994 | 91,798 | 410,000 |

SOURCE: Taken from the annual reports of the department on the work of Soviets of the Presidium of the USSR Supreme Soviet. *Sovety narodnykh deputatov*, No. 5, 1979–1983.

Using Soviet figures Jan S. Adams estimated that in 1975 there were 36.5 million Soviet citizens involved in public inspection activities, or 22 per cent of all adults.[19] These figures are no doubt somewhat inflated through double-counting, over-zealous plan-fulfilment by various volunteer organizations, but they would be impressive even if halved. Besides, they only cover one type of citizen involvement. The estimate of between one-fifth and a quarter of all adults participating is one borne out by Soviet research in the sixties and seventies.[20] By 1980 Soviet estimates gave 30 million participating in local government at various levels.

How does one judge the quality of such massive participation? Much of it is limited and not very effective, as Soviet critics willingly acknowledge. But the Soviet claim that it is improving in quality and increasingly effective is hard to disprove. And effectiveness is not the same as efficiency. Thus there were 43,319 deputy chairmen of local Soviets in 1982 who were non-staff (i.e., unpaid) as well as over half a million non-staff members of non-staff departments or non-staff members of staff departments of local government. Almost 50 per cent of all officials in Soviet local government are volunteers. No doubt the employment of more paid experts would increase the efficiency of local Soviets; it might also increase their bureaucracy.

In Table 7.1 I have set out several criteria to assist the evaluation of public participation at the level of local Soviets over recent years. They do not allow one to measure the relative importance of local Soviets and their executive committees but they do indicate a slow expansion of the work done in general sessions and in standing commissions (which normally exclude members of the executive committees). Many of the questions considered by local Soviets are centrally determined. This applies to questions relating to the economic plan, the local budget, agriculture, land utilization and forestry. It applies much less to other matters such as education and culture, fulfilment of electors' demands, the maintenance of public order, trade, public catering, local services, housing and town planning, and health and social insurance, which are also important in the discussions in local Soviets. In any case, most questions coming up before local Soviets these days come in the form of recommendations from the standing commissions rather than simply from the executive committee. There is bureaucratic supervision over the presentation of *nakazy* (mandates) and over their implementation. Executive committees are required to vet mandates to ensure that no wildly impossible demands are accepted. It is also the responsibility of the executive committee to pass a mandate to a higher level Soviet if local fulfilment is impossible. Nor are matters which are already covered by the local plan-budget accepted as mandates. Mandates are expected to stretch beyond the limits of the plan and their realization requires the mobilization of voluntary labour and resources made available by local enterprises. In this way extra facilities – streets, lighting, bus shelters, clubs, kindergartens, schools and shops – are provided for. Over the five years 1978–82 fulfilment of electors' mandates provided 5.6 per cent of all questions discussed at sessions of local Soviets.

I would argue that public participation, particularly although not exclusively at the level of local government, is steadily increasing in the Soviet Union. The rising levels of education of local governmental officials as well as of citizens generally is probably improving the level of local government and of citizen participation. This is so despite the relative decline in the proportion of the state budget spent at local levels in recent years. More resources would undoubtedly raise the level of local government. A change to a competitive electoral system would probably alter the tone of public participation. A reduction of Party involvement might strengthen local participation but it is by no means certain that it would. It is not simply the ineptitude of local Soviet officials that leads to Party *podmena* (substitution), for that is inherent in the system.

## Towards a model of communist politics

The rejection or revision of the totalitarian model provides the common starting point for most models of Soviet politics that have emerged over the past twenty years. We have seen how this was true for the advocates of a bureaucratic model. It was just as true for the advocates of revolutionary models. Thus Professor Robert Tucker of Princeton sought to retain the totalitarian model as a subclass within his 'mass revolutionary regime'.[21] Only the Stalin regime together with Nazi Germany is classified as totalitarian. Soviet Russia under Lenin and the post-Stalin USSR are classed as non-totalitarian. Almost any regime, provided it has some mobilized mass support, single-party leadership and revolutionary aspirations, is included under the concept 'revolutionary mass movement regime'. The concept was too wide-ranging to be useful.

Models of communist politics might be considered as a by-product of the development of courses in comparative communism which began in the USA in 1965–6 and spread to other parts of the English-speaking world before 1970.[22] But the early models for comparative communism were also explicitly linked to the rejection of the totalitarian model. Thus my own model (discussed below) was first presented to a second-year Soviet Politics class in October 1966 in a lecture entitled 'Totalitarianism Revisited'. It was published in an article the following year in the Melbourne journal *Arena*. The model was not widely distributed and had slight influence on overseas writers. It did however provide the basis for a very success-ful comparative communism course which ran at Melbourne be-tween 1969 and 1973. Although the model is deficient in some respects I think it is worth resurrecting.

The model was constructed not as an ideal type but as a historical model based on 'recurrent patterns' in existing communist-led societies. Since the USSR is the oldest of these communist regimes and has served – with some interruptions – as the basic model for the others, the historical experience of the Bolshevik Revolution is heavily embedded in my model. The model was deliberately con-structed so that it could accommodate changes that occur within the system. It needed to be flexible rather than rigid. It should also be a general model, i.e., it should take account of all the key features of the social and political system to which it is being applied.

Furthermore, it should be recognized that the model was con-structed as a Marxist model, not in the manner of the later Gripp model, but through drawing the process of social revolution into central focus. I did not seek to explain the political system or political changes as merely reflections to changes in the economic base but as something that was interdependent with it. At the time I set this model down in crude outline only. I later modified and extended it, but to preserve its historical context I reproduce it as originally drafted.

The characteristics of a communist political system are these:

1 It is established by means of a communist revolution, i.e., by the coming to power of a coalition of socialist and revolutionary forces led by a Communist Party.

2 Communist Party hegemony is used to refashion the existing social and political system in a fundamental way, in accordance with the accepted theory of Marxism-Leninism. Put briefly, this involves the expropriation of the former ruling classes, the socialization of the economy, central economic planning to accelerate and to direct economic growth, and the curtailment or elimination of peasant agriculture, and the systematic re-education of the community in the spirit of communism. The object of communist hegemony is not merely to maintain political power but to achieve socialism and eventually communism.

3 The transition from capitalism to communism is a revolutionary process which involves considerable use of coercion and violence but which also requires massive popular support, especially from industrial workers, poor farmers, and revolutionary intellectuals. The relative emphasis on violence and coercion on the one hand, and on persuasion and consent on the other, varies according to the material and social circumstances in which the revolution is carried out, and according to the leadership's estimate of the feasibility of alternative policies and tactics.

4 Marxism-Leninism becomes the official ideology and as the regime consolidates itself the ideology tends to become dogmatic and formalistic. The Party leadership establishes a monopoly over the interpretation of the ideology.

5 The Communist Party becomes the sole agency of power and tends to usurp the limited independent roles allocated to state agencies and to social organizations. The Communist Party, the state structure, and all important social organizations are arranged according to the principle of 'democratic centralism'. This principle is inherently ambiguous. The immensity of the revolutionary tasks set by the Communist Party tends to produce strict hierarchical or bureaucratic organizational structures but the residual democracy in the movement frequently reasserts itself and, under favourable circumstances, may even develop.

6 The typical leadership pattern in a communist state is either oligarchic or autocratic. The leadership theory is oligarchic but temporary equilibrium is often achieved at the expense of the collective. The ideological requirements of mass participation and 'communist self-administration' compel the leadership to overlap the institutional limits of top Party and state organs and to seek the advice and consent of increasing numbers of experts and activists.

7 Modifications to the political system of the communist state are the consequence of the interaction of objective sociological factors and political and subjective factors. Objective factors – such as the international situation, the degree of economic development of the country, the size and structure of its workforce, its educational and cultural level, etc. – provide the ultimate governor of its political development. Political (superstructural) factors – such as the personalities and qualities of its leaders, political traditions and political styles, the ideology, the evaluation of the historical experience of the revolution, etc., – will frequently retard and will often determine the pace of political change within the system.[23]

The above model has obvious defects even as an historical model. Certain elements in the historical experience of East European communism have not been included, especially the extent to which the socialist revolution in several countries (Poland, the GDR, Hungary, Rumania and Czechoslovakia) depended on the presence of the Soviet Army. Beyond this, the international element of the communist system, relations between communist states, has been excluded. The model would scarcely cover Cuba or China during the Great Proletarian Cultural Revolution. It underestimates political culture which is certainly of growing importance within communist states. The model was designed as a teaching aid and was not intended as a research aid.

Richard C. Gripp's *The Political System of Communism* (1973) also came out of attempts at teaching comparative communism. Again the framework is presented as a descriptive model rather than an ideal type. Gripp defines his model as one derived from Marxism-Leninism. Under this model a communist political system will be concerned with:

1 The inauguration of Marxism-Leninism.
2 The establishment of the Communist Party as the vanguard of the workers.
3 The organization of a socialist economic structure.
4 The establishment of a structure for popular worker rule.
5 The organization of an international association of Communist-Party states.

On the basis of this model Gripp advances five hypotheses to be examined in the book. These are set out as follows:

1 To be communist, a new political system is placed in power which is clearly labelled as 'Marxist-Leninist', and which has as its

main objective the bringing into full operation of a Marxist-Leninist, or communist, society.

2  In a communist political system, the Communist Party (a) assumes political control over the society; (b) serves as the spokesman for and represents the interests of the working class.

3  A communist system transforms an economy from private ownership to public socialist ownership and governmental control.

4  A communist political system (a) organizes structures for popular participation; (b) achieves viable worker rule through these structures.

5  A communist political system (a) supports a bloc of fellow communist states; (b) opposes capitalist governments; (c) supports anti-imperialist revolutionary movements.[24]

These hypotheses are found by Gripp to be only partly true in practice.

David Lane's *The Socialist Industrial State* (1976) has the subtitle *Towards a Political Sociology of State Socialism*. The emphasis is as much sociological as political. Besides setting out a comprehensive critique of theories of socialist society, it develops an alternative model which has certain similarities with both Churchward and Gripp. But to a far greater extent than these earlier writers Lane makes political culture a central element in his analysis. This will become clear from a single paragraph:

> While we shall consider important differences in the culture, the level of economic development and the political processes of state-socialist societies, the historical developments of these states share many common features. First, the communists came to power in alliance with other social-democratic or popular parties, and with the consolidation of the revolution such parties were weakened as independent political groups: they have been banned – as in Soviet Russia, amalgamated with the Communist Party – as was the fate of most social-democratic parties in East European countries, or reduced to the role of political interest groups subservient to the ruling party. Second, the process of revolution includes an attack on right-wing liberal-democratic groups: nationalization deprived the bourgeoisie of industrial property and land and was often accompanied by political violence – by civil war, by terror. Third, a land reform at first gave to the peasantry the rights over the land they worked, though this later gave way to the collectivization of agriculture: (Poland and Yugoslavia being two important exceptions). Fourth, political policy is decided within the Communist Party

and is often accompanied by internal conflict – by purges and political violence: politics remain endemic to state-socialist society. Fifth, economically, with the exception of Eastern Germany (GDR) and Czechoslovakia, all state-socialist countries were, relative to those of the advanced West, at a low level of economic development and they all pursued policies of rapid and extensive industrialization. Sixth, following the consolidation of political power and parallel to the industrialization drive, a cultural revolution was instituted which involved the introduction of mass education, widespread development of communications and the comprehensive development of social services.[25]

From their nature, models of communist systems or of state-socialist societies do not facilitate comparisons between communism and nazism or between socialist and capitalist systems. It is not surprising that Lane completely rejects convergence theory.[26]

Western images of Soviet reality vary widely and while this remains true, new models will be produced to assist the analysis of Soviet politics. Models are an aid to scientific analysis but they do not guarantee its achievement. They are influenced by the political passions that prevail at particular points in time, by the influence of fashion in the social sciences as well as by the personal prejudices and preferences of the author. All models discussed in this chapter reflect the improvement in Soviet-West relations after 1962 as well as the decline in the popularity of the totalitarian model. The decline in the popularity of the latter model was certainly assisted by its failure to accommodate the changes in Soviet society and politics that became evident in the Khrushchev years. The newer models reflect the greater availability of evidence from the Soviet Union itself about how the system operates. The popularity of the bureaucratic model after 1965 was certainly strengthened by the bureaucratic restoration that was so characteristic of the early years of the Brezhnev era.

In the last analysis however images and models vary in their appeal to individual scholars. The models of a communist political system developed after 1966 have in common the fact that they express a certain reluctance on the part of their creators to accept the completeness of a bureaucratic model. While they differ in their details they are all revolutionary models. They take as their starting point the historical revolutions in the communist countries and accept the fact that communist regimes are still influenced by revolutionary traditions, values and goals. They all emphasize the importance of the communist ideology in a way that the bureaucratic models do not. They also – though perhaps for different reasons – stress the importance of the class and social basis of communist politics. In the last analysis, whatever differences there are between the three writers discussed above, they are all residual Marxists.

## A note on the official Soviet approach to bureaucracy

Soviet writers draw a distinction between bureaucracy (*byurokratia*) and bureaucratism (*byurokratizm*). The former term is not normally used to describe either Party or state bureaucracies. The preferred term for the former is apparatus (*apparat*) while that for the state structure is apparatus or administration (*upravlenie*). Thus the 1958 *Political Dictionary* has no entry under *Bureaucracy* but gives the following definition of *Bureaucratism*:

> A method of administration or control of affairs distinguished by a predominance of red-tape, procrastination and care for the formal side of questions, by the absence of interest in the essence of things, by isolation from the people, by scorn for their needs and demands.
>
> The Communist Party and the Soviet socialist state, having smashed the bureaucratic apparatus of tsarist Russia, from the first days of the October Revolution carried on an uninterrupted struggle against every manifestation of bureaucratism preserved in surviving old structures.

The definition refers to various writings by Lenin in which the dangers of bureaucratism are analysed and remedies suggested. It concludes with a summary of means to combat bureaucratism:

> By means of the scientific organization of labour, accounting and control, strengthening the verification of decisions, by the widening of self-criticism and above all of criticism from below of the Party and the government, and by the systematic improvement of the work of the Soviet apparatus.[27]

There is nothing in the above formulations that would have upset Lenin. Public inspection and supervision of apparatuses from below were advocated from the 1920s onwards. Lenin's heirs have grown cold only on three remedies advocated by Lenin – the restriction of salaries of officials to the level of ordinary workers, the need to rotate officials at all levels, and the need to have two-thirds of the members of the Central Committee of the Party chosen from rank-and-file workers. Whether these additional measures would have restricted the growth of Soviet bureaucracy is another matter.

# 8 STALINISM

Stalinism is a complex political phenomenon. It is therefore not surprising that historians and political scientists have found it so difficult to define and to analyse Stalinism. Few would be satisfied with a simple dictionary definition such as 'the political theories and practices of Josef V. Stalin'.[1] But experts differ about its relation to Marxism and Leninism, about its relation to Russian traditions, about whether it was revolutionary or counter-revolutionary, about whether it was a Russian or an international phenomenon, and about its essential characteristics. These differences reflect the different political positions of their authors as well as different theoretical perspectives and preoccupations. This will become clear from a study of the definitions listed below:

> Stalinism, as an ideology and practice, gathers together in one tight knot, the authoritarianism that the workers were compelled to use in their efforts to revolutionize their situation in society; it develops these authoritarian means into absolutes which are then used as means against the very people they are supposed to serve . . .
>
> Stalinism is more than a purely Russian phenomenon.[2]

That statement was written by Jack Blake, an Australian worker who joined the Communist Party of Australia in 1924 at the age of fifteen. After many years as a Party functionary he became an oppositionist within the Party in the 1950s and has remained so ever since.

A few months before he died the Hungarian revolutionary, Georg Lukács, made the following definition of Stalinism:

> Stalinism is not only an erroneous interpretation and a defective application of Marxism; it is, in fact, its negation. There are no longer any theorists. There are only tacticians.[3]

Deutscher's Marxism (as well as his appreciation of Russian history) is reflected in the following extract:

> The transition from Leninism to Stalinism consisted in the abandonment of a revolutionary internationalist tradition in favour of the sacred egoism of Soviet Russia, and in the suppression of Bolshevism's pristine attachment to proletarian democracy in favour of an autocratic system of government. The isolation of the Russian revolution resulted in its spiritual and political adaptation to primordial Russian tradition. Stalinism represented the amalgamation of Western European Marxism with Russian barbarism.[4]

I give as a final example of definitions from a Marxist position that given by Ernest Mandel. In a review of the French communist historian Jean Elleinstein's book on *The Stalin Phenomenon* Mandel states:

> Stalinism is neither a 'deformation of the socialist state' nor the sum of the 'totalitarian institutions and practices' used to 'construct socialism by barbaric means'. Stalinism is the totality of political institutions, structures of rule, methods of governing and planning which secure the monopoly of power of the Soviet bureaucracy and which safeguard its privileges, in a society of transition from capitalism to socialism. This is the only explanation of the Stalinist phenomenon that conforms to the method of historical materialism and is capable of accounting for the *totality* of the contradictory aspects of the phenomenon.[5]

This is the most carefully phrased Marxist definition of Stalinism that I have come across. It is not surprising that it comes from an orthodox Trotskyist.

Political scientists, if they have bothered to define Stalinism, have usually done so within their favoured approach to Soviet politics. Thus writers who use a totalitarian model either take Stalinism as synonymous with totalitarianism or as a special type of totalitarianism. Such authors tend to emphasize the key role played by the state under Stalinism. Thus Robert C. Tucker has asserted that the essential meaning of Stalinism 'was the dynamic resurgence of *gosudarstvo*'.[6] T.H. Rigby, on the other hand, sees Stalinism as 'tyranny exercised under the conditions of a mono-organizational society'.[7] Jerry F. Hough is content to indicate key features of the Soviet political system under Stalin:

The great tour de force of Stalinism was the construction of a political system which combined the revolutionary and authoritarian heritage of Leninism, the traditional nationalism of tsarism, the stabilizing equilibrium of conservative social institutions, the dynamics of rapid industrialization, and the terror apparatus of a full-blown police state.[8]

## The essentials of Stalinism

The term Stalinism was invented by Trotsky in the mid-1930s. It has been widely used in the West for many decades but it has never had official acceptance in the Soviet Union and is not listed in Soviet dictionaries or encyclopaedias. It has currency among Soviet dissidents. As applied to the Soviet Union the term does not have a constant meaning. As Giuseppe Boffa has observed, Stalinism was not the same at all periods; it was different in 1930 to what it was in 1924, different in 1938 to what it was after 1945.[9] Although the term has international relevance within international communism its meaning has not conformed exactly to that within the Soviet Union. I will confine my discussion to the Soviet Union. I do not offer a new definition of the term but merely a listing of what seem to me to be key features of the system. The list is not meant to be comprehensive. Nor is it given in any particular order. Some features will be found in other political systems but not to the same degree.

Here then is my list of the essential features of Stalinism:

1  The personal autocratic rule of Stalin.
2  The Stalin cult.
3  Reckless alteration to the social structure through administrative means – revolution from above.
4  Mass terror.
5  Mendacity.
6  The politicizing of culture and the ideologizing of politics.
7  Excessive bureaucracy.

### 1  The personal autocratic rule of Stalin
Stalin exercised great power from November 1917 onwards. He was a member of the Politburo and of the Council of Peoples Commissars. He was Commissar of Nationalities and from 1918 to 1921 head of *Rabkrin* (the Workers and Peasants Inspectorate). He played a role second only to Lenin and Trotsky in the political direction of the Civil War. He was the first Chairman of the Orgburo of the Central Committee and became the leading Secretary of the Party in

April 1922. Though Lenin sought to remove him from office in 1923 he did not succeed. On Lenin's death in January 1924 Stalin emerged as one of three main leaders. Although he exercised enormous power through the Party positions he controlled he was forced to share power with other Party and state leaders.

The 'succession struggle' lasted from 1924 to the end of 1929. In a series of inner-party struggles (concerned with policy as much as power) Stalin defeated the Left, Trotskyist and Right opposition groups. By the end of 1929 his chief rivals, Kamenev, Zinoviev, Trotsky, Radek, Bukharin, Rykov and Tomsky had been removed from their leading positions. Between 1929 and the Seventeenth Party Congress early in 1934 Stalin exercised decisive leadership, although he still operated within a collective leadership and by virtue of the fact that he held a Party majority. He barely survived a challenge to his leadership at the Seventeenth Party Congress but used the assassination of his main rival Kirov on 1 November 1934 to unleash a campaign of terror. The terror continued, with only minor interruptions until early 1939. Stalin's personal tyranny could not have been attained without massive use of terror.

## 2 The Stalin cult

The 'personality cult' (*kult lichnosti*) of Stalin was the main focus of Khrushchev's attack on Stalin at the closed session of the Twentieth Congress on 25 February 1956. Indeed the 'personality cult' remained a Soviet synonym for Stalinism for years afterwards.

The Stalin cult was partly a natural growth but it became increasingly manipulated by Stalin himself and by the Party apparatus. Its popular basis lay chiefly in the popularity of his policies of building socialism in Russia and it was very strong amongst working-class recruits to the Party during the 1920s and early 1930s.[10] This spontaneous admiration of Stalin was also common in the 1930s amongst many sections of Soviet society. Stalin was taken as the cause and symbol of Soviet industrialization and 'modernization'. He was even presented in popular verse as a demi-god with cities growing with amazing rapidity wherever he planted his feet.[11] But the growth of the Stalin cult was above all a deliberate result of controlled propaganda. This 'routinizing of charisma' coincided with Stalin's achievement of decisive leadership in December 1929.[12] The occasion chosen to bring the Stalin cult to fruition was 21 December 1929, Stalin's fiftieth birthday. The entire Soviet press and radio network were mobilized to sing his praises. Stalin was hailed as 'the great continuator of Lenin's work', 'the great leader of his people', 'the leader of the international working class and of all progressive humanity' and a 'commander of genius'.

This formalizing and regularizing of the Stalin cult meant that it became part of the official ritual calendar. It became an essential part of all great public occasions such as Party Conferences and Congresses, the celebrations on May Day, Red Army Day, 7 November and Constitution Day (5 December) and Stalin's birthday. The cult grew unevenly; it reached its highest levels in 1936 with the adoption of the new (Stalin) Constitution and in the closing stages of World War Two.[13] It sank to very low levels, especially in the early months of the War, between June 1941 and November of the same year. Stalin's leadership was not apparent at this time and the emphasis in Soviet propaganda in 1941 and 1942 was much less on the great leader than on the entire Soviet people.

The formalized devotions to Stalin meant inevitably a great deal of insincerity. Few – and none in public view – could stand out against it. Officials, writers, artists and scientists felt compelled to worship Stalin on public occasions. The sycophancy was worst at the highest levels, of those who were closest to Stalin. The *Pravda* articles by Malenkov, Molotov, Beria, Voroshilov and Mikoyan on 21 December 1949 (Stalin's seventieth birthday) provide a clear example of this. I will limit my examples to a few extracts from the articles by Beria, Voroshilov and Mikoyan.

Beria's article begins as follows:

Since the great Lenin, there has not been nor is there any other name in the world so close to the hearts of millions of working people as the name of the great leader, Comrade Stalin. The name of Comrade Stalin is uttered with warm affection by the working peoples of all countries of the world who associate the name with the realization of their age-old hopes and aspirations.[14]

Marshal K.E. Voroshilov began his article thus:

On December 21, 1949, the Soviet people, together with all progressive mankind, is celebrating the seventieth birthday of the greatest man of our planet – their wise leader, teacher, indefatigable champion of peace and the independence of peoples, the builder of a new human society and the commander of genius.

Hundreds of millions of people labouring by hand and brain all over the world, of all races and nationalities, are in these days looking with hope and fraternal trust to the Soviet Union – to the country of victorious socialism – to Stalin, the wise and great friend of all the oppressed.[15]

A.I. Mikoyan opened his article by placing Stalin into the central place in the history of the revolution:

> On December 21, 1949, the peoples of the Soviet Union and the working people of the world, the whole of progressive mankind, celebrate Comrade Stalin's seventieth birthday. Comrade Stalin has devoted more than fifty years to the service of the working class, the achievement of proletarian dictatorship, the intense, tireless work of building Socialism in the Soviet Union, the international Communist movement.
>
> From the years of his youth, plunged in stormy revolutionary work in underground conditions under tsarism, Comrade Stalin immediately showed himself to be a professional revolutionary, an outstanding organizer and leader of the Leninist type. As Lenin's closest pupil and assistant, shoulder to shoulder with Lenin, Stalin reared and strengthened the Party of Bolsheviks, the Party of a new type, developing and enriching Marxism-Leninism.
>
> Together with great Lenin, Comrade Stalin led the working class of Russia to the October storm. After the victory of the Socialist Revolution, Comrade Stalin together with Lenin, was the creator and organizer of the first Soviet State in the world. On the direct assignment from Lenin, Comrade Stalin worked out the principles of a new military science and military art and headed the armed struggle of the young Soviet Republic against the horde of interventionists and the forces of counter-revolution at home, on all fronts of the Civil War where the fate of the October conquests was being decided.
>
> Together with Lenin, Comrade Stalin directed the work of the Party and the Soviet Government in restoring the war-ruined economy. After the death of Lenin, in fierce struggle against numerous enemies of the Party and of the people at home and abroad, Stalin brought our Motherland to the world historic victory of Socialism. Stalin is the great successor and continuator of the work of Lenin.[16]

This was all consistent with the official Party line as recorded in the official *History of the CPSU (B)* which Stalin had supervised and indeed partly written. But the inaccuracy of the claims made by Mikoyan and the others was well known. They contributed to this myth-history because Stalin expected it of them and they feared Stalin. Long before this time Stalin had ceased to be referred to merely as a leader (*rukovoditel*) for he was clearly the Leader (*vozhd*).

## 3 Revolution from above

From 1926 until 1928 Stalin worked in alliance with Bukharin. This made his approach to economic and social change cautious. The change came in 1928–9 when Stalin and the Party majority swung over to a program of accelerated industrialization and collectivization of agriculture. The reasons for this sudden change in strategy were partly based on fear – fear of the economic and political power of an independent peasantry and fear of capitalist encirclement. But it was also linked to the general acceptance that the revolution – and the Party – could not retreat. It must move towards the realization in practice of the slogan of 'socialism in one country'. Since peasant consciousness was clearly lagging behind the needs of the revolution the peasants would have to be coerced into joining collective farms. In the process five to seven million peasants (mainly but not exclusively *kulaks*) were driven from their lands. Displaced peasants helped to provide labour for the mills of industry. By 1935 most peasants had moved into collective or state farms. The working class (defined as those working in state enterprises) had grown to one-third of the workforce. The means of production had become socialized, even if the other prerequisites of socialism had not been attained.

The achievement of this restricted socialism gave the Soviet Union certain advantages when war came in 1941. The war became not only a patriotic war to defend Mother Russia but a war to defend the gains of the revolution. Most sections of Soviet society – workers, collective farmers, intelligentsia as well as most national groups – heroically supported the war effort. It also gave the Soviet government greater powers to mobilize resources and manpower than those possessed by most countries at war. Wholesale evacuations of industries and populations from the War zones began as early as July 1941. Industries and research institutes were relocated in the Urals, Siberia and Central Asia. The same factors assisted the Soviet Union in its post-War reconstruction which proceeded so rapidly 1945–8. At the same time Stalin and other Soviet leaders were often over-confident in their ability to control nature. Little came of Stalin's 1946 grandiose scheme to 're-make nature'. The scheme involved extensive landscaping and the planting of millions of trees in the semi-arid steppes, a task beyond the capacity of the Soviet government at that time. Similarly the ambitious plans to dam the north-ward flowing Siberian rivers and to divert their waters to irrigate the deserts of Central Asia had to be postponed for decades. Stalin's interest in and support for Lysenko was closely linked to his voluntarism, to his belief that a small investment in scientific research could change nature.[17]

## 4 Mass terror

The Soviet Union was a fully-fledged police state long before the Great Purge of 1936–8. What made the Stalin terror exceptional was its massive scale, its planned sequences and – as far as its victims were concerned – its complete arbitrariness.

Early arrests and trials were fairly selective. They were directed at engineers and specialists, often former Mensheviks. It is clear that many of these early victims were made scapegoats for mistakes in industrial development. The next stage was a major Party purge. No new members were admitted between January 1933 and November 1936. And more than a million members were expelled, mainly newer members lacking political conviction.[18] Few of these suffered immediate arrest.

The assassination of the Leningrad Party leader Kirov in November 1934 enabled Stalin to open up a new stage of the terror. There were hundreds of immediate arrests and executions and thousands more followed in following months. Many of these were prominent Party members and government officials. Leaders of national minorities were arrested and accused of 'bourgeois nationalism' and separatism. By 1936 the term 'enemy of the people' was in general use enabling the arrest of many local officials, journalists, academics, writers, artists, scientists, factory managers, engineers, army officers, as well as ordinary people. The terror was not confined to Moscow and Leningrad but extended to every republic, province, district and city. Evgenia Ginzburg, soon to become a victim of the terror, has described the atmosphere in 1936–7:

> The newspapers were red hot, the news clawed and stung. After each trial the screw was turned tighter. The dreadful term 'enemies of the people' came into use. By some lunatic logic, each region and every national republic had to have its own crop of enemies so as not to fall behind the others, for all the world as though it were a yearly campaign for deliveries of grain and milk.[19]

This suspicion was not misplaced. As Alexander Solzhenitsyn correctly noted in his *Gulag Archipelago*,

> The real law underlying the arrests of those years was the *assignment of quotas*, the norms set, the planned allocations. Every city, every district, every military unit was assigned a specific quota of arrests to be carried out by a stipulated time. From then on everything else depended on the ingenuity of the security operations personnel.[20]

Not only were regional Party and state bodies given targets for arrests but they were subject to direction from the top if they were thought to be lagging. Thus in September 1936 Stalin and Zhdanov sent telegrams to all Obkoms complaining that the political police were four years in arrears in unmasking enemies of the people and urging more action.[21] This was followed within days by the replacement of Yagoda by Yezhov as head of the NKVD. This unleashed an even greater and more savage terror, the *Yezhovshchina*, which lasted from September 1936 to March 1938.

There can be no doubt that Stalin engineered the *Yezhovshchina* in order to finally destroy his defeated opponents of earlier years and to remove all former oppositionists and potential oppositionists. At least 180,000 to 190,000 communists were purged in these years and many of these were executed.[22] Many more former communists excluded from the Party in earlier years were also victims of the Great Purge. The first of the great show trials was held earlier, in August 1936. Members of the former Left Opposition, Kamenev, Zinoviev and fourteen others were tried, confessed and were sentenced to be shot. In January 1937 came the turn of the Trotskyists. Seventeen former leaders, including Radek, Pyatakov and Sokolnikov, were tried, found guilty and executed. In June 1937 several top generals of the Soviet Army, including the great strategist Tukhachevsky, were tried by a military court, found guilty of treachery and espionage and promptly shot. In March 1938 came the trial of the former Right Oppositionists, Bukharin, Rykov and others. This time Bukharin did not confess to all the charges but this did not save his life. All twenty-one were sentenced to be shot.

Writing about the Great Terror much later, the Soviet historian, Roy Medvedev, declared:

It is obvious that Stalin's extermination of former oppositionists was not accidental; it was a premeditated, planned political act . . .

The scale of Stalinist terror was immeasurably greater. In 1936–9, on the most cautious estimates, four to five million people were subjected to repression for political reasons. At least four to five hundred thousand of them – above all the high officials – were summarily shot; the rest were given long terms of confinement. In 1937–8 there were days when up to a thousand people were shot in Moscow alone. There were not streams, but rivers of blood, the blood of honest Soviet people. The simple truth must be stated: not one of the tyrants and despots of the past persecuted and destroyed so many of his compatriots.[23]

The mass purge was scaled down during 1938 after Beria replaced Yezhov. It was criticized by Zhdanov (one of the main perpetrators of the mass purge) in his report to the Eighteenth Party Congress in March 1939. It was voted out of Party practice at that Congress in favour of individual purging. But mass terror remained endemic to Stalinism and it reached new heights in 1941 and in the post-War years. Stalin was about to launch another massive purge early in 1953 but it was prevented by his death.

The scale of Stalin's purge is difficult to estimate precisely. No official Soviet estimates have been published and court and police archives are still withheld. Estimates of purge executions range from a few hundred thousand to over a million while estimates of numbers in prison camps vary from four to five million to nine and a half million for 1938 and from a little over three million to between twelve and fifteen million in 1946.[24]

Why did Stalin carry out such drastic purges? Were they dysfunctional to the Soviet political system? Many have argued that Stalin organized the purge to consolidate the Party monopoly and his own domination of the Party. According to this line of reasoning the old guard in the Party wanted relaxation by 1934 so Stalin removed them and replaced them by younger and more servile men:

> Stalin did not stop half-way: he carried out a complete
> renovation of the party by the elimination of the generation
> which had made the revolution and won the civil war and the
> raising up of new men who owed everything to him. Thus,
> Stalin's revolution in agriculture and industry and his assault on
> the party which consummated this revolution must be seen as
> integrated parts of one and the same process.[25]

Certainly the new administrative elite was much less able or willing to challenge Stalin's leadership than the old one had been.[26] The new elite was less experienced than the old elite but not demonstrably less able. It included many who were to remain in the Soviet leadership until the late seventies and early eighties, men like Brezhnev, Podgorny, Kosygin, Tikhonov and Gromyko.

The purge was directed mainly at the upper and intermediate levels of administrators and officers, and at the intelligentsia, particularly the old intelligentsia. It did not damage ordinary workers and peasants to the same degree. It did not obviously weaken the security of the regime. The loss of many able administrators and officers was very serious, especially as the War broke out so soon after the purge. The war losses would have been less and the defeats fewer had more of them survived.

It has sometimes been argued that forced labour was essential to the rapid expansion of Soviet industry from 1930 right up to 1956. Thus Steven Rosefielde of North Carolina has recently calculated that forced labour grew from 3.8 per cent to 16.4 per cent of the non-agricultural workforce between 1929 and 1933 and that it rose to more than 20 per cent thereafter.[27] But this is much higher than the proportion commonly estimated by Western economists. The importance of *zek* labour is even less if the value of goods produced is considered. It still remains true that prison labour was crucial for the Stalin economy, especially in mining, forestry and construction, and especially in the Far North and in Siberia. It is still of marginal importance to the Soviet economy in the 1980s, especially in mining, lumbering and furniture manufacture. It is questionable whether conscript labour (a form of state slavery) has ever been very efficient and it is certain to be counter-productive in days of acute labour shortage as at present.

### 5 Mendacity

Mendacity or lying is part and parcel of all modern governments. It is usual for governments to deny that any actions they have taken have been in any way responsible for hostile reactions by other nations. Likewise all governments minimize the losses sustained by their armed forces during a battle just as they exaggerate the losses inflicted on the enemy. Nations are often secretive and often lie about the size of their armaments and the activities of their secret police. Propaganda involves a distortion or a withholding of truth. It was Hitler – taking his cue from British propaganda in the Great War – who held that the secret to success in propaganda was to use the biggest lie. Stalin followed the same pattern. While he did not lie on all matters he certainly lied steadily on all matters concerning his personal policies. He lied about the class relations in the countryside in 1929–30 and he lied later about the 'success' of collective agriculture. He lied about the success of the first two Five Year Plans and about the preparedness of the Soviet Armed Forces in 1939–41. He lied about the political actions of his opponents and happily sent them to their death for crimes he knew they had not committed. He wrote and caused others to rewrite history so that his own achievements were magnified and those of others deleted or obscured.

I take a single example of how Stalinism falsified history. It is taken from the official *History of the Communist Party of the Soviet Union (Bolsheviks)*, edited by Stalin:

The trials brought to light the fact that the Trotsky-Bukharin

fiends, in obedience to the wishes of their masters – the espionage
agents of foreign states – had set out to destroy the Party and the
Soviet state, to undermine the defensive power of the country, to
assist foreign military intervention, to prepare the way for the
defeat of the Red Army, to bring about the dismemberment of
the USSR, to hand over the Soviet Maritime Region to the
Japanese, Soviet Byelorussia to the Poles, Soviet Ukraine to the
Germans, to destroy the gains of the workers and collective
farmers, and to restore capitalist slavery in the USSR.

These Whiteguard pigmies, whose strength was no more than
that of a gnat, apparently flattered themselves that they were the
masters of the country, and imagined that it was really in their
power to sell or give away the Ukraine, Byelorussia and the
Maritime Region.

These Whiteguard insects forgot that the real masters of the
Soviet country were the Soviet people, and that rykovs,
bukharins, zinovievs and kamenevs were only the temporary
employees of the state, which could at any moment sweep them
out from its offices as so much useless rubbish.

These contemptible lackeys of the fascists forgot that the
Soviet people had only to move a finger and not a trace of them
would be left.

The Soviet court sentenced the Bukharin-Trotsky fiends to be
shot.[28]

Stalin's authorship of that passage is not indicated but the senti-
ments and imagery are clearly his. All this was lies: 'The truth is that
all these trials were completely fraudulent. They were a monstrous
theatrical presentation that had to be rehearsed many times before it
could be shown to spectators.' [29]

6 The politicizing of culture and the ideologizing of politics
The politicizing of culture began with the Bolshevik Revolution but
it was completed by Stalin after 1929. The 'Cultural Revolution'
launched in 1929 was directed mainly against 'bourgeois specialists',
the old intelligentsia. Although this cultural revolution was officially
terminated in 1931 its effects were felt right through the 1930s. Party
membership was increased amongst the creative and the scientific
intelligentsia. New single organizations under close Party control
replaced the previous competing autonomous groups. Thus the
Union of Soviet Writers was established in 1932 as was the Union of
Soviet Architects. The Union of Composers was established in 1932
and the Union of Artists in 1939.[30] The penetration of politics into
art was clearly evident at the First Congress of the Writers Union in

1934. The veteran socialist writer, Maxim Gorky, delivered a speech which suggested that the general approach of Soviet writers should be that of 'socialist realism', which he defined as 'a combination of realism and romanticism'. It was at once taken up by Stalin and converted to a rigid formula to be applied systematically to all future Soviet literature. It is not surprising that only really great writers such as Sholokhov, Panova, Fadeyev and Paustovsky could apply the formula and still produce good literature.

The same process of consolidation and coordination was applied to scientific research. Throughout most of the 1920s the Party did not interfere much with the Academy of Sciences, which had survived almost unchanged since tsarist times. Instead it had concentrated on building up a new competing academy directly controlled by the Central Committee of the Party. The Academy of Sciences was reorganized in 1927, enlarged and brought under government and Party control. The Academy suffered under the Cultural Revolution and many leading members (including the philosopher Deborin) were purged in 1929. A further reorganization followed in 1930 and in the years that followed the greatest expansion was in the Applied Sciences. Communist influence was increased, especially after the merging of the Communist Academy with the USSR Academy of Sciences in 1936.[31]

Ideology is inseparable from politics. After the Bolshevik Revolution communist ideology became the dominant ideology, but it was some time before it became a fully unified and integrated ideology or before competing ideologies were excluded from the political arena. The process of consolidating and formalizing the official ideology strengthened after Lenin's death and reached completion in the 1930s. In 1935 the sympathetic English writers Sidney and Beatrice Webb complained about 'the disease of orthodoxy' in Stalinist Russia. That this had come about was largely due to Stalin. In his absence the development would have been slower and less complete.

Was Stalin a Marxist? This question has vexed socialists inside and outside of the Soviet Union. While there has been some criticism of Stalin's theories in the Soviet Union since the Twentieth Congress and Stalin's works are seldom cited now by Soviet authors, he has not been entirely disowned as a Marxist. The 1958 Soviet political dictionary states that 'his name is inseparable from Marxism-Leninism'. Many – Lukács and Medvedev, for example – consider that Stalin was not a Marxist. I do not think that this is true. Stalin was, as Lukács observes, a tactician and not a theorist. Many Westerners have made the same evaluation of Lenin's Marxism. In comparison with Marx, Lenin appears as less a theorist than a strategist and tactician, more a practical politician. In comparison with Lenin, Stalin appears as a manipulator of concepts, a popularizer of basic Marxism and an organizer. He was not a 'creative Marxist' in the sense that Lenin or Mao were. Dogmatism weakens and distorts Marxism but rarely destroys it. It will be necessary to refer briefly to the process by which Soviet Marxism became formalized and rigidified under Stalin.

Before 1924 Stalin enjoyed small reputation as a theorist. His most important pre-1917 work was a substantial pamphlet, *Marxism and the National Question*, written under Lenin's supervision in 1913. It gave him the reputation which brought him the Commissariat of Nationalities in Lenin's first government of 1917. Most of his writing over the years 1917–23 related to practical organizational questions and to problems of national relations within the new Soviet state. At the beginning of 1924 he was rated as a theoretician far below Trotsky, Bukharin and Zinoviev.

Stalin's first achievement after Lenin's death, and his first victory over his rivals, was the establishment of Leninism as a new stage in the development of Marxism. It was typical of Stalin and a reflection of his early upbringing that he should establish the concept not merely theoretically but as a cult. On 26 January 1924, less than a week after Lenin's death, Stalin delivered an address to the Second All-Union Congress of Soviets 'On the Death of Lenin'. This was not presented in the style of a normal party obituary but as a litany, with Stalin providing both the utterances and the responses. It marked the establishment of a new secular religion and it began the codification of Leninism. I give only brief extracts:

> Comrades, we Communists are people of a special mould. We are made of a special stuff. We are those who form the army of the great proletarian strategist, the army of Comrade Lenin . . .

> *Departing from us, Comrade Lenin enjoined us to hold high and guard the purity of the great title of Member of the Party.* We vow to you, Comrade Lenin, that we shall fulfil your behest with honour!

> *Departing from us, Comrade Lenin enjoined us to guard the unity of our Party as the apple of our eye.* We vow to you, Comrade Lenin, that this behest, too, shall be fulfilled with honour!

> *Departing from us, Comrade Lenin enjoined us to guard and strengthen the dictatorship of the proletariat.* We vow to you, Comrade Lenin, that we shall spare no effort to fulfil this behest, too, with honour!

*Departing from us, Comrade Lenin enjoined us to strengthen with all our might the alliance of the workers and peasants.* We vow to you, Comrade Lenin, that this behest, too, we shall fulfil with honour!

*Departing from us, Comrade Lenin enjoined us to strengthen and extend the Union of Republics.* We vow to you, Comrade Lenin, that this behest, too, we shall fulfil with honour!

*Departing from us, Comrade Lenin enjoined us to remain faithful to the principles of the Communist International.* We vow to you, Comrade Lenin, that we shall not spare our lives to strengthen and extend the Union of the Working People of the whole world – the Communist International![32]

The veneration of Lenin was to be carried much further in future years with the erection of a mausoleum in Red Square to hold the preserved body of the former leader.

In April 1924 Stalin delivered a series of lectures at the Sverdlov University 'On the Foundations of Leninism'. As Roy Medvedev has pointed out, Stalin used the manuscript of a book prepared in the previous year by a historian of that university F.A. Ksenofontov, borrowing extensively from it without acknowledgement.[33] Stalin's lectures were immediately published in a pamphlet which had a massive sale. It was in this work, in speeches that followed it and in *On Problems of Leninism* (1926) that Stalin developed his theory of 'socialism in one country'. Writing about this theory much later Roy Medvedev wrote this:

Stalin also blighted the concept of the socialist revolution. He took Lenin's thesis about the possibility of socialism in one country and proclaimed it a new and complete theory of revolution. In this way a rigid limit was imposed on the further development of the theory of socialist revolution and an essential element of Leninism was separated from Marxism . . .
    If it is possible to speak of a Stalinist stage in the theoretical field, then it is one of temporary decline and stagnation . . .
    Stalin's few original works contain more incorrect than correct views. The list of his theoretical achievements is short, the list of his theoretical errors is long.[34]

While these views are accurate they are somewhat one-sided. It is not so much the correctness of a theory as its acceptance that counts. In one area at least, Stalin made an original and enduring contribution to the development of Soviet Marxism, namely, on the theory of the state. He restored the state both in theory and in practice.[35]

The ideologizing of politics carried out under Stalin remains a feature of Soviet politics to this day. One has only to read any *Pravda* editorial to sense this.

## 7 Excessive bureaucracy

In one sense, as Trotsky recognized, Stalin was as much the product of Soviet bureaucracy as its creator. The General-Secretaryship of the Party came into being in 1922 because the Party organization was already so large and complex as to require it. Its growth after 1922 shaped Stalin's political style further in its initial direction. It also provided the basis for his power during the years after 1924. But Stalin once in power was no longer dependent on the formal structure of the Party apparatus. He continued to use the Party apparatus to gain information about how people were reacting to his policies, and to allow him to modify policies in mid-stream and to shunt the blame onto others, preferably onto lower level officials. In periods of acute crisis Party officials, particularly *obkom* and *raikom* secretaries, would often exercise increased powers. This happened 1934–9 and during the War and early post-War period. But with the setting up of many new commissariats after 1930 the state bureaucracy tended to grow more quickly than that of the Party.*This not only provided Stalin with additional means of control but with additional sources of information.

From the mid-1930s onwards Stalin had the advantage of being at the head of a complex of hierarchical, parallel but interlocking apparatuses. This allowed him to play off one against another so that none could challenge him. He relied increasingly on the various state police agencies. He largely ignored the Leninist concept of 'collective leadership'. The Central Committee met infrequently and no Party Congress was held between March 1939 and October 1952. Even the Politburo did not meet regularly and did not function as a collective. Stalin replaced it by cronyism, the practice of summoning a handful of special cronies to his dacha whenever he wanted their company or advice. He also set up numerous little *ad hoc* committees to carry out the work of the Politburo.[36]

The two sides of Stalin's social revolution, collectivization of agriculture and industrialization both led to greater bureaucracy. The network of village and rural district Soviets was expanded to allow more effective supervision of a disgruntled peasantry. Not only were more and more industrial commissariats (ministries)

---

* The number of ministries and departments included in the USSR Council of Ministers (People's Commissars) rose from 12 in 1936 to 15 in 1935, to 26 in 1938 and to 64 in 1946.

established but the network of planning, supply and control agencies had to be steadily enlarged. It is of course difficult to measure the size of the bureaucracy under Stalin. In 1940 there were 1,837,000 persons employed in the apparatus of state and economic administration and in the administrative organs of cooperatives and social organizations (including the Party, trade unions and the Komsomol) out of a workforce in the public sector of 33,926,000. That represented 5.4 per cent of the total. In 1950 there were 40,420,000 employed in the public sector of whom 1,831,000 (or 4.5 per cent) were employed in administration. In 1960 out of 62,032,000 working in the public sector only 1,245,000 were employed in administration, a mere 2.0 per cent of the total. This percentage fell to 1.9 in 1965 but rose to 2.2 in 1975. The number of administrators was 2,411,000 in 1979 or 2.2 per cent of a public sector workforce of 110,592,000.[37] These figures do not give a complete picture of the size of the bureaucracy relative to that of the entire workforce.* Nor do they include military officers serving in field units.

Could Stalinism have been avoided? I do not believe that there was any inevitability about the pattern of Soviet history between 1920 and 1953. Had Lenin's health not broken down in 1922–3 and had he lived for another ten or fifteen years Stalin would probably have been reduced in power and influence. Other policy decisions would have been taken. It is impossible to tell whether Lenin would have veered towards Trotsky's or Bukharin's policies; he might well have found a third alternative. Under whatever leaders, the Party would have striven to maintain its political monopoly and to move the revolution forward. Modernization of the economy could not have been achieved on the basis of a peasant economy so that – sooner or later – the New Economic Policy would have had to be abandoned. Perhaps a 'revolution from above' would have come later and with more emphasis on raising peasant consciousness and the general cultural level of the entire society coming as a prerequisite. In any case some coercion would have been necessary. And, despite all efforts, bureaucracy and bureaucratism would have increased. But without Stalin, the Stalin cult and Stalin's tyranny there would not have been Stalinism. Stalinism represents not simply Soviet bureaucracy and communist ideology but the coincidence of these things with Stalin's personal power and ruthlessness. Stalinism is first a tendency operating within the Soviet political system, in competition with other tendencies between 1924 and 1929; establishing its supremacy between 1930 and 1934; and dominating and

---

* Collective farm management is not included.

transforming the entire system after that.[38]

If full blown Stalinism operated only between the end of 1934 and Stalin's death in March 1953 Stalinism has survived as a tendency both within the Soviet Union and in international communism. My next chapter will discuss the process and the limits of de-Stalinization in the Soviet Union since 1953.

# 9 DE-STALINIZATION

The term 'de-Stalinization' as applied to Soviet politics means the process by which the Stalinist elements have been extracted from Soviet politics. This has not been a simple process, for neither in the Soviet Union nor elsewhere is there clear agreement on the precise meaning of the Stalinist elements which need to be eliminated nor on the extent of the required changes. For some, the criticism of Stalin made at the Twentieth Congress of the CPSU and in the months that followed represented the entire process. For others, these events signified the beginning of a protracted political struggle that will end only with the complete restoration of Leninist norms.

The process of de-Stalinization in the Soviet Union has been largely managed by the political leaders. It is they who have determined the elements to be attacked and those to be preserved in Stalinism. Their factional struggles have largely determined the speed of de-Stalinization, its unevenness, reversals and limited success. But the Soviet people and above all special sections of it have influenced the process at crucial stages. While de-Stalinization is primarily a Soviet process it is also international. Foreign communists intervened – with limited success – in the Soviet debates during the second half of 1956. Beyond that de-Stalinization has been a movement within all communist parties and within other communist-led organizations.

How important is de-Stalinization to the politics of the post-Stalin period? An early answer to this question was given by Robert C. Tucker in July 1957 when he described it as:

> The issue around which Soviet politics and Soviet history have largely revolved ever since Stalin died . . . The death of the dictator exposed the integral relationship between Stalin as the ruling personality and Stalinism as the system of rule.[1]

Not everyone would agree with this evaluation now. It became the central issue in Soviet politics (and then only for some within the leadership) only in 1956–7, and more briefly, late in 1961. Since 1965 the Soviet leaders have done their best to exclude it from Soviet politics, treating it as something completed in 1956–7 and now only meriting occasional brief mention. This is not to say that the process has ceased to operate. It has only ceased to be an issue of factional struggles within the leadership.

## Aspects of de-Stalinization

In this section I shall analyse briefly four aspects of de-Stalinization: its role in leadership factional struggles, the role of the Soviet public, the Marxist critique of Stalinism as an element of de-Stalinization, and the development of polycentrism within the communist world.

To what extent was de-Stalinization a major issue in factional struggles within the Soviet leadership? It was not an immediate issue but it emerged as a central issue in the succession struggle in the weeks leading up to the Twentieth Congress in February 1956. If Robert Tucker was right when he stated that 'the first and essential act of de-Stalinization was the death of Stalin' [2] the fact was not immediately apparent to Stalin's successors. Nobody had the capacity to replace Stalin, so some form of a collective was necessary. The immediate attempt by Malenkov and Beria to establish a duumvirate was scotched by the rest of the Party Presidium. This was followed by a steady stream of articles in *Pravda* and elsewhere emphasizing collective leadership as central to Leninism. Malenkov was forced to give up the top Party position although he retained the Chairmanship of the Council of Ministers. N.S. Khrushchev took over the First Secretaryship of the Party by mid-1953. Beria – whose control of the police apparatus threatened the survival of the collective – was arrested in July and subsequently executed. He was accused of collaboration with capitalist countries as an intelligence agent since 1918. Later he was to be blamed, even more than Stalin, for the excesses of the purge after 1938.

The removal of Beria was followed by a reduction of the powers of the police. The single police ministry which had been established in March 1953 was dismantled early in 1954 with the establishment of the Committee of State Security (KGB) and the re-establishment of the Ministry of Internal Affairs (MVD). Both were placed under close Party supervision.* The MVD lost its powers to exile political prisoners and many prisoners were released from concentration camps.

---

* The Special Security Tribunal, which had sentenced thousands to death without formal court trial, was abolished in 1953.

Talking about this in his reminiscences Khrushchev admits that before the Twentieth Congress the leadership withheld part of the truth:

> For a while we gave the Party and the people incorrect
> explanations about what had happened; we blamed everything
> on Beria. He was a convenient figure. We did everything we
> could to shield Stalin, not yet fully realizing that we were
> harbouring a criminal, an assassin, a mass murderer! Not until
> 1956 did we set ourselves free from our subservience to Stalin.[3]

Khrushchev claims that he first became aware of Stalin's responsibility when he was in Yugoslavia in 1955 and that he then brought it up repeatedly at the Party Presidium. Eventually the Presidium set up a special commission under Pospelov to investigate. This report became available to the Presidium on the eve of the Twentieth Congress early in the following year.

There can be little doubt that Khrushchev took the initiative on the question of reporting on this to the Party Congress. According to his own account, after he had delivered the report of the Central Committee to the Congress on 17 February, he forced the Presidium to consider the matter and was eventually (against the opposition of several senior colleagues) authorized to make a report to a special 'closed session' of Congress. The report was prepared by Khrushchev, with the assistance of Pospelov. It was presented right at the end of the Congress on 25 February.[4] The decision to make the secret report was thus a compromise; it represented the most that the more conservative members of the leadership would accept. The report was hastily prepared, not fully reviewed by the Party Presidium, and presented by the First Secretary so that his own reputation was not endangered while that of the opposition was. But Khrushchev was not honest in denying all knowledge of Stalin's crimes until 1955. Like others in the leadership he was actively involved in those criminal activities.

The secret speech was a very incomplete exposure of Stalin's criminal activities. It was even less satisfactory as a Marxist explanation of how Stalin came to dominate the Soviet Union for so long. It coined the phrase 'cult of the individual' and blamed Stalin's shortcomings and criminal mistakes largely on personality defects, defects which Lenin had warned against in 1922–3.[5]

There can be little doubt that one consequence of the secret speech was a hardening of the opposition against Khrushchev which came to a head late in 1956 and early in 1957. Common opposition to open de-Stalinization brought together individuals and groupings who were not united in opposing the full range of Khrushchev's domestic and foreign policies. The defeat of the 'anti-Party group' at the June–July plenum (1957) was followed more than four years later by a series of condemnations and confessions before the delegates assembled at the Twenty-second Party Congress. This time the links between the discredited oppositionists and Stalin (and resistance to de-Stalinization) were made even more explicit.

The collective which displaced Khrushchev in October 1964 was less enthusiastic about de-Stalinization. Most of the new leaders seemed to consider it a diversion while a few, most notably Shelepin, thought the time ripe for restoring Stalin's reputation. Brezhnev steered a middle course and in his speech at the military parade in Red Square on 8 May 1965, he partially restored Stalin's reputation as a war leader but stopped short of reversing the de-Stalinization process.[6] Factional conflicts continued amongst the leaders but they were not directly related to de-Stalinization. As far as Brezhnev and his associates and rivals were concerned, de-Stalinization was no longer an issue.

The second aspect of de-Stalinization I wish to comment on is the role of the people in the process. The leaders were united in seeking to preserve as much of the system as they could, but differed among themselves only over the tactics they employed. A few – Khrushchev among them – seem to have realized that some fairly basic changes were necessary. But how did ordinary people, Party members and non-Party persons, participate in the process?

There was no public criticism of Stalin prior to the Twentieth Congress but the process of de-Stalinization had already commenced. Although Stalin was not yet criticized many features of Stalinism were being questioned by Soviet writers. Ilya Ehrenburg's novel *The Thaw* was published in Moscow in 1954 and it immediately produced a powerful reaction and provided the label for the period up to the Twentieth Congress. While not really a great novel it did criticize some of the worst features of Stalinism, especially its tendency to assess performance of lower managers and officials in terms of very narrow success criteria. It began a trend in Soviet literature of criticism and exposure of bureaucracy and of 'little Stalins', of men who modelled themselves on the dictator and showed scant consideration for people. These criticisms were taken up in various ways between 1954 and 1957 by writers such as Ovechkin, Dudintsev and Tendryakov. Such works prepared the Soviet public for worse shocks to come.

The review of Soviet prisons and labour camps had reached an advanced stage by late 1955. Many thousands of victims of Stalin's purges were being released and exonerated, readmitted to the Party, to the capitals and to intellectual life. Stories and sketches about prison life were written in hundreds, especially after the publication of Solzhenitsyn's *One Day in the Life of Ivan Denisovich* in 1962. Returned ex-prisoners constituted a growing pressure on the Party leaders, forcing them to take steps to expose past crimes and mistakes and to restore damaged reputations. Khrushchev gave this as a main reason why he insisted on there being an exposure of Stalin's crimes* at the Twentieth Congress.[7]

The speech 'On the Cult of Personality and its Consequences', delivered at the Twentieth Congress on 25 February 1956 was not published, although it is referred to in a resolution passed at the Congress.[8] Copies of the report were made available to members attending the special session and to the delegations from ruling parties in other communist states. Soviet delegates returning from the Congress reported on the secret session along with the rest of the Congress. Copies of the secret speech were available in all regional and district Party offices where members could read them. They were also read out and discussed at special meetings of Primary Party Organs. Within weeks millions of Soviet citizens were involved in considering the speech. Discussion soon spread to the non-Party majority of the population. Something of the impact of this speech on ordinary Party members is conveyed in the following passage from a young Soviet poet:

> The Twentieth Congress at which the Party showed its confidence in the people and, unafraid of hostile misinterpretation abroad, gave out the story of Stalin's crimes, strengthened the conviction that the people want only the truth and that to keep it from them is to insult them by distrust.
>
> Although I had some idea of Stalin's guilt, I could not imagine, until Kruschev made his speech, how tremendous it was. Most people had the same experience. After the text was read to them at Party meetings they went away in distress, their eyes on the ground. Probably many among the older people tortured themselves with the question: had they lived their lives in vain? The gifted writer Fadeyev shot himself with the gun he had carried as a partisan in the Civil War. His death was another of Stalin's crimes.
>
> A part of the younger generation naturally looked with suspicion not only on Stalin but on the past as a whole, and this doubled the distress of their parents. But there were parents and parents, children and children.

---

* Khruschev referred to 'abuses' and 'mass repression' in 1956 but to 'crimes' in 1961.

The older generation split in two: the genuine, dedicated communists who continued to work without losing courage but ready to remember past mistakes in order to correct them; and the dogmatists who naturally regarded themselves as the most dedicated communists of them all.

The dogmatists only paid lip service to the resolutions adopted by the Twentieth Congress to 'restore the Leninist norms of life.' The very word 'restore' was an idictment of Stalinism – you can only restore what is in ruins. But they had not the civic courage to admit this fact, so terrified were they for their jobs.

They did their tricky best to balance the accounts of the Stalin era, in practice to sabotage economic reconstruction; they opposed the abolition of privileges for high officials, such as the 'blue packets' and the 'private' cars. They grumbled and accused the younger generation of having no respect for the traditions of the Revolution. That young men wore narrow trousers and liked jazz, or even that they read Hemingway and liked Picasso, was evidence of their 'nihilism' – and, upon a sociological basis, proved the disintegrating effect of bourgeois infiltration . . .

The best of the young Soviet generation came through their difficult moment of doubt and reappraisal without becoming cynical. Their experience tested and strengthened their courage not only to oppose the repetition of their fathers' mistakes but also to fight for the carrying forward of their fathers' great achievements. The antagonism between the old and the new generations in the Soviet Union has been very much exaggerated in the Western press. There are many communists old enough to be my father whom I have always felt to be my contemporaries – and I have contemporaries who reek to me of mothballs.[9]

Soviet scholars had begun to criticize some of Stalin's theoretical formulations as early as 1955 but they were stimulated to greater activity by both the Twentieth and the Twenty-second Congresses. For the most part they kept within the limits established by the Party leaders but on some theoretical points – as with Stalin's theory of the state under socialism and his theory and practice of the national question – they pushed the criticism further.[10] Soviet scholars began a re-examination of the writings of Marx, Engels and Lenin, and Stalin's works were less often cited. Soviet historians began a painful and slow revision of the history of Bolshevism, of the 1905 and 1917 Revolutions, of the Civil War and of the Second World War. Stalin's role in Soviet history was being scaled down and his mistakes laid bare and criticized.

The victims of the purge who had survived and the surviving

relatives of those who had perished put increasing pressure on the Party leadership to extend the de-Stalinization process. This reached a peak in 1961 when the Twenty-second Congress was in session. There was strong demand to remove Stalin from the mausoleum and to erect a monument to the victims of the purge. The leaders equivocated and only the former was carried out – Stalin was removed from the place beside Lenin and reburied in the Kremlin wall. There were rumours before the Twenty-third Congress in 1966 that the de-Stalinization campaign was to be reversed. There were many protests against this, including a letter signed by many of the top scientists, writers and artists of the country. Nothing was publicly reversed at the Congress.

It will be clear from what I have written above that the Soviet people did not control the pattern of Soviet de-Stalinization but they were not totally excluded from it. The widespread popular assumption that Stalin's death would initiate changes in many features of the regime, that it would bring in new policies directed to raising living standards, that it would bring greater personal security and more freedom of movement, clearly influenced the leaders in their search for new policies.[11] And once the leadership was committed to a policy of open and progressive de-Stalinization, it proved difficult to reverse it. Conservative views also had popular basis. These were strongest within sections of the Party and state apparatus but they were also common amongst ordinary people. There were riots in Georgia when Stalin was denounced in 1956 and even today many Georgians hold dear his memory. There are still monuments to him in Tbilisi.

How far did the CPSU succeed in developing a Marxist critique of Stalinism? The answer is that they had very limited success in this enterprise. All that the Twentieth Congress did was to condemn the cult of Stalin's personality as alien to Marxism-Leninism, to criticize Stalin's crimes and to suggest some revisions to his theory. It was only after a number of foreign communists had criticized the secret speech for its inadequacies that an attempt was made to develop a Marxist critique.

The first important intervention by a foreign communist party was the publication in Peking on 5 April 1956 of the article 'On the Historical Experience of the Dictatorship of the Proletariat'. This was followed in December of the same year by the publication of a second article, 'More on the Historical Experience of the Dictatorship of the Proletariat'. This second article sought to redress the balance of Soviet criticism. Stalin was condemned for his mistakes but the Stalin phenomenon was placed in historical perspective. The harsh objective circumstances in which the Bolshevik Revolution occurred and developed, the isolation of that revolution, the weakness of the Russian proletariat, capitalist encirclement and intervention, were given new emphasis. On balance, the Chinese argued that Stalin played a positive role in the Russian Revolution.

The intervention of Western communist parties came only in June 1956, after the publication by the United States Department of State of an unauthorized text of the Khrushchev speech. All the major communist parties of Western Europe as well as those of the USA and Canada were soon involved in the debate.[12] Some but not all of these contributions were reported in the Soviet press or in the resolution of the Central Committee of the CPSU of 30 June 1956. The latter statement was clearly influenced by the foreign contributions, especially those by the Chinese and the Italian Communist, Palmiro Togliatti.

The first and most important intervention by Togliatti was the interview to the journal *Nuovi Argomenti* that appear on 16 June 1956 under the title *9 Domande sullo Stalinismo*. In this article Togliatti declared forthrightly:

> As long as we confine ourselves, in substance, to denouncing the personal faults of Stalin as the cause of everything we remain within the realm of the 'personality cult'. First, all that was good was attributed to the superhuman positive qualities of one man: now all that is evil is attributed to his equally exceptional and even astonishing faults. In the one case, as well as in the other, we are outside the criterion of judgement intrinsic in Marxism. The true problems are evaded, which are why and how Soviet society could reach and did reach certain forms alien to the democratic way and to the legality which it had set for itself, even to the point of degeneration. This study must be made following the various stages of development of this society, and it is our Soviet comrades above all others who have to do it because they know the limitation better than we, who might err because of partial or even erroneous knowledge of the facts.[13]

Needless to say the Soviet Party did not fully take up this challenge. To recall the thrust of this interview I will quote two further passages:

> Stalin was at the same time the expression and the maker of a situation, because he had shown himself the most expert organizer and leader of a bureaucratic-type apparatus at the time when this got the better of the democratic forms of life, as well as because he provided a doctrinal justification of what was in

reality an erroneous line and on which later was based his personal power, to the point of taking on degenerate forms. All this explains the consensus (solidarity) which surrounded him, which lasted until his demise, and which still perhaps has retained some effectiveness.[14]

We have said several times that it is the duty of our Soviet comrades to face some of the questions raised by us and to furnish the necessary elements for a comprehensive answer. Thus far they have developed the criticism of the 'personality cult' above all by correcting the erroneous historical and political judgements of facts and people and destroying the myths and legends erected for the purpose of exalting one single person. This is very good, but it is not all that one must expect of them. What is more important today is to reply correctly, by a Marxist criterion, to the question of how the mistakes which have been denounced today were interwoven with the development of socialist society, and whether there did not intervene at a certain moment in the very development of this society certain elements of disturbance, mistakes of a general character, against which the whole camp of socialism must be put on guard – I mean all those who are already building socialism according to a path of their own and those who are still seeking their own path.[15]

The resolution of the Central Committee of the CPSU of 30 June 1956 attempted to take up some if not all of these questions. For the first time it attempted to place the criticism of Stalin into a Marxist framework:

In the struggle against the personality cult the Party leadership is guided by the known tenets of Marxism-Leninism on the role of the masses of the people, the Party, and specific individuals in history, on the inadmissibility of the cult of a political leader, however great his merits.[16]

The document maintained that the focus on Stalin and the personality cult was necessary because this cult put a brake on the further development of Soviet society towards communism. Despite its condemnation of Stalin's errors and crimes the Central Committee endorsed the entire political line of the Party since 1917. It excused the leadership for not acting sooner: during the periods of building socialism, defending the country against hostile imperialist enemies and post-War reconstruction any criticism of Stalin would have been regarded as a hostile act by the entire people. The statement recognized the value of the Chinese and American contributions but took

Togliatti to task for asking wrong questions:

> In particular, one cannot agree with the question posed by
> Comrade Togliatti as to whether Soviet society may have reached
> 'certain forms of degeneration'. There is no foundation for
> posing such a question.[17]

Togliatti was firmly rebuked for asking this question which the
Russians said contradicted the answer to another question where
Togliatti had argued that the essence of the socialist system had not
been lost under Stalin. Despite the fact that he had been repri-
manded, Togliatti expressed general satisfaction with the Soviet
statement.[18] Others were not so satisfied.

The 30 June statement was the first and last attempt at a Marxist
evaluation made by the Soviet leadership. It was theoretically incomplete since it provided no basis for identifying incorrect policies and
methods of rule. It did not make it possible to separate out the
necessary from the avoidable elements in Soviet historical development. To say that the masses and not individuals make history tells
us very little. If the masses and the Party rather than Stalin produced
the successes of the Soviet Union over more than thirty years why are
Lenin's achievements still venerated? As an attempt at a Marxist
explanation of Stalinism the Soviet statement is inferior to the
general discussion by Plekhanov in *The Role of the Individual in
History* (1898). But it is better to assess the document as a deliberate
exercise in political legitimization. To have suggested that the main
line of the Party was ever erroneous would have weakened the
political authority of Stalin's heirs.

What I have written above is not to suggest that a satisfactory
Marxist explanation of such a complex historical problem as the
relation between Stalinism and Soviet socialism is possible. Some
elements of this relationship are better approached from other
theoretical perspectives: organizational or psychological theories.
For example, Weber's theories of bureaucracy and charismatic
authority provide some insights for the understanding of Stalinism.

My fourth aspect, that of polycentrism within the communist
world, requires only a brief comment. The term was coined by
Togliatti in June 1956, but the phenomenon was present earlier. As
used by Togliatti the term meant the recognition of the fact that each
communist party must find its own road to socialism and not be tied
to the Soviet model. It was recognized that the Chinese and Yugoslav
Parties had done this and that other parties were beginning to do so.
Khrushchev's official report to the Twentieth Congress had floated
the proposition that there was more than one road to socialism and

that some countries might achieve socialism through peaceful means. This endorsed the stand taken up by Italian communists since 1944. It is not surprising therefore that Togliatti should give it added emphasis in his articles and speeches in 1956. Thus in his report to the Central Committee of the PCI on 24 June 1956, Togliatti stated:

This was not the original position of Marx and Engels; it was the position which they arrived at after the experience of the Paris Commune and which was developed in particular by Lenin. Is this position still entirely valid today? Here is a subject for discussion. When, in fact, we state that it is possible to proceed toward socialism not only through democracy but also by using parliamentary forms, it is evident that we are correcting something in this position, taking into consideration the changes which have taken place and which are still taking place in the world.[19]

The Twentieth Congress was not only a stimulus to this polycentrist tendency within the communist world but the very manner in which the Soviet Party unilaterally decided to denounce Stalin produced new grounds for difference. This was clearest with the Chinese Communist Party which came out by late 1956 as a defender of Stalin. The Twentieth Congress became a central issue in the ideological dispute which developed between the USSR and Communist China in April 1960. Although it was possible to get delegations from eighty-one Communist Parties to agree to a common declaration in Moscow in November 1960 it was a unity around over-general and sometimes contradictory propositions. It meant different things in Moscow, Peking, Rome and Paris.

## The limits of de-Stalinization

From what I have written above it will be clear that the process of de-Stalinization has been very uneven. It began slowly, obliquely and haltingly. It reached a level of openness after the Twentieth Congress but it was already waning by the end of 1956. It reached a second high level in 1961 in the months leading up to the Twenty-second Congress in October, during the Congress itself and through to the early 1960s. It was already waning when Nikita Khrushchev was ousted from office in October 1964. It has been quietly shelved since the Twenty-third Congress in 1966.

How are these modifications and limits to the process of de-Stalinization to be explained? What are the determinants of the process? The first thing to notice is the lack of full agreement on the need for the policy among the Soviet leaders. Older members of the original post-Stalin collective, such as Molotov, Voroshilov and Kaganovich, opposed the exercise altogether. This opposition was not simply due to their desire not to have their close association with Stalin exposed to public criticism. It was linked to their general conservatism on almost all policy questions and their adherence to the status quo. Younger leaders such as Malenkov, Saburov and Pervukhin, were prepared to make policy changes in areas such as economic management, agriculture and consumer goods but they did not easily accept all of Khrushchev's initiatives.[20] This combination of different degrees of support for de-Stalinization and differences over a wide range of domestic and foreign policy issues produced inconsistencies in the application of Khrushchev's de-Stalinization program. Nor was it in periods of maximum authority that the policy flourished. Rather it was emphasized when Khrushchev's position was under threat, when the First Secretary used de-Stalinization to whip up support for the whole range of his policies. Linked to the state of leadership factional struggles was the question of resistance within state and Party apparatuses to a campaign which threatened their particular sectors of power and privilege. Police officials, especially top-level and middle-level officers, objected to the policy of reorganization and reduction carried out over 1953–5. There was also bureaucratic opposition to industrial de-centralization, reduction in the size of state and Party apparatuses, reduction in higher level salaries and privileges and other administrative reforms, all of which were essential elements in the de-Stalinization process.

Changes in the international situation, especially within the communist world, also affected the process of de-Stalinization. Rioting in the GDR and Czechoslovakia in 1953 influenced the Soviet leaders and helped to confirm their preference for oblique de-Stalinization which characterized their approach up to February 1956. The political crisis in Poland and the open revolt in Hungary in October 1956 strengthened the conservatives in the Soviet leadership. It was obviously not the time to rock the boat in Moscow. Although there were still some reformist elements present in the Central Committee of the CPSU resolution of 30 October 1956, it must be remembered that this document coincided with the partial withdrawal of Soviet forces from Hungary. The policy was reversed within days and by 4 November Soviet troops were again on the offensive. The strengthening of polycentrism also influenced the pace of de-Stalinization. From 1956 onwards the Soviet leaders could no longer expect to have universal communist support for whatever policies they followed. On the contrary they had to adjust to the uncomfortable situation where most parties were criticizing them for their conservatism while a few accused them of radicalism.

A fourth determinant of the speed and extent of de-Stalinization was the changing balance of domestic politics. For years after Stalin's death the Soviet leaders felt unsure of themselves. Khrushchev's 'adventurism' had limited support within the collective. Most felt that the risks were too great and the rewards too uncertain. Despite Khrushchev's populism he wanted to retain central Communist Party control over policy and administration. He wanted mass public participation to relieve the strain on local officials (and thus to justify substantial reduction in their numbers) as well as to increase pressure on industrial managers and middle-level officials so that they would better carry out central policies.[21] But the dismantling of much of the police apparatus meant a reduction in the efficiency of control over people. From 1955 it became possible for Soviet citizens to group themselves around specific policies which the leadership was considering. These 'issue-oriented' groups lacked any lasting organizational structure but they linked together important officials, Party secretaries, academics, scientists, economists, lawyers and other professional people. Such temporary groupings occurred across the whole spectrum of Soviet politics, especially on those issues that were formally opened up to public debate by organized country-wide discussions. These shifting alliances of opinion influenced and sometimes limited the ability of the leadership to carry through agreed policies. Other things also restrained the leadership. Stalin was not unduly perturbed by the weather but the impact of the weather and other factors on the grain harvest became a source of uncertainty in the reform policies introduced by his successors. A bad harvest could mean the deferment or even abandonment of a scheduled reform elsewhere. All these factors tended to influence the ability of the leadership to carry out consistent policies of de-Stalinization.

It will be useful at this point to again refer to the seven features of Stalinism discussed in the previous chapter. Which of these features continued into the post-Stalin period and which were replaced? Where essential features continued, how far were they changed?

The first two essential features of Stalinism – the personal autocratic rule of Stalin and the cult of Stalin – would seem to have disappeared with the death of Stalin. Yet this was not fully the case. No one could exercise Stalin's power and a form of oligarchy replaced his autocracy. But as after Lenin the collective soon disintegrated and by July 1957 Khrushchev was the dominant leader. When he ousted Bulganin from the Chairmanship of the USSR Council of Ministers in April 1958 Khrushchev combined in one person the top state position with the top Party positions of First Secretary of the Central Committee and Chairman of the Bureau on the RSFSR. But Khrushchev never enjoyed Stalin's full measure of power and his policies were often challenged, usually modified and sometimes reversed during his leadership.

The removal of Khrushchev ushered in a new era of collective leadership with Brezhnev taking over his Party positions, Kosygin the Chairmanship of the Council of Ministers and Podgorny the Presidency. Besides these three, Suslov and other leaders exercised considerable power in particular areas. To guarantee the survival of the collective and to prevent further reversion to autocracy certain rules were established. The top Party and state positions were not to be held by the same person and no Party leader was to secure a monopoly of patronage relating to senior appointments. In this way power and influence were to be shared.*

Brezhnev was less impetuous than his predecessor and more respectful of the collective. Nevertheless he gradually increased his power and had a clear majority of supporters in the Politburo at least from 1975 until his death in November 1982.[22] Although he never upset the 1964 'rule' by becoming Chairman of the Council of Ministers he did become President in May 1977. He had earlier become Chairman of the Defence Council, a Marshal of the Soviet Union and Commander-in-Chief of the Armed Forces. When Yuri Andropov succeeded Brezhnev to the General Secretaryship of the Party in November 1982 he did not immediately become President of the Presidium of the Supreme Soviet. By the following May he held both offices.

Chernenko was elected General Secretary of the Party on 13 February 1984, four days after the death of Andropov. Despite his age and uncertain health he quickly secured formal recognition of his leadership. He became Chairman of the Defence Council a few weeks later and Chairman of the Presidium of the USSR Supreme Soviet the following April. Thus these three recent General Secretaries have also held two key state positions but not the Chairmanship of the Council of Ministers. By April 1984 it seems to have been decided that the General Secretary would normally hold the posts of Chairman of the Defence Council and President. But this arrangement was not allowed to settle. When Chernenko died in March 1985, he was immediately replaced by Gorbachev as General Secretary. While Gorbachev became Chairman of the Defence Council soon after, he did not become President (Chairman of the Presidium

---

* The Bureau on the RSFSR, which gave Khrushchev so much control over appointments in the Russian federation was abolished a few months after his downfall.

of the Supreme Soviet). That position went to A.A. Gromyko, the most long-standing and experienced Politburo member, in July 1985. At the same time E.A. Shevardnadze was promoted from candidate membership to full membership of the Political Bureau on becoming the new Foreign Affairs Minister. So yet another step was taken to prevent undue concentration of state power in the hands of the General Secretary of the Party.

The experience of the last thirty years has demonstrated that autocracy is not the normal pattern of Soviet leadership. Collective leadership is the form that has constitutional and theoretical justification. Nevertheless oligarchic leadership is inherently unstable because individual oligarchs are always trying to increase their power and this must be at the expense of rival oligarchs and eventually at the expense of the collective.

Has the leadership cult been eliminated? One cannot say that this is the case. Certainly Stalin's personality cult has been largely eliminated although some residual elements remain. Stalin's theoretical leadership has been transferred back to Lenin. What survives, actual political and tactical leadership, remains to be competed for between the present leaders. There has been a mild form of collective leadership cult operating over many years. The collective leaders (members of the Party Politburo and Secretariat) often appear in public on ceremonial occasions and at the opening of sessions of the USSR Supreme Soviet. The names are listed together in press reports of these occasions, the General Secretary first, full members of the Politburo in alphabetical order, then candidate members and members of the Secretariat, also in alphabetical order. Huge portraits of collective leaders, of equal size and prominence, are displayed in Soviet parades and during election campaigns. Members of the collective are given birthday honours and awards when they turn sixty or seventy.

Within the cult of the collective there is a tension as individual leadership cults strive to develop. There was a well-developed leadership cult around Nikita Khrushchev, especially in the years 1961–4. However it never reached the level of the Stalin cult, not even to that enjoyed by Stalin at the close of 1929. The Brezhnev cult grew more slowly and reached its peak only in 1976–7. In this period Brezhnev presided over the Twenty-fifth Party Congress, became Marshal of the Soviet Union, had his seventieth birthday, became President of the USSR and presided over the launching of a new Constitution. He also secured a Lenin Prize in literature. All these and other occasions were the pretext for exaggerated praise for the leader. He was frequently compared to Lenin and was sometimes referred to as *vozhd*. His seventieth birthday was honoured in a manner not afforded to other leaders and somewhat reminiscent of Stalin's seventieth birthday in December 1949. Party leaders published glowing comments in national and republican newspapers. A television film on Brezhnev was viewed by tens of millions. And the praise was clearly sycophantic. Thus the First Secretary of the Communist Party of Georgia, Shevardnadze, declared after the Twenty-fifth Party Congress:

> The Twenty-fifth CPSU Congress once again convincingly displayed to the entire planet that in the modern world which is full of dialectical contradictions – a complex world with many problems – there is in the international arena no more eminent a political figure and statesman; no more farsighted and wise politician; no more vivid personality for whom people of good will throughout the world harbour such sincere feelings of sympathy and love, gratitude and trust; no other person seen as a more outstanding fighter for peace and universal progress . . . and as the outstanding organizer and inspirer of this sacred struggle than Leonid Ilyich Brezhnev.[23]

It was a sorry imitation of the Stalin cult but disturbing nonetheless. It seems to be self-generating in the Soviet political system and must be regarded as an inevitable consequence of the struggle for power within the collective leadership. It is perhaps also deliberately promoted by the collective as a device to present a united voice to the public. This might explain the muted leadership cults of Andropov and Chernenko after they became General Secretary. After Mikhail Gorbachev became General Secretary in March 1985 there was a renewed emphasis on collective leadership. This was reflected in the amendment to Rule 19 of the Rules of the CPSU at the Twenty-seventh Congress early in 1986. As a result of this amendment, collective leadership became incorporated as an element of democratic centralism. Yet this renewed emphasis on collective leadership did not prevent the consolidation of the personal power of the new General Secretary and the beginnings of a new leadership cult.

Has the post-Stalin regime been characterized by reckless alteration to the social structure? It would be difficult to argue this. On the contrary the post-Stalin period has seen the gradual and partial reassertion of Soviet society over the state.* But although the state has not attempted to re-make the social structure in Stalin's manner it has continued to undertake massive programs of social engineering

---

* Cf. the chapter by Jerry Hough in Susan Solomon, ed. 1983.

such as the Virgin Lands campaign under Khrushchev and the BAM railway and industrial development of Siberia under Brezhnev. The Soviet state was largely created to run and develop the economy and this continues to be its major – although not its exclusive – function.

The fourth essential feature of Stalinism – mass terror – has not survived. While mass terror has not been applied at any stage in the post-Stalin period selective terror has been used. It was used for the last time against the leadership in 1953 when Beria and his close associates were removed from office and executed. Since then it has been used against dissidents, especially since early 1966. The police apparatus, which was partly dismantled and decentralized under Khrushchev, has been recentralized and expanded since 1966. Both the MVD and the KGB have increased their staffs over recent years.

In the previous chapter I identified mendacity as an essential element of Stalinism. Does this remain characteristic of Soviet politics? Has the truth been told about the Stalin period? The answer is clearly 'no'. Stalin's crimes and mistakes have been criticized in general terms on a number of occasions but they have not been fully listed or examined. Stalin's historiography has been modified but in the process new distortions and omissions have crept in. I will illustrate this by quoting briefly from the 1960 and 1970 editions of the official *History of the Communist Party of the Soviet Union*, edited by B.N. Ponomarev,* candidate member of the Politburo and a Doctor of Historical Science. The first passage from the 1960 edition may be compared with the passage from Stalin's history cited in the previous chapter:

> On the other hand in 1937, when Socialism was already victorious in the USSR, Stalin advanced the erroneous thesis that the class struggle in the country would intensify as the Soviet State grew stronger. The class struggle in the Soviet country was at its sharpest stage in the period when the question 'Who will beat whom?' was being decided. When the foundations of Socialism had been won, after the exploiting class had been eliminated and political unity had been established in Soviet Society, the thesis of the inevitable sharpening of class struggle was an erroneous one. In practice it served as a justification for mass repression against the Party's ideological enemies who had already been routed politically.
>
> Many honest Communists and non-Party people, not guilty of

---

* Ponomarev was dropped from the Politburo but was re-elected to the Central Committee of the CPSU at the 27th Congress in March 1986.

any offence, also became victims of the repressions. During this period the political adventurer and scoundrel Beria, who did not stop short at any atrocity to achieve his criminal aims, worked his way into responsible positions in the State, and, taking advantage of Stalin's personal shortcomings, slandered and exterminated many honest people, devoted to the Party and the people.

In the same period a despicable role was played by Yezhov, the then People's Commissar for Home Affairs. Many workers, both Communists and non-Party people, who were devoted to the cause of the Party were slandered with his assistance and perished. Yezhov and Beria were duly punished for their crimes.

The victims of unjustified persecutions were fully exonerated in 1954–5.[24]

The following quotations give the different versions of the criticism of Stalin at the Twentieth Congress:

On the initiative of N.S. Khrushchov, the Party and its Leninist Central Committee laid bare the harm caused by the cult of Stalin's personality and the mistakes and shortcomings arising from it, and began energetic efforts to eliminate them.[25]

An important place in the work of the Twentieth Congress of the CPSU was taken up with overcoming the personality cult of Stalin and its consequences. In taking these revealing resolutions the Central Committee worked energetically for the restoration of Leninist norms of Party life and the restoration of inner-Party democracy. The Congress recommended that the C.C. continue to carry out measures providing for the complete overcoming of the consequences of the cult of the individual, so alien to Marxism-Leninism, and liquidating its consequences in all branches of Party, State and ideological work, firmly observing Leninist norms of Party life and the principle of collective leadership.

In criticizing the personality cult the Party was guided by the leading propositions of Marxism-Leninism concerning the role of the masses, the Party and leaders in history, concerning the inadmissibility of the personality cult of a political leader, no matter how great his services.[26]

The above quotations are fairly good examples of the rewriting of history that is going on all the time. Each generation of leaders writes its own history and central figures of one generation become nonentities for the next. This is falsification but not mendacity.

My sixth element of Stalinism – the politicizing of culture and the ideologizing of politics – remains, although the success of the regime in managing to do this remains much less than it was under Stalin. The Union of Soviet Writers remains the single organization of Soviet writers but many writers operate outside of it. Even within the writers' union there are sometimes divisions between editorial boards controlling particular literary magazines. There is also a significant underground oppositionist literature.

Party saturation of scientists is higher than it was in the Stalin period but scientists through the various branches of the Academy of Sciences as well as through individual research institutes and through representation on the Central Committee are able to exert increasing pressure on the Party leadership.[27] While some scientists – especially social scientists – are dismissed because of political nonconformity they are seldom dismissed because of their political opinions alone. It is far easier for Soviet scientists and academics to hold conflicting opinions and to carry out their own research work than it was under Stalin.

The ideologizing of politics is still a main concern of the Party but the results are less complete than they were under Stalin. The ideology has been manipulated by various leaders, most successfully by Khrushchev and Brezhnev. These modifications have involved the alteration of several of Stalin's theories and the abandonment of others. More rarely, Lenin's theories have been modified on the grounds that they are no longer adequate. However on many subjects (such as the building of socialism, the nature of the Soviet state and the basic laws of socialist economic development) the ideology is still basically Stalinist. Very often what is ascribed to Lenin really derives from Stalin.

Finally, does excessive bureaucracy remain a feature of Soviet politics? How far, if at all, has bureaucracy been curbed? The evidence is contradictory and far from conclusive.[28] The most persistent attempt to reduce the size and cost of government and economic administration was under Khrushchev, particularly over the years 1957 to 1962. Beginning in 1957 there was a substantial reduction in the staff of local government, particularly at the district and town levels. But even here the trend was contradictory. While the administrative structure of central ministries was drastically cut in 1957, entirely new structures were set up to operate the regional economic councils (*Sovnarkhozy*) and there was some expansion of regional state and Party apparatuses. There was also a steady expansion in Gosplan staff during these years, especially at the republican level. Nevertheless there was an overall reduction. The number of leading administrators and economic managers fell by almost 600,000 between 1950 and 1960 and their percentage of the public sector workforce fell from 4.5 to 2.0. The expenditure on public administration in the state budget fell from 3.9 per cent of the total in 1940 to 1.2 per cent in 1965. For several years after 1954 there was an annual reduction in the amount being spent on public administration. The decision to divide Party and state organs into separate agricultural and industrial structures (taken in November 1962) meant a further increase in the size of regional administration although it was counter-balanced somewhat by the drastic reduction at the rural district level. Still the number of persons employed in senior administration and management began to increase in 1963. It increased by more than 200,000 between 1960 and 1965 and by a further 423,000 over the next five years. But in terms of the larger number employed in the public sector workforce the increase was less startling. Senior administrators and managers constituted only 1.9 per cent of the public sector workforce in 1965 and only 2.1 per cent in 1970. The figure stabilized at 2.2 per cent of that workforce during the late 1970s.

The Brezhnev record on this matter is also contradictory. Throughout the Brezhnev period there was a greater emphasis on professionalism and a lesser emphasis on amateurism in public administration. The emphasis included stricter attention to selection of officials, higher and more specialized levels of training, less use of cooptation and Party generalists.[29] In 1965 the administrative structure was restored to roughly the shape it had at the beginning of 1957 and Khrushchev's special agencies in both Party and state structures were abolished. The number of paid officials in local government again began to increase although non-staff personnel continued to be important. Nor did the economic reform in the Brezhnev years do much to reduce the size of the bureaucracy. The restoration of the industrial ministries late in 1965 transferred many thousands of administrators from the provinces back to Moscow but it also provided the basis for expanding the central bureaucracy as existing ministries were bifurcated and new ministries established. The reform of April 1973 establishing production and industrial combines was intended to rationalize (by redistributing administrators) rather than reduce numbers. It was hoped that administrators would be moved out from the main departments (*glavki*) in the ministries and attached to the new combines which were to combine management and research with production. It was resisted both from the ministries and from the enterprises. In many cases production combines have not been established and the industrial combines have been little more than the old *glavki* under a different name. Ministries have sometimes refused to have successful plants consolidated and amalgamated with less successful plants.

What general conclusions can be drawn from the above uneven record? It is obvious that Soviet leaders since Stalin have been conscious of the problems of excessive bureaucracy and have sought various means to control it. They have conducted campaigns against excessive bureaucracy and have reduced bureaucratic privileges. They have encouraged communist party organizations to exercise control over industrial managers and the administrators of research institutes. They have revived and extended the practice of citizens' control and considerably enlarged the sphere of public participation, especially at the local level. But the Soviet Union is still highly bureaucratized and is likely to remain so.

The overall slowness and unevenness of Soviet de-Stalinization is not to be wondered at. The leaders who replaced Stalin right through to the 1980s had their political apprenticeship and early careers under Stalin. The system had given them careers and promotion to positions of great power and influence. They sought to modify it, not to destroy it. The successive leaderships have not sought 'a systematic and consistent democratization of the whole . . . political and social life on a socialist basis' as Medvedev and others have urged.[30] But they have all the same fostered slow adjustment to the inherited system so that within a few years of Stalin's death it was no longer recognizable as the same system. It had ceased to be Stalinist but remained a communist-led, state socialist society.

How far will it change in the future? It is difficult to answer this question with any certainty. Power will continue to be dispersed and is unlikely to be reconcentrated into the hands of a single leader. As younger persons, recruited to the Party since Stalin died, come into top and middle leadership positions the attachment to old forms and policies will probably change more quickly.[31] One can only guess at how radical these changes will be.

# 10 SOVIET DEMOCRACY RECONSIDERED

Is the USSR a democracy? The question has taxed my mind since student days. I remember being confronted by this question on a Final Honours examination paper in December 1939. I handled the question by outlining the Webbs' argument in *Soviet Communism: A New Civilisation* and then demolishing it. I argued that notwithstanding its socialist elements the USSR could not be considered a democracy because it was a one-party system, because of its neglect of individual and minority rights, because of police terror and because of its intolerance towards dissent. This line of argument was not surprising in the aftermath of the purges and the Nazi-Soviet Pact. My opinions at the time were liberal democratic and neither Marxist nor Leninist. They were strongly influenced by university teachers such as W. Macmahon Ball and R.M. Crawford, as well as by the writings of A.D. Lindsay, Harold J. Laski, J. Bryce, I. Jennings, C. De Lisle Burns and L. Basset. And behind all these writers stood John Stuart Mill.

I moved to the left during the War and also became a close student of the Soviet Union. I read Lenin, Trotsky and Stalin with greater attention and moved to a less critical appreciation of the Webbs. While I developed a more positive evaluation of Soviet democracy in these years I still had some reservations. The Stalin cult, Stalin's autocratic power, the failure to call a Party Congress, the neglect of inner-party democracy and continued police terror, provoked many doubts about official Soviet claims regarding democracy. From 1954 I came increasingly under the influence of the socialist optimism of writers such as Isaac Deutscher and Rudolf Schlesinger. In 1956 I began a reappraisal of Soviet democracy placing particular emphasis on the grass-roots level and on local government. The articles I published between 1957 and 1966 were characterized by a critical optimism. The restoration of legality to the Soviet political system seemed to me to foreshadow the development of a more genuine democracy. I argued – somewhat mechanically – that the moderniza-tion of Soviet society would necessarily lead, sooner or later, to a reordering of the political system along more democratic lines.

My most detailed exploration of Soviet democracy published to date appeared in Chapter 17 of *Contemporary Soviet Government*. This was written at the end of 1965 after my return from the USSR where I had worked as a guest of the USSR Academy of Sciences for three months. Since the material in the present chapter is closely linked to that in the earlier book it will be necessary for me to recapitulate my earlier argument. I sought to explain the Soviet conception of democracy and how it was related to Western parliamentary democracy and to measure the Soviet practice against the Soviet theory of democracy.[1] The analysis covered only the first twelve or thirteen years after the death of Stalin. The present chapter will look more closely at Soviet developments since 1977. In the earlier chapter I summarized Soviet theory of Soviet democracy in the following propositions:

1 Soviet democracy is a variety of socialist democracy and is therefore more democratic than any bourgeois parliamentary democracy.
2 Soviet democracy, being based on a socialist society, guarantees individual social and political rights more effectively than any capitalist democracy.
3 Soviet society, unlike bourgeois society, is fully united so that Soviet democracy reflects the moral and political unity of Soviet society.
4 The political monopoly of the Communist Party does not belie but confirms the claim that the Soviet state is democratic.
5 Soviet democracy, like any system claiming to be democratic, accepts the concept of popular sovereignty.
6 The Soviet concept of democracy insists that representative government must be matched with direct popular participation. The masses must participate directly in deciding major questions and in government administration.
7 The Soviet concept of democracy includes the principle of accountability and removability of office holders although it does not contain the British principle of ministerial responsibility.[2]

A reading of Soviet discussion of democracy over the past decade shows no important shift in the argument. The concept of the 'state of the whole people' which is incorporated in the 1977 Constitution underlines the principle of popular sovereignty. The leading and directing role of the Communist Party is recognized much more explicitly in the 1977 than in the 1936 Constitution. The rights and duties of citizens are set out in the same manner but they have been extended. The new Constitution combines the principles of representative and direct democracy. The linkage between socialism and democracy has been given new emphasis as has the claim about the moral and political unity of Soviet society. The following passages from recent Soviet writing should bring this out.

An early Soviet book celebrating the new Constitution contains this passage:

> The main direction in the development of the Soviet state, as in all political systems of the USSR, was and remains the all-round development of democracy, of the broadest involvement of all citizens in the administration of the affairs of society and state. All these processes are led by the Communist Party of the Soviet Union.[3]

On the first anniversary of the adoption of the new Constitution, *Pravda* published an editorial with the title 'The Creativity of Full People's Power'. It contained the following statement:

> Socialism and Democracy cannot be separated. Just as full democracy is impossible without socialism, so socialism is impossible without the continued development of democracy.[4]

The above statements are consistent with the underlying theory. Just as socialism involves a higher form of democracy than capitalism so 'developed socialism' involves further improvement of socialist democracy. And since the transition from socialism to advanced socialism does not necessitate any revolutionary change to society or polity, movement into and through this higher stage will also require Party tutelage.

Consider the following passages.

> Socialist democracy affords the working class and all working people an ample and real chance to participate in administering the affairs of the state and society, including economic, political and social problems. Socialist democracy presents a unity of rights and duties, genuine freedom and civil responsibility . . .
>
> The guidance of society by the Marxist-Leninist Party is the supreme expression of the democratic character of the socialist system and a decisive condition for the further all-round development of socialist democracy . . .
>
> Soviet experience shows that society can enter the stage of developed socialism without essential formal changes in its

political system. In the main, the political system society had at
the previous stage continues to function . . .
   Socialist democracy is a system of organization and
functioning of the state and the whole political system of
socialism which is based on granting citizens and people's
associations broad rights and freedoms and providing conditions
in which they can really be recognized, drawing the masses into
vigorous social and political activities, and systematically
improving the mechanism of social regulation so as to
consolidate the position of socialism and build a communist
society.[5]

The Twenty-seventh Congress saw nothing new in the approach to
Soviet democracy. The new Party Rules prohibited individual leadership cults and wrote in collective leadership as an essential ingre-
dient of democratic centralism. Communist self-administration was
re-emphasized as the goal towards which Soviet society was developing.

## Democracy in action – the making of a Constitution

The 1977 USSR Constitution was not passed without due care and
deliberation. It was first mooted by Nikita Khrushchev in his report
to the Extraordinary Twenty-first Party Congress in January 1959.
The USSR Supreme Soviet appointed a Constitutional Commission
to consider the matter in April 1962. It was rumoured to be ready by
early 1964 but the draft was not published. A meeting of the
Constitutional Commission held on 16 July 1964 (following a
meeting of the Supreme Soviet) was reported in *Izvestia* the following day. The report indicated that reports had been given by Khrushchev (the Chairman) and by Brezhnev, Kosygin and Mikoyan.
Unfortunately no summary of these reports or of the debate on them
was given in *Izvestia*. Following the downfall of Khrushchev the
Constitutional Commission was reconstituted in December 1964
with Brezhnev as Chairman. There were no reports of its activities
over the following eight years. On the occasion of the fiftieth
anniversary of the founding of the USSR in December 1972 it was
announced that the draft Constitution would be presented to the
Twenty-fifth Party Congress scheduled for early 1976.[6] Yet when
the Twenty-fifth Congress met, Brezhnev was forced to apologize for
the non-appearance of the draft. It had, he said, proved more
difficult to complete than had been anticipated.[7] It was only after the
removal of Podgorny from the Soviet Presidency and from the
Politburo in May 1977 that the text of the draft Constitution was

published in the Soviet press on 4 June. A general public discussion followed, similar to but more extensive than that which preceded the adoption of the Stalin Constitution in 1936. Four-fifths of all adults were said to have taken part in this four-month discussion – 140 million people.[8] One and a half million meetings were held in industrial enterprises. There were 450,000 open Party meetings in which over three million people spoke in discussion. The draft was discussed in Soviets at all levels, in trade union meetings, Komsomol meetings, cooperatives, collective and state farms, schools, universities, colleges, research institutes, flat meetings, village meetings and many other places. Thousands of letters on the draft Constitution were published in the daily press and over 400,000 amendments were suggested. This mass of material was reviewed by the Constitutional Commission which recommended changes – mostly minor but some substantial – to 110 out of 173 articles in the draft and the inclusion of one new article dealing with electors' mandates. Following a report on the draft Constitution and the public debate on it by L.I. Brezhnev to the Supreme Soviet on October 4, there was a brief discussion over two days during which an editorial commission (under Brezhnev's chairmanship) met to prepare the final draft. This was passed unanimously by a joint sitting of both chambers of the Supreme Soviet on 7 October.

It is difficult for outsiders to judge the effectiveness of this exercise in Soviet democracy. Most published contributions to the debate were adulatory, praising the Party and the Soviet state for past achievements. Many anticipated a strengthening of Soviet democracy coming from the expansion of sections dealing with the rights and duties of citizens. Many contributions expressed national pride in the Soviet Union and in its achievements. Contributions which accepted the basic lines of the draft and clearly had massive support had the most chance of receiving official approval and adoption. Thus three amendments were made to the wording of Article 35 (dealing with women) and the extensive discussion of Article 8 (dealing with public participation and public opinion) led to its being moved (to form Article 9) while Article 16 of the draft (dealing with workers' collectives) was substantially rewritten and extended to become the new Article 8. But amendments suggesting the abandonment of Article 35 or the alteration of the balance of power between republican and local government on the one hand, and central government on the other, were rejected as being inconsistent with the basic principles of the Constitution. In like manner, those who advocated the retention of the wording of the old Constitution for particular articles (because of the simplicity and clarity of the language) got short shrift. One gets the impression that the leadership largely succeeded in producing an orchestrated discussion which legitimated the new Constitution but that spontaneous enthusiasm quickly evaporated. I found it difficult to get much serious discussion of the new Constitution in Moscow in January 1978, notwithstanding continued publicity on radio and in newspapers.

The 1977 Constitution is much longer than the one it replaced. Unlike the 1936 Constitution it has a lengthy preamble, twenty-one chapters and 174 articles as against thirteen chapters and 146 articles (in 1971). New chapters in the Constitution cover foreign affairs, defence of the socialist motherland and people's deputies. Other chapters have been split into two new chapters. The preamble established the basic theories of developed socialism and the state of the whole people. Basic organizational principles are stated early in the Constitution: 'democratic centralism' in Article 3 and Communist Party leadership in Article 6.

Rights and duties of citizens are set out in greater detail and in a revised form in Chapter 7, and those relating to equal citizenship in Chapter 6. The basic features of the contemporary Soviet economic system are set out in Chapter 2, and those relating to social development and culture in Chapter 3. The Constitution describes more carefully the existing political institutions and reflects the changing balance of power between the Presidium of the Supreme Soviet and the USSR Council of Ministers over recent years. Unlike the old Constitution, it does not delineate the entire Council of Ministers, thus avoiding the need for a constitutional amendment each time a ministry is established, subdivided or abolished. Consistent with current political theory all Soviets have been renamed 'Soviets of People's Deputies' instead of 'Soviets of Working People's Deputies', and 'National Areas' have been renamed 'Autonomous Areas'.

If the public debate on the Constitution was protracted the Supreme Soviet debate was truncated, as it usually is in the Soviet system. Likewise the preparation of the final text was done with undue speed so that the text is often carelessly drafted. In this respect it is inferior to its predecessor.

## Variety of opinions in the constitutional debate

Opinions expressed on various aspects of the Constitution varied considerably. I will illustrate this by citing a few of the letters published in *Pravda* dealing with women's rights. On 25 July 1977 *Pravda* published a provocative letter entitled 'Do We Need Article 35?'. I quote the letter in full:

Having become acquainted with the draft Constitution of the

USSR I have noticed some things with which I am not in agreement. Article 34 states that 'Citizens of the USSR are equal before the law irrespective of origin, social and property position, race, Party membership or sex.' But I turned the page of the newspaper and on the second page I read through Article 35 which is specially concerned with women.

Do we need this article? Our women head enterprises, lead scientific research, and often direct male collectives. In a word, the equal rights of women are fully operative in our society. Yes, and the position of men in the family has changed; there rests on them today a considerable share of the care of bringing up children. The husband helps the wife in the housework. In general, it isn't necessary to achieve equal rights and we can be proud of this.

But Article 35, although it speaks of the equal rights of women and men, has been formulated in such a way that, wittingly or unwittingly, it places women, to a certain extent, in a privileged position.

I suggest that this article should be excluded altogether or reformulated thus: 'Men and women in the USSR have equal rights.' That means that the subsequent points in this article concerning the guaranteeing of equal rights, as is necessary, will have the same relevance whether they apply to men or to women.

V. Kutsyi, Locksmith
Kabeln Factory, Odessa

The same issue contained the following letter headed 'Care Inspires':

We have read the draft of the new Constitution of the USSR with interest. Proudly we have discussed each article of this historic document. Who cannot but be proud of their motherland that she has achieved such a level of development which our people could only dream of earlier?

All women are talking a great deal about Article 35 in which it is written: 'Women in the USSR have equal rights with men . . .' Certainly, the realization of these rights has already been secured for some women by equal opportunities for the gaining of education and professional training in work, in awards and in many other things. It's a very important article of the draft! All these rights will be fully guaranteed. The care of the Party and of our State for Soviet women is an inspiration to work.

Right now we are outstripping our targets. We declare that we will fulfil the Five Year Plan of the sixtieth anniversary of the

Great October, and that we will keep our word.

N. Barkova, G. Kubanova
Textile operatives, Pskov Oblast

A week later on 31 July *Pravda* published a very long and moving letter from a woman in Central Asia under the heading 'Once More on Equal Rights'.

Locksmith V. Kutsyi from Odessa (in *Pravda*, 25 July) came up with the proposal to exclude Art.35 which states, 'Women in the USSR have equal rights with men', from the new Constitution.

In support of his proposal he stated: 'Our women head enterprises, lead scientific research, and often direct male collectives.' In a word, women have equal rights – things for us are customary, firm and always sure. And therefore it is not necessary to formulate it in the new Constitution.

The proposal has called forth a lively discussion. I and my girl friends at work don't agree with it. It's not at all as simple as Kutsyi claims.

First of all, in our Constitution there are not a few rights which are daily exercised; they are for us habitual and natural. Take the article of the draft where it states: 'Soviet citizens of different nationalities and races have equal rights'. Really, isn't that right and obvious for the people of our Soviet land?

Yet for all that, we want to have it in the Fundamental Law, and we are proud of this achievement. And its consolidation is still another witness of the democracy of the Soviet system. The adoption of the new USSR Constitution will have international significance.

Those countries which are choosing their own path of development may clearly make certain of the heights attained by the first government of socialism, and how the rights of Soviet people are guaranteed by the state.

The equality of women and men in our country hasn't happened of its own accord, it has been won in difficult struggle.

The women of Central Asia have taken an active part in this revolutionary transformation. Tursui Usmanova and Batrachka Meri Khodzhaena served as medical sisters in the Red Army and volunteered for the front in 1919. Zainab Kasymova from the town of Osk was a scout and agitator in the camp of the enemy.

But the tasks of revolution continued in the years of restoring a disorganized economy. And these skirmishes, in terms of their intensity, were no less heated than cavalry clashes. In Central

Asia women were from olden times excluded from public work. On them fell the yoke of *shariat* and *adat*, the religious fanaticism of the mullah, the imam and the bey. It was necessary to fight against these pressing inequalities. The transformation to the economic and social equality of women was not simple. Lenin wrote about it: 'To overcome this was difficult for the task here concerned an alteration striking fully at habitual, hardened, ossified "traditions".'

The class enemies gave support to the resistance and incited shady and backward men to persecute women activists. Thus the *Zhenotdel* delegate Kurbandzhan Zadubaeva from Tashkent-Guzera was killed.

But the struggle against polygamy, against bride abduction and against other survivals developed more quickly.

The return of the women of the East to the feudal order was already impossible. The former farmhand Surakan Kainazarova is today a double Hero of Soviet Labour. The road marked out by Kainazarova has become the route of thousands and thousands of women of socialist Kirgizia. Many of them are occupying government positions. Take our own corporation. Its director is D. Zaretskaya, famous for her leadership. The Sewing Factory '40 Years of October' is headed by Sh. Sherkulova. Seamstress Ainek Aitkulova has risen from an apprentice to a master worker, to being master of a section. She has won the award of Hero of Socialist Labour. There are thousands of women workers in various branches of industry, science, literature and art. I could list their names. But is it necessary? It's not about that that I want to speak.

Six decades of Soviet power have passed and the woman of the East has become an equal, and her rights are fully guaranteed. Gone is the old making of roads out of dung. However, its champions, while not open but hidden, are still continuing their stealthy, creeping activity. Today no-one openly defends bride-money. But really its variant has become '*achun basar*', 'quietening' the relatives of the bride . . . The old and obsolete still hold tenaciously in many families.

The Soviet state is doing a great deal for working women. The words of comrade L.I. Brezhnev addressed to women workers at the Twenty-sixth Congress of Soviet TUs are close to our hearts: 'I say frankly: we men are indebted to them. We are still far from having done everything to lighten the double burden which they carry in the home and in production.'

Returning to the draft Constitution and to the proposals of V. Kutsyi, I say this: I agree with that part of his letter where he speaks about the actual successes we have had in equalizing men and women in our country, but I don't agree that we have already done everything on that plane. Not so, quite a little remains to be worked over in order to strengthen what has already been achieved. Therefore I insist that Article 35 stay in the new Constitution of the USSR.

There is in truth one wish. At the end of that article there is a phrase about state aid to single mothers. As it happens I myself have brought up two children without a husband. But have I been isolated? I couldn't say that. Around me are my women friends, acquaintances, kind neighbours. The social responsibility I carry has been shared by all. And I don't stay out of work; my personal five-year plan I fulfilled in four years, and I will fulfil two years' tasks for the sixtieth Anniversary of the Great October. And my wish is that the Constitutional Commission consider if the words 'single mother' could not be changed for others less offensive.

K. AIDAROVA, Seamstress
Komsomol Silk Corporation, Frunze

The debate on Article 35 continued into September. I quote only two of the later letters, taken from *Pravda*, 3 September 1977.

In the pages of *Pravda* readers have sent in various contributions to the editor on Article 35: 'Women in the USSR have equal rights with men.' Opinion has been polarized on this issue. Locksmith V. Kutsyi from Odessa suggested the removal of this article from the Constitution, and seamstress K. Aidarova from Frunze proposed retaining Article 35 in the new Constitution.

Without distinguishing between the views of these comrades I propose that Article 35 should start thus: 'In the USSR men and women have equal rights.'

V. BROVKO, Lecturer
All-Union Correspondence Institute
of the Food Industry, Rostov-on-Don

The draft Constitution of the USSR fixes already established humane principles of our life. That applies to Article 35 which consolidates the political, social and other rights of Soviet women. I'm for all of it. In addition I suggest several worthwhile changes to the editor concerning the phrase which speaks of state aid to single mothers.

The expression 'single mother' is in my opinion unsatisfactory.

In socialist society based on collectivism there is not, nor can there be, loneliness as a social and political category. Therefore the phrase 'single mother' should be deleted.* To replace it I would suggest this to the editor, 'state aid to unmarried mothers'.

V. LEVCHENKO, Cand. of Legal Sc.
Moscow

Other correspondents suggested a reduction of the working day for working mothers with young children. The latter point was taken up by Soviet woman cosmonaut, Nikolaeva-Tereshkova, in the editing commission and accepted.

## How influential was the public debate?

The fact that two-thirds of the articles in the draft Constitution were revised is not an accurate measure of the effectiveness of the public debate. Many of the amendments were marginal. Others, which might appear of minor importance to a Westerner, were regarded as basic by many Soviet citizens. Major adjustments to the social or political system were not possible and even minor adjustments to the operating political system proved unacceptable to the leadership. Most of the decisions about wording were made by the Constitutional Commission (and its sub-committees) and the editing committee of the Supreme Soviet. Hundreds, possibly thousands, were involved in the process, not millions.

I take as examples of substantial revision through the public debate Articles 8 and 102 and as an example of minor (yet important) amendment Article 35.

*Article 8*

DRAFT (Article 16)
Collectives of working people and public organizations shall participate in the management of enterprises and associations in deciding matters concerning the organization of labour and everyday life, and the use of funds allocated for the development of production and also for social and cultural requirements and material incentives.

CONSTITUTION
Work collectives take part in discussing and deciding state and

---

* The Russian word 'odinokie' means 'lone' and 'lonely' as well as 'single'.

public affairs, in planning production and social development, in training and placing personnel, and in discussing and deciding matters pertaining to the management of enterprises and institutions, the improvement of working and living conditions, and the use of funds allocated both for developing production and for social and cultural purposes and financial incentives.

Work collectives promote socialist emulation, the spread of progressive methods of work, and the strengthening of production discipline, educate their members in the spirit of communist morality, and strive to influence their cultural level and qualifications.

*Article 102*
It was not in the draft.

CONSTITUTION
Electors give mandates to their Deputies.

The appropriate Soviets of People's Deputies shall examine the electors' mandates, take them into account in drafting economic and social development plans and in drawing up the budget, organize implementation of the mandates, and inform citizens about it.

*Article 35*

DRAFT
In the USSR women shall have equal rights with men.

Exercise of these rights shall be assured by according to women equal opportunities for education and professional training, for employment, remuneration and promotion, social, political and cultural activity, and likewise by special measures for the protection of the labour and health of women; by legal protection, material and moral support of mother and child, including paid leaves and other benefits to mothers and expectant mothers, and state aid to single mothers.

CONSTITUTION
Women and men have equal rights in the USSR.

Exercise of these rights is ensured by according women equal access with men to education and vocational and professional training, equal opportunities in employment, remuneration and promotion, and in social and political and cultural activity, and by special labour and health protection measures for women; by providing conditions enabling mothers to work, by legal protection and material and moral support for mothers and children, including paid leaves and other benefits for expectant mothers and mothers, and gradual reduction of working time for mothers with small children.

These modifications to the draft Constitution were sometimes based on the recognition of recent legislation or practices but they sometimes anticipated legislation. Thus Article 8 went beyond existing law and it had to be matched by a new Statute on Work Collectives passed by the USSR Supreme Soviet in June 1983. Again the draft Statute was made the basis of a broad public discussion in which 110 million were said to have participated and 130,000 proposals submitted. These were reviewed by the Legislative Proposals Commissions of the USSR Supreme Soviet before the Statute was passed by the Supreme Soviet. Changes were made to 21 out of 23 articles in the draft.[9] Electors' mandates had operated for many years before they were written into the Statute on Deputies of Soviets in September 1971. Thus the inclusion of Article 102 in the 1977 Constitution did not vary the practice in any way; it merely incorporated it into the Fundamental Law. Most of what went into Article 35 reflected established practice. Even the amendment providing for shorter hours without loss of pay for working mothers recognized a practice which already operated in some sectors of the economy. But the incorporation of this into the Constitution made it a general principle and this required early legislation. In March 1981 the Central Committee of the CPSU and the USSR Council of Ministers published two joint decisions, 'On the Means for Improving State Help for Families with Children', and, 'On the Means for Further Improvement of the Social Security of the Population'. This legislation extended the period that mothers could stay away from work after the birth of a child without loss of pay or status to eighteen months (and in some cases to three and a half years), provided child-minding subsidies to full-time mothers of between 35 and 50 roubles a month, a reduction of the working day for mothers to six hours without loss of pay, and other improvements to pensions.[10] In early September 1981 a combined decision of the Central Committee, the Presidium of the Supreme Soviet, the Council of Ministers and the Trade Unions vastly extended the March legislation. This new measure made the three-day rest period for mothers with children under twelve years general and introduced a system of maternity allowances beginning at the first child. It extended the existing assistance for women with large families of five or more children.[11]

A great deal of other consequential legislation followed the adoption of the USSR Constitution on 7 October 1977. This included the new Constitutions of the Union Republics, the Electoral Law of the USSR and the Statute on the Council of Ministers (all passed by July 1978) and the Statute on the Basic Powers of Krai, Oblast, Autonomous Oblast and Autonomous Okrug Soviets passed in June 1980.[12]

Does the new Constitution represent an expansion of Soviet democracy? I believe that it does this through extending both the rights and duties of citizens, through enlarging the process of public participation and through a number of adjustments to Soviets and administrative agencies. The public debate on the new Constitution was, within limits, an exercise in direct democracy. The new Constitution does not represent the 'perfecting' of Soviet democracy because the authorities kept close guard over its key bureaucratic features which act to restrict, and at times, to contradict the democratic process. These restrictions will be explored in the following section of this chapter.

## Is the USSR a democracy?

The Communist Party of the Soviet Union has always claimed to believe in democracy and has frequently sought to promote it in practice. This objective of a democratic society has been subordinated to the objective of building socialism and communism. The pursuit of these various objectives has not been free from contradictions. The Soviet conception of democracy is not identical with that held in the West but it is historically related to the latter. It represents a variant of socialist theories of democracy which first developed in Western Europe in the 1840s. Lenin sometimes distinguished democracy as a system of government (*demokratia*) from democratic behaviour in political practice (*demokratizm*). The distinction has not been altogether abandoned but the latter term is seldom used nowadays. There is a similar blurring of the distinction between democracy as a method of government and democracy as a set of ideals (or aspirations) in recent Western theory.

I do not think Soviet democracy can be measured against Western theories of democracy. I do not think that democracy is synonymous with a bi-party or a multi-party system, with the operation of ministerial responsibility, with the operation of a system of separation of powers between legislative, executive and judicial bodies, with judicial review, with referenda, or with a popularly elected President. Yet clearly a certain political climate and practice is required for the operation of democracy anywhere. I would accept the following statement by Roy A. Medvedev as providing a useful operational framework for discussing the question of Soviet democracy:

Real democracy cannot exist (and socialist democracy is no exception) unless the rights of both majority and minority are guaranteed, unless there is a place for dissent and opposition and the possibility of forming independent social and political associations. There must also be freedom of conscience, freedom of movement, free elections by secret ballot, and absolute equality before the law. In Soviet conditions, socialist democracy should provide greater rights for the Union Republics. There is a need to reduce irrational centralization in all areas of economic, political, and cultural life, and to ensure effective popular control over all activities of government . . .[13]

All of the above are claimed to exist in the Soviet Union and are provided for in Soviet legislation. Soviet practice is another matter. Minority rights are permitted only if they are considered not to challenge any aspect of the existing order. Private dissent is tolerated but public dissent is discouraged and penalized. While Soviet elections are secret and serve to involve millions in the process of selecting and electing candidates they do not allow for the voter to choose between candidates at the poll. There is greater freedom of movement in the Soviet Union than there was thirty years ago but the internal passport system still restricts movement within the country, especially as between rural and urban areas, while travel abroad is confined to a privileged few. Despite repeated attempts to decentralize the system it remains one of the most centralized, if not the most centralized, political systems in the world. Union republican and local governments have received additional powers over recent decades; in practice, very little has changed.

Some of the changes advocated by Medvedev seem to be inappropriate. Separation of powers, for example, is against a basic principle of the Soviet system. Thus we find him suggesting that:

Ministers and people in basic positions of responsibility in the government should be selected by the Supreme Soviet from among the most outstanding and capable men in the country. But if a person appointed to a government post happens also to be a deputy he should resign from the Supreme Soviet, and conversely, if a minister is elected deputy he should give up his ministerial office. Needless to say, the party would continue to exercise a decisive influence on the Supreme Soviet . . .[14]

Consistent with this opinion Medvedev favours very long sessions and much more debate in the Soviets.[15] No doubt longer sessions of all Soviets would allow for greater debate of legislation and, at least at city and regional levels, there is already a trend to increase the number of Soviet sessions and to make them longer. But this is a long way from the permanent sitting of the Supreme Soviet as recommended by Medvedev. What would happen then to the principle that deputies must continue in their normal employment or to the practice (steady since 1966) of having the main work of legislative preparation exercised by the Standing Commissions? There is a distinct tendency in Medvedev, as with many other Soviet dissidents, to wholesale copying of the USA.

How effective is public participation in the Soviet political system? I have discussed this matter in earlier chapters and in previous writing. Yet there still remain some points needing clarification. The scale is impressive. By mid-1984 there were over eighteen million members (and candidate members) of the Communist Party, over forty million members of the Komsomol and 135 million members of trade unions.[16] Millions more participate in other social organizations, cultural and educational associations. Thirty million people are said to participate directly in the work of local Soviets. Significant extensions to this process have taken place over the past two decades through such bodies as Collective Farm Councils (operating from the district level upwards), NOT (Scientific Organization of Labour) Councils operating in industrial enterprises and farms, Knowledge Society activities (over three million members in 1984), Societies for the Preservation of Nature, Historical Monuments, etc. The figures are undoubtedly exaggerated since totals do not allow for overlapping memberships. But they represent a massive public participation. This is mobilization by the Party to enable the realization of Party goals. Yet public participation is an end in itself and not merely a means to an end. Nor is the participation devoid of decision-making. Decisions have to be taken at all levels in a political system and in the Soviet Union even if most decisions are centralized and Party-dominated they are usually made in outline and consequential decisions of all types have to be taken at republican and local levels. These decisions relate to economic, social and cultural matters; they involve the preparation of decisions, plans for development, policy recommendations to executive bodies and supervision over administrative agencies.

Who then takes these decisions? At the central level it is mainly the Politburo, the Secretariat, the Central Committee and its apparatus, the Council of Ministers and individual Ministries and State Committees, the Presidium of the Supreme Soviet and the Standing Commissions of both Chambers. Some decisions involve social organizations such as trade unions and the Komsomol. Many thousands are involved in the central decision-making process.

Millions are involved at the local government level. The figure of thirty million is not meaningful; it is more like six to seven million of whom perhaps 5 per cent hold paid administrative positions in local government. The most effective agencies of this local Soviet *aktiv* are the Standing Commissions, serviced by almost five million deputies and non-deputies. Every year the Standing Commissions of local Soviets prepare between 500,000 and 600,000 questions for Soviet sessions and between 800,000 and 900,000 matters for recommendation to Executive Committees.[17]

To argue that public participation is meaningful in the Soviet system is not to argue that it is as effective as it might be if some structural reforms were carried out along the lines I will shortly suggest. Although the research carried out on very small samples of former Soviet citizens now resident in Israel is interesting, it does not afford any basis for measuring its effectiveness.[18]

For the remainder of this chapter I wish to examine what I call the structural limitations to Soviet democracy. These are limitations which follow from the organizational principles of the Soviet political system, which are part of the historical experience of the socialist revolution carried out under adverse conditions. For the most part, these structures have limited but not prevented democratic development. Even democratic centralism — both as principle and practice — is capable of modification.

The structural features I will examine here are four: party leadership, democratic centralism, dual subordination and bureaucracy. This is far from being an exhaustive list but it is sufficient for the purposes of my argument.

The principle of Communist Party leadership is set out in Article 6 of the 1977 Constitution.

*Article 6*
The leading and directing force of Soviet society and the nucleus of its political system and of all state and social organizations is the Communist Party of the Soviet Union. The CPSU exists for the people and serves the people.

The Communist Party, armed with Marxist-Leninist theory, determines the general course of development of society and the course of domestic and foreign policy of the USSR, directs the great constructive work of the Soviet people, and provides a planned, systematic and scientific formulation to their struggles for the victory of communism.

All Party organizations act within the framework of the Constitution of the USSR.[19]

The final sentence was not in the original draft.

The trouble with Party leadership of the entire society and polity is that it always leads to *podmena*, substitution. This tendency was criticzed as early as the Eighth Party Congress in March 1919 but it is impossible to check. Party organs are meant to lead and direct but not to administer Soviets or economic agencies. But if state agencies are neglectful of Party directions, Party committees are inclined to step in in order to retrieve the situation. This practice of supplanting Soviets and economic agencies has always been criticized by the Party leaders. As recently as March 1984 K.U. Chernenko, in a speech made to workers in the Party *apparat* in the Kremlin warned that Party committees must not overstep their functions: 'They organize the fulfilment of tasks not apart from economic and Soviet organs, but through them.' [20] But the practice persists. It is not surprising that Soviets are often criticized for tardiness, 'for sheltering behind the broad back of the Party'. This is not to say that Soviets never show initiative for they clearly do on many matters. The central Party organs and apparatus seek to direct all spheres of economic, social and political life but intermediate level committees are mainly concerned with economic direction. Thus in 1983 regional Party committees issued, on average, 1270 letters and telegrams of instruction on economic matters but only twenty-two on questions of organization and education.[21] Clearly, the Party is not able to effectively direct the entire society.

A key mechanism the Party uses to establish its leadership is by control over personnel not merely within the Party organization itself but in state agencies and social organizations. Stalin was fond of saying that 'Cadres decide everything'. Indeed the modern *nomenklatura* system (outlined in Chapter 3) dates from Stalin's domination of the Central Committee apparatus in the early 1920s. The modern *nomenklatura* system is really a series of central, republican, regional, city and district 'job lists' controlled by Party, state agencies and social organizations. There are probably more than two n.illion nomenklatured positions in the USSR today. These include many positions which are nominally elective positions. Thus Chairmen and Secretaries of Executive Committees of Village Soviets are nominally elected by the Village Soviet. They are in fact appointed by the District Party Committee and approved by the Soviet. The system sometimes causes clashes with local Soviets but not often.[22] There is clearly a contradiction between the *nomenklatura* system and the elective principle of a democracy. Appointment of key office holders from above is a normal procedure in many administrative structures but few modern countries carry it to the degree practised in the Soviet Union. It is possible that some positions (chiefly in areas such as education and science) have been 'de-classified' over recent years but the system has undergone no major reduction. Clearly, a substantial reduction in the size and scope of the *nomenklatura* system and a reduction in the size of the Central Committee apparatus would strengthen Soviet democracy.[23]

To my mind a single-party system is not necessarily incompatible with democracy, provided that it is able to ensure democracy within itself and is willing to tolerate freedom of opinion and association outside of the party. The latter condition does not exist in the Soviet Union. The former exists only in part. It has not been possible to restore inner-Party criticism. Individual Party members are guaranteed the right to take criticism direct to the Central Committee but they may get short shrift if they do. Some attempt was made to guarantee minority rights within Primary Party Organizations in 1956 but they are still fragile and uncertain. It is hard to see how a party as large as the CPSU could be fully democratic. It is organized along hierarchical lines, it operates according to the principle of democratic centralism and it carries a large professional apparatus. It has its own *nomenklatury* right down to the district level. Secretaries of Primary Party Organizations are not really elected by the membership; they are appointed by the District Committee.

The term 'democratic centralism' seems to have been first used by Lenin in 1906.[24] It soon became part of the organizational theory of the Bolshevik Party and has been part of the theory and practice of Bolshevism since 1918–19. Its classic exposition is that in Rule 19 of the current (1986) Rules of the Communist Party of the Soviet Union.

19. The guiding principle of the organizational structure of the life and activities of the Party is democratic centralism, which signifies:

(a) election of all leading Party bodies from the lowest to the highest;

(b) periodical reports of Party bodies to their Party organizations and to higher bodies;

(c) strict Party discipline and subordination of the minority to the majority;

(d) the decisions of higher bodies are obligatory for lower bodies.

(e) collectivity in the work of all organizations and leading organs of the Party and the personal responsibility of every communist for the implementation of his duties and Party commissions.

The principle was not stated explicitly in the 1936 Constitution but it was clearly implicit and was invariably discussed in detail by Soviet legal texts of that period. It is explicit in Article 3 of the 1977 Constitution.

> *Article 3.* The organization and activity of the Soviet state is constructed on and conforms to the principle of democratic centralism: the election of all organs of state power from the lowest to the highest, their accountability to the people, and the obligation of lower bodies to observe the decisions of higher ones. Democratic centralism combines united leadership with initiative and creative activity in the localities and with the responsibility of each state organ and official for fulfilling their tasks.[25]

This is an admirable principle for a party seeking to direct the entire course of development of a society. In the government sphere it means that the Supreme Soviet and its agencies direct the activities of lower Soviets and their Executive Committees and departments. In the large cities, City Soviets direct the activities of District Soviets within the city. In the rural areas Provincial Soviets or Territorial Soviets direct the rural District Soviets which in turn direct the Village Soviets. With few exceptions departments of local Soviets are matched by departments and ministries in higher Soviets. Decisions taken by the USSR ministries are communicated through this network to the appropriate departments in local government. While local Soviets have wide responsibilities and powers they generally act as subordinate agencies of central organs. This is particularly so in the budget-planning area. The USSR operates a unified state budget and economic plan. Under this system the budgets of Union Republics are incorporated into the State Budget of the USSR. In like manner the Budget of the RSFSR will include the budgets of the local governments directly subordinate to it. The Moscow City Budget will include the allocations for revenue and expenditure of the 32 City Districts into which Moscow is divided. The same system operates with the Economic Plan. This centralized budget and plan place severe restrictions on the activities of local government. While budgets have expanded at all levels of government during the post-Stalin years they have expanded most rapidly at the All-Union level since the mid 1960s. Local government expenditure as a percentage of the USSR budget was 15.9 per cent in 1950, 19.7 per cent in 1960. Despite continued rapid growth in urban population it had fallen to 18.7 per cent by 1970 and 17.9 per cent by 1975.[26]
The principle of democratic centralism is supposed to combine

democracy and centralism. This could make some sense in a small and relatively homogeneous community but in a country as large, populous and diverse as the USSR the centralism tends to crowd out the democracy. This tendency is heightened by the centralized appointment system and by the operation of the related principle of dual subordination.

Dual subordination (*dvoinoe podchinenie*) is a basic organizational principle in Soviet administration although it is not explicitly stated either in the 1936 or the 1977 Constitution. It is really an aspect of democratic centralism although it is often set out in Soviet texts on constitutional law as a separate principle. The following is a typical definition.

> Dual subordination means that the organ is subordinated to two lines: (a) to *vertical* (i.e., to control from above) in order to provide for the unity of the activities of all similar local organs, subordinating that activity to the unified plan and the directives of the centre, and (b) to *horizontal* subordination, which gives the possibility to the state apparatus to have direct ties with the population and so to provide guarantees against the transformation of local organs into bureaucratic apparatuses.[27]

Dual subordination has proved more effective in maintaining control from above than control by local Soviets. This can be illustrated by the limited success of the USSR government's attempts to transfer control over housing, retail trade and everyday services from the ministries to local Soviets. In August 1967 the USSR Council of Ministers directed that all housing controlled by ministries be transferred to local Soviets. But by 1979 local Soviets controlled only 40 per cent of the public housing in their areas.[28] The 1971 regulations on District and City Soviets provided for the transfer of all retail trade and services in the area to the control of District and City Soviets. But this was not achieved in all cases. The rationalization of the industrial structure carried out in April 1973 and following months also weakened local Soviet control over local industries since many plants were transferred from local control and absorbed into combines which were mainly under Union Republican or All-Union control. Since the profits from such transferred establishments no longer went into local budgets, local government was further weakened.[29]

The limitations on local government mentioned in the previous paragraph were frequently referred to in the public discussion on the new Constitution in 1977. I will cite only a few passages from one of the longer letters, written by a machinist in a railway workshop, a

Hero of Socialist Labour and a member of his City and Territorial Soviet.[30]

Take the Krai Soviet. It is called on to plan and coordinate the development of economic and social-cultural construction throughout the territory of the Krai. However, in fact it plans the development only of the economy directly subordinate to it. What concerns the enterprise subordinated to a higher authority and their managers almost always is to automatically include the economic plan in the form in which the Soviet organs received it from the ministries and the Western Siberian Railway. Our organization has Union Republican as well as zonal subordination. Major problems arising from the development of arterial transport are decided by the USSR Ministry of Railways. But it's a major worry to realize the production program, and the section of the plan on social-cultural-welfare is postponed to the last. As a result we don't have enough housing, cultural-enlightenment, kindergartens, creches, sporting and entertainment facilities. As a deputy I have already taken up these questions repeatedly in the Zheleznodorozhny *raiispolkom*, Barnaul Town Soviet and in the Krai Soviet. As far as possible we have given help with flats, with expanding kindergartens, general schools and music schools . . .

One could cite several other examples, where the ministry has not acted jointly and concertedly with the Krai organs concerning social questions, beginning with municipal problems and ending with problems concerning the protection of local resources . . .

By the way, it is the obligation of the local organs of power to exercise control over housing construction. But we have very little power to do that – there are no proper levers of influence, economic or administrative . . . It's time to stop the departmental approach to the solution of social problems. It would be a good thing if Article 146 said something about that and contained the supplementary words, 'Ministries and departments are closely interdependent with local organs of power with the aim of the integrated development of the territories and provinces, economic regions and branch industries' . . .

It follows that it is necessary to regulate the interdependence of local Soviets and enterprises, branches and combines, and administrations situated in neighbouring territories and provinces. That is so in the Altai where a majority of the divisions of the RSFSR Ministry of Light Industry are so situated. Practically all of their products go to meet local needs. Moreover, many of them (in particular, clothing manufactures) don't comply with set tasks. Several are even cutting back their production. But the Krai Soviet and its Executive Committee haven't any power to influence these activities. They are not even able to influence the assortment of the goods produced, although that is necessary.

What's the way out? Obviously, several of these enterprises could be transferred so that they are directly controlled by the Krai Soviet. Perhaps there's another variant: put them under dual subordination: enterprise-combine and territory (province). To the Soviet should be left the ultimate power within the limits of its authority to take decisions which are obligatory for the leaders of the enterprises and which take into account the appropriate ministries and departments. In that case, in Article 147, after the words, 'Decisions of local Soviets must be fulfilled by all enterprises, branches and organizations in the territory of the Soviet, as well as by individual citizens', should be added, in my opinion, making it more precise, 'independently of their subordination'.

Further changes were recommended to the draft of Article 149, changes designed to strengthen the position of Territorial Soviets. But to no avail; the Constitution accepted the principle of dual subordination but did nothing to ensure that horizontal subordination would be effective.

Throughout this book I have several times discussed the problem of Soviet bureaucracy and the restraints it imposes on democracy. The Soviet system contains many agencies of popular control designed to check bureaucratic behaviour by officials. But the inherent contradiction between the rules governing the appointment of officials and the democratic principle of election are never admitted. It is true that any bureaucratic structure tends to contradict democracy. The contradiction is less however when many positions at all levels are filled by election or by open competition. Neither of these safeguards is characteristic of the Soviet system. Very few Party, state or social organization positions are elective in the full sense of the term. There is no open competition for positions even between those already holding nomenklatured positions. While new people are frequently co-opted into the *apparat*, once in the *apparat* they are seldom dropped. They may be displaced from a particular position, demoted, transferred or promoted, but they are seldom excluded altogether. There is a mechanism for electing leaders in the Soviet Union but the domination of the Party *apparat* ensures that the

Central Committee will endorse the Politburo member already chosen by that body. It is not possible for the public, even through representative bodies like the Soviets, to influence this choice.

The Soviet Union is in some ways a democratic society. From one point of view Soviet political history over the past thirty years has been concerned with establishing and re-establishing the democratic basis achieved by the 1917 Revolution but largely lost during the Stalin dictatorship. In this process, the Soviet leadership has played the directing role. This has meant a slow fumbling movement towards greater democracy. Even when the process has been accelerated as in 1956–7, 1961–2, 1977–8 and since 1983, it has always been a guided democracy, guided from above by the Party leadership. But the process has had massive support from the public, for the public, much more than the leadership, feels the need for broader democracy.

Soviet society is more co-ordinated than most capitalist societies but that does not make it undemocratic. There is a great deal of democratic activity in Soviet society and its scope is expanding. In some respects (workers' collectives, public participation, people's control, etc.) the society has greater democracy than its capitalist counterparts. There is also, at many levels, greater social equality. Passivity and isolation are still problems but to a lesser extent than in many Western societies.

The Communist Party aims to direct the development of the entire society. Yet this direction is less than complete. Indeed it is doubtful if the Party really tries to direct in detail many aspects of the public activity of citizens. Thus the Party (in this case the District Party Committee) no longer keeps close control over such agencies as citizens' militia and comrades' courts. In so far as such agencies are supervised, the supervision comes more from local Soviets and local trade union committees than from the District Committee. What keeps such agencies going is not Party direction but the enthusiasm and initiative of the activists, Party and non-Party.

The Soviet Union is an imperfect and unfinished socialist society. Its political system is more authoritarian than democratic but the democratic elements are growing and will eventually become dominant.

# Notes

## Chapter 1   The Soviet approach to socialism and its Marxist critics

1   Cited in Marcel Liebman (1975), p. 213.
2   V.I. Lenin, 'Better Fewer, But Better' (1923); Leon Trotsky, 'The New Course' (1923).
3   Cited in T.H. Rigby (1972b), p. 133.
4   V.I. Lenin (1946), *Selected Works*, Vol. 9, p. 403.
5   J. Stalin (1945), espec. pp. 156–63.
6   *Op.cit.*, p. 157.
7   Leon Trotsky, *The Permanent Revolution*. Excerpt in V.V. Calverton (1937), pp. 421–6.
8   *The USSR Economy: A Statistical Abstract*, USSR Council of Ministers, Moscow (1956). London: Lawrence and Wishart (1957), pp. 45–8, 55–8.
9   *Narodnoe khozyaistvo SSSR za 60 let* (1977), p. 8. My category 'working class' includes both manual workers and white-collar workers.
10   J. Stalin, 'Report to the 18th Congress of the CPSU (B)', in J. Stalin (1945), pp. 631–8.
11   J. Stalin (1950).
12   L.G. Churchward (1961), (1975, Ch. 6).
13   Kanet was incorrect in his 1968 evaluation. See Roger E. Kanet (1968), M.P. Shedrik (1970) and Alfred B. Evans (1977).
14   *Constitution (Fundamental Law) of the Union of Soviet Socialist Republics*, October 7, 1977, Moscow (1977), pp. 13–14.
15   A good example is the article by P. Fedoseev (1976).
16   James Burnham (1945), Ch. xiv.
17   Milovan Djilas (1957), pp. 47, 58, 165.
18   Thesis 10. *Critique* No. 3 (1974), p. 19f.
19   David Lane (1976), p. 42.
20   H.H. Ticktin (1973).
21   Leon Trotsky (1965), pp. 111–12.
22   H.H. Ticktin (1973) *Critique* Nos. 1 and 2. The percentage of working class first-year day tertiary students rose from 38.7 in 1965 to 45.5 in 1975–6. See the tables in M.N. Rutkevich (1978), pp. 46, 110.
23   H.H. Ticktin (1973), *Critique* No. 1, p. 41.
24   Tony Cliff (1974), Martin Nicolaus (1976).
25   The concept of 'social imperialism' was developed by Chinese writers in

the years after 1961. It has been gradually abandoned since 1976 and largely replaced by that of 'Soviet hegemony'.
26 Tony Cliff (1974), pp. 153–4, 167–70.
27 Martin Nicolaus (1976) *passim.*
28 Alec Nove (1977), p. 317.
29 Mary McAuley (1977), pp. 241–3; Henry Norr (1968). See also *Pravda,* 26 July, 1978, editorial.
30 Mervyn Matthews (1972), p. 78. Matthews cites a Soviet survey of 888 family budgets in Sverdlovsk in 1966–7 which showed that 46.4 per cent of the incomes of the poorest families came from 'social funds' while only 11.5 per cent did so in the case of the richest families.
31 *Narodnoe khozyaistvo SSSR v 1979g.* (1980), p. 394.
32 Alec Nove (1977), p. 42.

## Chapter 2   The social structure of the Soviet Union

1 Terence M. Cox (1979), p. 29; V.S. Semenov (ed.), (1968).
2 Yu. V. Arutyunyan (1971).
3 M.N. Rutkevich (1977), p. 48f.
4 F. Burlatsky, A. Galkin (1974), pp. 68–9.
5 Yu. V. Arutyunyan, *op.cit.,* pp. 109–12.
6 Alex Inkeles (1968). His ten class-status groups represent a blurring of Weber's distinction between class and status.
7 Mervyn Matthews (1972), David Lane (1982).
8 *Nar. khoz. SSSR v 1979g.,* p. 9.
9 Boris Rumer (1981).
10 Here I follow S. Ossowski (1963).
11 *Nar. khoz. SSSR v 1979g.,* p. 292f.
12 Calculated from information given in *Nar. khoz. SSSR v 1979g.* The average payment in state farms per labour-day was 6.36 roubles while the average payment to collective farmers (in money and produce) per labour-day was 5.35 roubles. Collective farmers however were only paid for the number of days worked.
13 Alec Nove (1982).
14 David Lane (1982), p. 41.
15 David Lane and Felicity O'Dell (1978) pp. 18–20.
16 *Op.cit.,* p. 41.
17 For a Soviet article in English, see T.I. Oiserman (1965).
18 Zvi Gitelman (1977).
19 Wolfgang Teckenberg (1978).
20 Leslie Dienes (1975).
21 Figures taken from 1970 census material. *Itogi vsesouznoi perepisi naselenia 1970 goda,* III, p. 368f.
22 *Vestnik statistiki,* No. 2, 1981, p. 11.
23 Christel Lane (1978), espec. pp. 149–51.
24 *Zhenshchiny v SSSR* (M.1982), p. 8.
25 Figures from 1970 census material.
26 Murray Yanowitch (1977), p. 168.

27 See in particular, Alastair McAuley (1981b). See also, Mervyn Matthews (1972) and Gail Lapidus (1978).
28 Z.A. Yankova (1978), pp. 156–7.
29 Leslie Dienes (1975). 1970–9 figures from *Nar. khoz. SSSR v 1979g.*, p. 11.
30 *Zhenshchiny v SSSR* (1982), p. 8.
31 Nancy Lubin (1981).
32 Cf. the table in V.M. Selunskaya (ed.), (1982), p. 35.
33 Yu. V. Arutyunyan (1971), espec. Ch. VIII; Terence M. Cox (1979), p. 40f.

## Chapter 3 Ruling class or power elite?

1 Herman F. Akhimov (1958); Ivan Szelenyi (1978).
2 Alec Nove (1975).
3 Michael Voslensky (1980).
4 Based mainly on Jerry F. Hough (1969).
5 Alec Nove (1975), p. 630.
6 Michael Voslensky (1980), p. 32.
7 *Op.cit.*, pp. 76–92.
8 *Op.cit.*, p. 101.
9 *Op.cit.*, p. 125.
10 *Op.cit.*, pp. 217, 236.
11 *Op.cit.*, p. 362.
12 *Op.cit.*, pp. 400–3.
13 *Op.cit.*, p. 413.
14 G. Mosca (1965, 1895), p. 50; V. Pareto (1966, 1916).
15 Mervyn Matthews (1978), p. 180.
16 *Op.cit.*, p. 90.
17 Murray Yanowitch (1977), pp. 157–9. This was a central element in the reform experiment at the Akchi state farm in Kazakhstan over the years 1968–70.
18 C. Wright Mills (1957), FN p. 217.
19 *Op.cit.* (1959), espec., pp. 27, 54, 78, 168.
20 Most notably H. Gordon Skilling and Franklyn Griffiths (eds), (1971).
21 Cf. Hélène Carrère d'Encausse (1980), p. 181f. The American political scientist, Jan S. Adams has also used this term. See Jan S. Adams (1980), pp. 122–4, 140. The term was first used by Jerry F. Hough in 1972.
22 T.B. Bottomore (1964), p. 26.
23 *Op.cit.*, p. 14; cf. p. 20.
24 Mervyn Matthews (1978), p. 30.

## Chapter 4 The intelligentsia revisited

1 L.G. Churchward (1973), Introduction and Chapter 1.
2 *Op. cit.*, p. 6.
3 See the review by A.K. Sokolov in *Istoria SSSR*, No. 2, 1975, pp. 191–3. See also the comments by M.N. Rutkevich (1977), p. 67. M.N. Rutkevich, *et al.* (1978), pp. 49–50.
4 M.N. Rutkevich (1977), p. 35.

5  E.g., M.R. Zezina (1982). Thus she estimates the Soviet intelligentsia in 1970 at 23,206,700 but there were only 16,840,700 specialists with tertiary and secondary specialist qualifications in the workforce at that time.
6  A.K. Sokolov, *op. cit.*
7  Antonio Gramsci discusses the intelligentsia at various places in his *Prison Notebooks*. See Antonio Gramsci (1957), pp. 118–25; and Antonio Gramsci (1971), *passim*. The distinction between 'traditional' and 'organic' intellectuals is somewhat blurred in Gramsci.
8  Antonio Gramsci (1957), p. 122.
9  Mervyn Matthews (1982), p. 117. The number of specializations in tertiary establishments (*VUZy*) was reduced to 274 in 1964 but the total had risen to 449 by 1979.
10  Cf. the review of *The Soviet Intelligentsia* by A.K. Sokolov in *Istoria SSSR*, No. 2, 1975.
11  *Op. cit.*, pp. 48–9.
12  Calculated from tables in *Nar. khoz. SSSR v 1979g.*, pp. 397–8.
13  I have not been able to find any discussion of this in either Western or Soviet sources. It was probably an unplanned consequence of the Education Act of 1958 which made 'work experience' an essential qualification for most applicants seeking admission to *VUZy* or technicums. The main beneficiaries of this reform would appear to have been 'working-class' males.
14  *Zhenshcheny v SSSR* (1982), p. 12.
15  Antonio Gramsci (1957), p. 122.
16  I use the term here not in the Gramscian sense but in the sense in which it is commonly used in the West and sometimes in the Soviet Union. An intellectual in this sense is one whose intellectual interest is broad, who is concerned with the criticism of the entire society. For the 'semi-intelligentsia' see L.G. Churchward (1973), p. 5.

## Chapter 5   Social mobility in the Soviet Union

1  Mervyn Matthews (1982), p. 99.
2  *Nar. khoz. SSSR 1922–1972*, p. 9.
3  M.N. Rutkevich and F.R. Filippov (eds), (1978), p. 46.
4  David Lane (1982), p. 19.
5  *Zhenshchiny v SSSR* (1982), p. 10.
6  *Nar. khoz. SSSR 1922–1972*, p. 9. *Nar. khoz. SSSR v 1979g.*, p. 7.
7  M.N. Rutkevich and F.R. Filippov (eds), (1978), p. 46.
8  I.M. Muminov (1979), pp. 177, 183.
9  *Pravda* 19 August 1982, editorial, 'Universal Secondary Education' in which the rural areas of Central Asia and also the Yakut, Udmurt, Komi and Dagestan ASSRs are criticized.
10  *Nar. khoz. SSSR v 1979g.*, pp. 489, 493–4.
11  Mervyn Matthews (1982), pp. 55, 130.
12  M.N. Rutkevich and F.R. Filippov (eds), (1978), p. 125.
13  Calculated from the table in *Nar. khoz. SSSR 1922–1982*, p. 49.
14  Yu. V. Arutyunyan (1971), p. 196 and (1969).
15  K. Akhmuradov (1972), p. 77.

16 Yu. V. Arutyunyan (1971), p. 329.
17 *Ibid.*, pp. 312–15.
18 L.G. Churchward (1973). See the table on p. 28.
19 *Nar. khoz. SSSR 1922–1982*, p. 485.
20 David Lane (1982), p. 112.
21 M.N. Rutkevich and F.R. Filippov (eds), (1978), p. 105.
22 David Lane and Felicity O'Dell (1978), p. 102.
23 *Partiinaya zhizn*, No. 14, 1981.
24 Murray Yanowitch (1977), p. 118.
25 Alex Inkeles (1968), pp. 156, 409.
26 To a certain degree both Mervyn Matthews (1982) and David Lane (1982) do this.

## Chapter 6 Towards an analysis of Soviet politics

1 Konrad Grigor Suny (1983).
2 Walter Laqueur, *Survey*, No. 41, April 1962, p. 58.
3 *Op. cit.*, Preface, p. vii.
4 Jerry F. Hough (1976); Theodore H. Friedgut (1979).
5 L.G. Churchward, 'Continuity and Change in Soviet Local Government', *Soviet Studies*, ix, 1958, pp. 256–85. Later articles appeared in *Australian Outlook*, Sept. 1959, *Osteuropa* No. 1, 1960, and in *Soviet Studies*, April 1966.
6 *Op. cit.*, Preface, p. viii.
7 Samuel N. Harper and Donald Thompson (1949), Preface.
8 Cf. Leonard Schapiro (1972), p. 14.
9 Franz Neumann (1942) p. 46f.
10 E.g., C. Grant Robertson, *Religion and the Totalitarian State* (1936).
11 Rudolf Schlesinger (1947), p. 67.
12 *Op. cit.*, see the Preface to the first edition.
13 *Op. cit.*, second edition, 1958, p. 323.
14 *Op. cit.*, p. 379.
15 *Op. cit.*, p. 323.
16 Daniel Bell, 'Ten Theories in Search of Reality: The Prediction of Soviet Behaviour' (1957), in Bell (1961), Ch. 14.
17 Max Weber, *Basic Concepts in Sociology*, p. 52f.
18 C.J. Friedrich and Z.K. Brzezinski (1956), Ch. 1.
19 *Op. cit.*, p. 5.
20 *Op. cit.*, p. 211.
21 Cf. T.H. Rigby's review of the later history of totalitarian theory: T.H. Rigby (1972).
22 John S. Reshetar Jr. (1971), pp. 338–41.
23 Z.K. Brzezinski (1962), pp. 19–20.
24 Z.K. Brzezinski and S.P. Huntington (1964).
25 *Op. cit.*, p. 20.
26 Leonard Schapiro (1965), p. 13.
27 Hough and Fainsod (1979), Preface to the third edition.
28 Merle Fainsod (1953). Quotes from pp. 152f, 327, 483.

29  *Op. cit.*, p. vii.
30  Merle Fainsod (1963), p. 421.
31  *Ibid.*
32  *Op. cit.*, *p. 451.*
33  *Op. cit.*, p. 577.
34  Hough and Fainsod (1979), p. 277.
35  *Op. cit.*, pp. 519–23.
36  *Op. cit.*, p. 420.
37  *Op. cit.*, table, p. 217.
38  *Op. cit.*, p. 278.
39  *Op. cit.*, pp. 215f, 272–8.
40  It soon became a world trend reaching the Soviet Union by 1970. Cf. F.M. Burlatsky (1970), p. 55f. See also Stephen White (1979).
41  *Op. cit.*, pp. 13, 34.
42  *Op. cit.*, p. 214.
43  The best known example of this in Australia was the late Professor Hugo Wolfsohn (1918–1982) of La Trobe University who for many years ran a most successful first year comparative politics course based on totalitarian theory. The main emphasis in this course was on Nazi Germany and the USSR.

## Chapter 7    Bureaucracy and communist politics

1  Jerry F. Hough (1969) p. 240.
2  *Op. cit.*, pp. 282–3.
3  See T.H. Rigby (1972a, 1972b, 1977). See also Rigby and Miller (1976).
4  On the latter, see Stephen Fortescue (1977).
5  Allen Kassof (1964), p. 558f.
6  Alfred G. Meyer (1961, 1965).
7  *Op. cit.*, Ch. XXIII.
8  The analogy is not original. It was earlier developed and discussed at considerable length by David Granick (1960), Ch. 12. For a more detailed discussion of this point, see L.G. Churchward (1968b).
9  Jerry F. Hough (1969), p. 97.
10  *Op. cit.*, p. 296.
11  Merle Fainsod (1963b), Carl Friedrich (1952).
12  Jerry F. Hough (1976).
13  *Op. cit.*, pp. 5–6.
14  *Op. cit.*, pp. 18–19.
15  Rigby and Miller (1976) p. 9.
16  T.H. Rigby, 'Hough on Political Participation in the Soviet Union', *Soviet Studies*, XXVIII, April, p. 258.
17  *Op. cit.*, p. 288. Cf. the conclusion to Jan S. Adams (1977), p. 205.
18  For a fuller discussion of the Soviet theory of public participation, see L.G. Churchward (1983).
19  Jan S. Adams (1977), p. 138f.
20  See, for example, Kallion and Schneider (1967).
21  Robert C. Tucker, 'On Revolutionary Mass Movement Regimes, *Amer-*

*ican Political Science Review*, June 1961. Also included in Tucker (1963).

22  A course was being taught at York (Toronto) in 1968. A somewhat similar course was taught at Melbourne University 1969–73 while at least one such course was taught in New Zealand from 1969 onwards.

23  *Arena*, No. 12, 1967, p. 38f.

24  *Op. cit.*, p. 18.

25  *Op. cit.*, p. 13f. For a later attempt at defining a communist political system, see Stephen White, *et al.* (1982).

26  David Lane (1976) pp. 59–62.

27  *Politichesky slovar* (1958), pp. 63–4.


## Chapter 8   Stalinism

1  *The Concise Oxford Dictionary* (1960), p. 1515.

2  J.D. Blake (1971), p. 52f.

3  G. Lukacs (1972).

4  Isaac Deutscher (1953), p. 34. Cf. Deutscher (1967), p. 34.

5  Ernest Mandel (1978b), pp. 76–7.

6  Robert C. Tucker (1963), p. 82. See also Ch. 3.

7  T.H. Rigby (1977), p. 64.

8  Jerry F. Hough and Merle Fainsod (1979), p. 192.

9  Giuseppe Boffa and Gilles Martinet (1977), p. 13.

10  Roy A. Medvedev (1971), p. 430f.

11  Cf. Davies and Steiger. *Soviet Asia*, p. 118.

12  Giuseppe Boffa and Gilles Martinet (1977), p. 97. Graeme Gill (1973, 1980).

13  Graeme Gill (1980).

14  *Seventieth Birthday of Joseph Vissarionovich Stalin, Pravda Articles, Soviet News* Booklet, London, 1950, p. 27.

15  *Op. cit.*, p. 41.

16  *Op. cit.*, p. 59f.

17  See Robert C. Tucker (1963), Ch. 5, 'Stalin and the Uses of Psychology'.

18  T.H. Rigby (1968b), pp. 210–12.

19  Evgenia Ginzburg (1967), p. 27.

20  Alexander Solzhenitsyn (1974), p. 71. Cf. Roy A. Medvedev (1971), p. 294.

21  T.H. Rigby (1968), p. 214.

22  T.H. Rigby (1968), p. 212, estimates 180,000. Rudolf Schlesinger (1977) estimates 190,000.

23  Roy A. Medvedev (1971), pp. 190, 239.

24  See Hough and Fainsod (1979), p. 177; Steven Rosefielde (1981); S.G. Wheatcroft (1981).

25  Leonard Schapiro (1970), p. 434.

26  Hough and Fainsod (1979), p. 177.

27  Steven Rosefielde (1981), p. 76.

28  *Op. cit.*, p. 347.

29  Roy A. Medvedev (1971), p. 179.

30  L.G. Churchward (1973), p. 65f.

31 Loren R. Graham (1968).
32 J. Stalin, *Works*, Vol. 6, pp. 47–53.
33 Roy A. Medvedev (1971), p. 509f. F.A. Ksenofontov's book was published in 1925 under the title *Uchenie Lenina o revolyutsii*.
34 Roy A. Medvedev (1971), pp. 514, 522, 512.
35 L.G. Churchward (1975), Ch. 6.
36 See T.H. Rigby (1968); N.S. Khrushchev (1977), Vol. 1, *passim*.
37 Based on tables in *Nar. khoz. SSSR 1922–1972*, pp. 346–7; *Nar. khoz. SSSR za 60 let*, p. 463; and *Nar. khoz. SSSR v 1979g.*, pp. 387–8.
38 Cf. T.H. Rigby (1977), pp. 70–4.

## Chapter 9   De-Stalinization

1 Robert C. Tucker, 'The Politics of De-Stalinization', *World Politics*, July 1957. Reprinted in Tucker (1972). Quotation from p. 173.
2 *Op. cit.*, p. 183f.
3 N.S. Khrushchev (1977), Vol. 1, p. 368.
4 *Op. cit.*, pp. 369–72.
5 The best edited text of this speech is that in T.H. Rigby (1968).
6 Paul J. Murphy (1981), p. 259f.
7 N.S. Khrushchev (1977), Vol. 1, p. 371f.
8 For the text of this resolution see T.H. Rigby (1968), p. 91.
9 Yevgeny Yevtushenko (1963), p. 102f.
10 On the theory of the state, see L.G. Churchward (1975), Ch. 6. On the national question, see G.V. Tadevosyan (1964).
11 Hough and Fainsod, (1979), p. 192f.
12 The best collection of these articles is in *The Anti-Stalin Campaign and International Communism*, published by the Columbia University Press late in 1956.
13 Palmiro Togliatti (1956), pp. 120–1.
14 *Op. cit.*, p. 126. The false theory referred to is that which held that the class struggle inevitably intensified as socialism was being developed.
15 *Op. cit.*, p. 128.
16 *The Anti-Stalin Campaign and International Communism*, p. 281.
17 *Op. cit.*, p. 300.
18 *The Anti-Stalin Campaign and International Communism*, p. 307f.
19 *Op. cit.*, p. 234.
20 Cf. George W. Breslauer (1982), Seweryn Bialer (1980).
21 George W. Breslauer (1982), p. 125f.
22 Paul J. Murphy (1981), p. 318f.
23 *Zarya vostoka* (Tbilisi), March 17, 1976. Quoted from Paul J. Murphy (1981), p. 306f.
24 B.N. Ponomaryov (ed.), (1960), p. 513.
25 B.N. Ponomaryov (ed.), (1960), p. 655.
26 B.N. Ponomarev (ed.), (1970), p. 577. Trans. by L.G. Churchward.
27 Stephen Fortescue (1983).
28 L.G. Churchward (1975), pp. 96–9, 301.
29 Seweryn Bialer (1980), p. 117f.
30 Roy A. Medvedev (1975), p. 332.

31 By 1971 almost 70 per cent of members of the CPSU had joined since Stalin died. See Peter Frank (1975), p. 109.

**Chapter 10    Soviet democracy reconsidered**

1 L.G. Churchward (1968a), p. 257f.
2 *Op. cit.*, pp. 262–7.
3 N.S. Gudkova (ed.), (1978), p. 21.
4 *Pravda*, 7 October 1978.
5 The passages cited are from E. Chekharin (1977), pp. 14, 41, 219, 224.
6 *Pravda*, 22 December 1972.
7 Report of the C.C. of the CPSU to the Twenty-fifth Party Congress. *Pravda*, 25 February 1976.
8 See E. Schneider (1979).
9 *Pravda*, 21 June 1983.
10 *Pravda*, 31 March 1981.
11 *Pravda*, 6 September 1981.
12 Text of the regulations in *Sovety nar. dep.*, No. 8, 1980.
13 Roy A. Medvedev (1975), pp. xv–xvi.
14 Roy A. Medvedev (1975), pp. 139–40.
15 *Op. cit.*, p. 138.
16 Trade Union membership from *Pravda*, 31 July 1984.
17 Exact figures are not always published. In 1978 the figures were: 516,000 questions prepared for Soviets and 900,000 for Executive Committees. In 1981 Standing Commissions prepared 594,000 questions for local Soviets and 900,000 for submission to Executive Committees. *Sovety nar. dep.*, No. 5, 1979 and 1982.
18 Theodore H. Friedgut (1983); A. Unger (1981).
19 Author's translation from Russian text of the Constitution of the USSR.
20 Quoted in *Pravda* editorial, 'Organs of Political Leadership', 30 March 1984.
21 *Ibid.*
22 For an example of this see L.G. Churchward (1975), p. 185.
23 Roy A. Medvedev (1975), p. 300.
24 The term 'democratic centralism' was in the Rules of the Communist League, 1847. Lenin popularized this term in the weeks leading up to the Fourth Congress of the RSDLP. My criticism of the concept is similar to that in David Lane (1978), p. 163f.
25 Author's translation from the Russian text.
26 Local Soviet expenditure taken from Everett M. Jacobs, (ed.), (1983), p. 63. The amount of expenditure directed through Union Republican budgets has varied widely over recent years. It reached 54.9 per cent in 1963 but had fallen to 44.2 per cent by 1970. It rose again after 1973 to reach 59.8 per cent in 1976. It sank to 39.1 per cent under Andropov in 1983 but rose to 44.2 per cent of USSR budget for 1984.
27 V.A. Vlasov (1959), p. 266.
28 Henry W. Morton (1983), p. 197f.
29 Everett M. Jacobs, (ed.), (1983), p. 177.
30 V. Dokukin, *Pravda*, 28 August 1977, p. 3.

# BIBLIOGRAPHY

Adams, Jan S. (1977) *Citizen Inspectors in the Soviet Union: The People's Control Committee*, New York, Praeger.

Adams, Jan S. (1980) 'Political Participation in the USSR: The Public Inspector', Ch. 4 in Daniel N. Nelson (ed.).

Aitov, N.A. (1969) 'An Analysis of the Objective Prerequisites for Eliminating the Distinctions between the Working Class and the Peasantry', Ch. 10 of G.V. Osipov (1969).

Akilov, K.A. and Gulyamova, M.A. (1978–9) *Sovetskaya intelligentsia Uzbekistana*, 2 vols, Tashkent.

Akhimov, Herman F. (1958) 'The Soviet Intelligentsia', included in *Soviet Society Today*, pp. 64–87.

Akmuriadov, K. (1979) *Izmenenie sotsialnoi struktury obshchestva v period ot sotsializma k kommunizmy*, Ashkhabad.

Albrow, Martin (1970) *Bureaucracy*, London, Macmillan.

Almond, Gabriel A. and Verba, Sidney (1965) *The Civic Culture*, Boston and Toronto, Little, Brown & Co.

Almond, Gabriel A., Powell, Jr. and Ingham, G. (1966) *Comparative Politics: A Developmental Approach*, Boston and Toronto, Little, Brown & Co.

Amelin, P.P. (1970) *Intelligentsia i sotsializm*, Leningrad.

Anderson, Perry (1983) 'Trotsky's Interpretation of Stalinism', *New Left Review*, No. 139, pp. 49–58.

Aptheker, H. (ed.), (1965) *Marxism and Alienation*, New York, Humanities Press.

Arendt, Hannah (1951) *The Origins of Totalitarianism*, Cleveland, World Publishing Co.

Armstrong, John A. (1959) *The Soviet Bureaucratic Elite*, New York.

Armstrong, John A. (1965) 'Sources of Administrative Behavior: Soviet and Western European Comparisons', *Am. Pol. Sc. Rev.*, LIX, 3, pp. 643–55.

Arutyunyan, Yu. V. (1966) 'The Social Structure of the Rural Population' (in Russian), *Voprosy filosofii*, No. 5, pp. 51–61.

Arutyunyan, Yu. V. (1969) 'Rural Social Structure', Ch. 17 in G.V. Osipov (1969).

Arutyunyan, Yu. V. (1971) *Sotsialnaya struktura selskovo naselenia*, Moscow.

Aspaturian, V.V. (1968) 'Foreign Policy Perspectives in the Sixties', Ch. 6 of

A. Dallin and T.B. Larson (1968).

Azrael, J.R. (1967) *Managerial Power and Soviet Politics*, Harvard University Press.

Bacon, Elizabeth (1967) *Central Asia Under Russian Rule*, Cornell University Press.

Bahme, S. (1962) 'Trotsky on Stalin's Russia', *Survey*, No. 41, April, pp. 27–42.

Barghoorn, Frederick C. (1966) *Politics in the USSR*, Boston and Toronto, Little, Brown & Co.

Bell, Daniel (1961) *The End of Ideology*, New York, Collier Books.

Bell, Daniel (1961) 'Ten Theories in Search of Reality: The Prediction of Soviet Behavior', Ch. 14 in *The End of Ideology*.

Bialer, Seweryn (1980) *Stalin's Successors: Leadership and Change in the Soviet Union*, Cambridge University Press.

Blake, J.D. (1971) *Revolution From Within – a Contemporary Theory of Social Change*, Sydney, Outlook.

Blake, Jack (1983) 'The Soviet Union and the Movement Against Nuclear War', *Arena*, No. 63, pp. 138–47.

Blau, Peter (1956) *Bureaucracy in Modern Society*, New York, Random House.

Boffa, Giuseppe (1960) *Inside the Khrushchev Era*, London, Allen & Unwin.

Boffa, Giuseppe and Martinet, Gilles (1977) *Dialogue sur le Stalinisme*, Paris, Stock.

Boldyrev, V.A. (1972) *Itogi perepisi naseleniia SSSR v 1970g.*, Moscow.

Bottomore, T.B. (1964) *Elites and Society*, London, Watts.

Bottomore, T.B. (1965) *Classes in Modern Society*, London, Allen & Unwin.

Brezhnev, L.I. (1971) 'Report of the Central Committee to the 24th Congress of the CPSU', *XXIV Sezd Kommunisticheskoi Partii Sovetskovo Soyuza*, I, pp. 26–131.

Brezhnev, L.I. (1976) 'Report of the Central Committee to the 25th Congress of the CPSU, 24–25 February, 1976, *Stenograficheskii otchet*, I, pp. 26–115.

Brinkley, G.A. (1961) 'The Withering Away of the State Under Khrushchev', *The Review of Politics*, XXII, pp. 37–51.

Brown, Archie (1975) 'Political Developments: Some Conclusions and an Interpretation', Ch. 10 in Brown and Kaser.

Brown, Archie and Kaser Michael (eds), (1975) *The Soviet Union Since the Fall of Khrushchev*, London, Macmillan.

Brown, Robert (1979) 'Bureaucracy: the Utility of a Concept', Kamenka and Krygier, Ch. 6.

Brutents, K.N. (1977) *National Liberation Revolutions Today*, 2 vols, Moscow, Progress Publishers.

Brzezinski, Z.K. (1962) *Ideology and Power in Soviet Politics*, New York.

Brzezinski, Z.K. (1966) 'The Soviet Political System: Transformation or Degeneration?', *Problems of Communism*, XV, Jan.–Feb., pp. 1–15.

Brzezinski, Z.K. and Huntington, S.P. (1964) *Political Power: USA/USSR*, London, Chatto & Windus.

Bukharin, Nikolai (1972) *Imperialism and World Economy*, London, Merlin Press.

Burlatsky, F., *The State and Communism*, Moscow, n.d.

Burlatsky, F.M. (1970) *Lenin, gosudarstvo, politika*, Moscow.

Burlatsky, F. and Galkin, A. (1974) *Sotsiologia, politika, mezhdunarodnye otnoshenia*, Moscow.

Burnham, James (1945) *The Managerial Revolution*, London, Pelican.

Burns, Tom and Stalker, G.M. (1959) *The Management of Innovation*, London, Tavistock Publications.

Calverton, V.V. (ed.), (1937) *The Making of Society*, New York, Modern Library.

Carr, E.H. (1946) *The Soviet Impact on the Western World*, London, Macmillan.

Chamberlin, William H. (1935) *The Russian Revolution 1917–1921*, 2 vols, New York, Macmillan.

Chekharin, E. (1977) *The Soviet Political System under Developed Socialism*, Moscow, Progress Publishers.

Churchward, L.G. (1957) 'Contemporary Soviet Government', *Soviet Studies*, IX, No. 2, Oct., pp. 191–9.

Churchward, L.G. (1961) 'Contemporary Soviet Theory of the Soviet State', *Soviet Studies*, XII, pp. 404–19.

Churchward, L.G. (1962) 'Soviet Revision of Lenin's *Imperialism*', *Australian Journal of Politics and History*, VIII, pp. 57–65.

Churchward, Lloyd (1967) 'Theories of Totalitarianism', *Arena* No. 12, Autumn, pp. 36–47.

Churchward, L.G. (1968a, 1975) *Contemporary Soviet Government*, London, Routledge & Kegan Paul.

Churchward, L.G. (1968b) 'Bureaucracy – USA: USSR', *Coexistence*, Vol. 5, pp. 201–9.

Churchward, L.G. (1973) *The Soviet Intelligentsia*, London, Routledge & Kegan Paul.

Churchward, L.G. (1983) 'Public Participation in the USSR', Ch. 2 in Everett M. Jacobs, pp. 34–47.

Cliff, Tony (1964, 1974) *State Capitalism in Russia*, London, Pluto.

Cohen, Stephen (1975) *Bukharin and the Bolshevik Revolution*, New York, Vintage Books/Random House.

Cohen, Stephen (1977) 'Bolshevism and Stalinism', Ch. 1 of Robert C. Tucker (ed.), pp. 3–29.

Cole, G.D.H. (1937) *Practical Economics*, London, Penguin.

Conolly, Violet (1975) *Siberia Today and Tomorrow*, London and Glasgow, Collins.

Conquest, Robert (1968, 1971) *The Great Terror*, London, Macmillan.

Cox, Terence M. (1979) *Rural Sociology in the Soviet Union: Its History and Basic Concepts*, London, Hurst.

Crankshaw, Edward (1966) *Khrushchev*, London, Collins.

Cummins, Ian (1980) *Marx, Engels and National Movements*, London, Croom Helm.

Dallin, Alexander and Larson, Thomas B. (eds), (1968) *Soviet Politics Since Khrushchev*, NJ, Prentice-Hall.

Davies, R.A. and Steiger, A.J. (1943) *Soviet Asia*, London, Gollancz.

Davisha, Adeed and Karen (eds), (1982) *Perspectives on Soviet Policy in the Middle East*, London, RIIA and Heinemann.

Deutscher, Isaac (1953) *Russia after Stalin*, London, Hamish Hamilton.

Deutscher, Isaac (1966) *Ironies of History: Essays on Contemporary Communism*, London, Oxford University Press.

Deutscher, Isaac (1967) *The Unfinished Revolution: Russia 1917–1967*, London, Oxford University Press.

Dienes, Leslie (1975) 'Pastoralism in Turkestan: Its Decline and its Persistence', *Soviet Studies*, XXVII, No. 3, pp. 343–65.

Djilas, Milovan (1957) *The New Class*, New York, Praeger.

Dornberg, John (1974) *Brezhnev: The Masks of Power*, London, André Deutsch.

Dyker, David A. (1981) 'Planning and the Worker', Ch. 3 of Schapiro and Godson, 1981.

Efrat, Moshe (1983) 'The Economics of Soviet Arms Transfers to the Third World – A Case Study: Egypt', *Soviet Studies*, XXXV, No. 4, Oct., pp. 437–56.

Elleinstein, Jean (1976) *The Stalin Phenomenon*, London, Lawrence & Wishart.

d'Encausse, Hélène Carrère (1980) *Le Pouvoir Confisqué*, Paris.

Evans, Alfred B. (1977) ' "Developed Socialism" in Soviet Ideology', *Soviet Studies*, XXIX, July, pp. 409–28.

Evans, Alfred B. (Jr) (1986) 'The Decline of Developed Socialism? Some Trends in Recent Soviet Ideology', *Soviet Studies*, XXXVIII, No. 1, pp. 1–23.

Fainsod, Merle (1953, 1963a) *How Russia is Ruled*, Harvard University Press.

Fainsod, Merle (1963b) 'Bureaucracy and Modernization: the Russian and Soviet Case', in J. La Polombara, 1963.

Fedoseev, P. (1976) 'Theoretical Problems of Developed Socialism and of Communist Construction', (in Russian), *Kommunist*, No. 15, pp. 40–54.

Fedotov, M.A. (1980) 'National Discussion and the Press' (The experience of content analysis of press material devoted to the Draft Constitution of the USSR, 1977), (in Russian), *Sovetskoe gosudarstvo i pravo*, May, pp. 32–40.

Filippov, F. (1973) 'The Soviet Intelligentsia – Active Builder of Communism', (in Russian), *Kommunist*, No. 16, Nov., pp. 89–99.

Fisher, Wesley (1977) 'Ethnic Consciousness and Intermarriage: Correlates of Endogamy among the Major Soviet Nationalities', *Soviet Studies*, XXIX, No. 3, pp. 393–408.

Fleron, Frederic J. (1969) *Communist Studies and the Social Sciences*, Chicago, Rand, McNally & Co.

Florinsky, Michael T. (1939) *Toward an Understanding of the USSR*, New York, Macmillan.

Fortescue, Stephen (1977) *The Primary Party Organizations in Non-Production Institutions*, Ph.D. thesis, Australian National University, Canberra.

Fortescue, Stephen (1983) *The Academy Reorganized: The R & D Role of the Soviet Academy of Sciences Since 1961*, Canberra, Australian National University.

Frank, Peter (1975) 'The Changing Composition of the Communist Party', Ch. 5 of Brown and Kaser.

Frankland, Mark (1966) *Khrushchev*, London, Penguin.

Frederiksen, O.J. (ed.), (1958) *Soviet Society Today: A Symposium*, Munich.

Friedgut, Theodore H. (1974) 'Community Structure: Political Participation and Soviet Local Government: The Case of Kutaisi', Ch. 7 of Morton and Tokes.

Friedgut, Theodore H. (1979) *Political Participation in the USSR*, Princeton University Press.

Friedgut, Theodore H. (1983) 'The Soviet Citizen's Perception of Local Government', Ch. 7 in Everett Jacobs (ed.).

Friedrich, Carl J. (1952) 'Some observations on Weber's analysis of Bureaucracy', Robert K. Merton (ed.), pp. 27–33.

Friedrich, C.J. and Brzezinski, Z.K. (1956) *Totalitarian Dictatorship and Autocracy*, Harvard University Press.

Gedilaghine, Vladimir (1974) *Les Contestataires en URSS*, Paris, Casterman.

Gerth, H.H. and Mills, C. Wright (eds), (1947) *From Max Weber: Essays in Sociology*, London, Kegan Paul, Trench, Trubner.

Gill, Graeme J. (1973) *The Cult of the Individual and the Search for Legitimacy: The Case of Mao and Stalin*, M.A. thesis, Monash University, Melbourne.

Gill, Graeme (1980) 'The Soviet Leader Cult: Reflections on the Structure of Leadership in the Soviet Union', *British Journal of Political Science*, 10, pp. 167–86.

Gill, Graeme (1985) 'Institutionalisation and Revolution: Rules and the Soviet Political System', *Soviet Studies*, XXXVII, No. 2, April, pp. 212–26.

Ginzburg, Evgenia (1967) *Into the Whirlwind*, London, Penguin.

Gitelman, Zvi (1977) 'Soviet Political Culture: Thoughts from Jewish Emigrants', *Soviet Studies*, XXIX, No. 4, pp. 543–64.

Glezerman, G.E. (1968) 'The Social Structure of Soviet Society', (in Russian), *Kommunist*, No. 15, pp. 28–39.

Graham, Loren R. (1968) *The Soviet Academy of Sciences and the Communist Party 1927–1932*, Oxford University Press.

Gramsci, Antonio (1957) *The Modern Prince and Other Writings*, London, Lawrence & Wishart.

Gramsci, Antonio (1971) *Selections from the Prison Notebooks*, New York, International Publishers.

Gripp, Richard C. (1963) *Patterns of Soviet Politics*, Illinois, Dorsey Press.

Gripp, Richard C. (1973) *The Political System of Communism*, New York, Dodd, Mead.

Gu, Guan-Fu (1983) 'Soviet Aid to the Third World: An Analysis of its Strategy', *Soviet Studies*, XXXV, No. 1, January, pp. 71–89.

Gudkova, N.A. (ed.), (1978) *Konstitutsia razvitovo sotsializma*, Moscow.

Gulyamova, M. (1962) *Iz istorii formirovania Uzbekskoi sovetskoi intelligentsii (1933–37)*, Tashkent.

Gvishiani, D.M., *et al.*, (1976) *The Scientific Intelligentsia in the USSR*, Moscow, Progress Publishers.

Hallas, Duncan (1979) *Trotsky's Marxism*, London, Pluto Press.

Halliday, Fred (1980) 'War and Revolution in Afghanistan', *New Left Review*, No. 119, Jan.–Feb., pp. 20–41.

Halliday, Fred (1981) *Threat From the East*, London, Penguin.

Hammer, Darrell P. (1974) *USSR: The Politics of Oligarchy*, Illinois, The Dryden Press.

Hanak, H. (1972) *Soviet Foreign Policy Since the Death of Stalin*, London, Routledge & Kegan Paul.

Harper, Samuel N. (1937) *The Government of the Soviet Union*, New York, Van Nostrand.

Harper, Samuel N. and Thompson, Donald (1949) *The Government of the Soviet Union*, second edn, New York, Van Nostrand.

Hazard, John N. (1957) *The Soviet System of Government*, University of Chicago Press.

Hill, Ian H. (1975) 'The End of the Russian Peasantry?', *Soviet Studies*, XXVII, pp. 109–27.

Hirszwicz, Maria (1976) 'Is there a Ruling Class in the USSR? – A Comment', *Soviet Studies*, XXVIII, No. 2, pp. 262–71.

Hodges, D.C. (1963) 'Class, Status and Intelligentsia', *Science & Society*, XXVII, pp. 49–61.

Holmes, Leslie (1986) *Politics in the Communist World*, Clarendon Press, Oxford.

Holubenko, M. (1976) 'The Soviet Working Class', *Critique*, No. 4, pp. 5–25.

Hough, Jerry F. (1969) *The Soviet Prefects: The Local Party Organs in Industrial Decision-Making*, Harvard University Press.

Hough, Jerry F. (1976) 'Political Participation in the Soviet Union', *Soviet Studies*, XXVIII, No. 1, pp. 3–20.

Hough, Jerry F. and Fainsod, Merle (1979) *How the Soviet Union is Governed*, Harvard University Press.

Iman, Zafar (1983) 'Soviet Treaties with Third World Countries', *Soviet Studies*, XXXV, No. 1, January, pp. 53–70.

Inkeles, Alex (1950) 'Social Stratification and Mobility in the Soviet Union, 1940–1950', *Am. Soc. Rev.*, XV, pp. 465–79.

Inkeles, Alex (1968) *Social Change in Soviet Russia*, Harvard University Press.

Iskenberov, A.A. *et al.* (1964) *Rabochii klass stran Azii i Afriki*, Moscow, Nauka.

*Itogi Vsesoyuznoi Perepisi Naselenia 1970 goda* (1972–3), 7 vols, Moscow.

Jacobs, Everett M. (ed.), (1983) *Soviet Local Politics and Government*, London, Allen & Unwin.

Jancar, Barbara Wolfe (1974) 'Women and Soviet Politics', Ch. 3 in Morton and Tokes.

Jukes, Geoffrey (1973) *The Soviet Union in Asia*, Sydney, Angus & Robertson and AIIA.

Kabyshev, V.T. (1980) 'Social-psychological aspects of popular power in the USSR', *Sovetskoe gosudarstvo i pravo*, March, pp. 22–7.

Kallion, I. Kh. and Shneider, Kh. Kh. (1967) 'Social Control and its Effectiveness', *Sovetskoe gosudarstvo i pravo*, No. 3, pp. 65–72.

Kamenka, Eugene and Krygier, Martin (eds), (1979) *Bureaucracy: The Career of a Concept*, Melbourne, Edward Arnold (Australia).

Kanet, Roger (1968) 'The Rise and Fall of the "All-People's State": Recent Changes in the Soviet Theory of the State', *Soviet Studies*, XX, July, pp. 81–93.

Kassof, Allen (1964) 'The Administered Society: Totalitarianism without Terror', *World Politics*, XVI, 4, pp. 558–75.

Keller, Suzanne (1963) *Beyond the Ruling Class*, New York, Random House.

Khalzamov, K. Kh. (1965) *Formirovania kadrov natsionalnoi intelligentsii v avtonomykh respublik Siberi*, Moscow.

Kharchev, A.G. (ed.) (1977) *Izmenenie polozhenia zhenshchiny i semya*, Moscow.

Khrushchev, N.S. (1977) *Khrushchev Remembers*, 2 vols, London, Penguin.

Kim, M.P. (1966) *Iz istorii sovetskoi intelligentsii*, Moscow.

Koestler, Arthur (1946) *Darkness at Noon*, London, Penguin.

Kolakowski, Leszek (1977) 'Marxist Roots of Stalinism', included in Robert C. Tucker (ed.), pp. 283–98.

Komkov, G.D., *et. al.* (1968) *Akademie Nauk SSSR: shtab sovetskoi nauki*, Moscow.

Kornhauser, William (1959) *The Politics of Mass Society*, New York.

Kugel, S.A. (1969) 'Changes in the Social Structure of Socialist Society under the impact of the scientific and technological revolution', (in Russian), *Voprosy filosofii*, No. 3, pp. 13–22.

Kuryleva, V.K., *et al.* (1969) *Iz opyta konkretnykh sotsiologicheskikh issled-ovanii*, Moscow.

Kusin, Vladimir (1976) 'Apropos Alec Nove's Search for a Class Label', *Soviet Studies*, XXVIII, No. 2, pp. 274–5.

Lane, Christel (1978) *Christian Religion in the Soviet Union*, London, Allen & Unwin.

Lane, Christel (1981) *The Rites of Rulers*, London, Cambridge University Press.

Lane, David (1976) *The Socialist Industrial State*, London, Allen & Unwin.

Lane, David (1978) *Politics and Society in the USSR*, second edn, London, Weidenfeld & Nicolson.

Lane, David (1982) *The End of Social Inequality?* London and Sydney, Allen & Unwin.

Lane, David and O'Dell, Felicity (1978) *The Soviet Industrial Worker: Social Class, Education and Control*, London, Martin Robertson.

Lapidus, Gail W. (1978) *Women in Soviet Society*, Berkeley, University of California.

La Polombara, J. (ed.), (1963) *Bureaucracy and Political Development*, Princeton University Press.

Lenin, V.I. (1917) *Imperialism: The Highest State of Capitalism, Selected Works*, Vol. 5, pp. 3–119.

Lenin, V.I. (1939–46) *Selected Works*, London, Lawrence & Wishart.

Lenin, V.I. (1957) *The National Liberation Movement in the East*, Moscow: FLPH.

Leonhard, Wolfgang (1968) 'Politics and Ideology in the Post-Khrushchev Era', Ch. 3 in Dallin and Larson (eds).

Lewin, Moshe (1975) *Political Undercurrents in Soviet Economic Debates*, London, Pluto Press.

Lewis, Philippa (1976) 'Peasant Nostalgia in Contemporary Russian Literature', *Soviet Studies*, XXVIII, No. 4, pp. 549–69.

Liebman, Marcel (1962) 'The Webbs and the New Civilisation', *Survey*, No. 41, April, pp. 58–74.

Liebman, Marcel (1975) *Leninism Under Lenin*, London, Cape.

Liely, Helen (1979) 'Shepherds and Reindeer Nomads in the Soviet Union', *Soviet Studies*, XXXI, No. 3, pp. 401–16.

Lipset, Seymour M. (1952) 'Bureaucracy and Social Change', included in Robert K. Merton (ed.), pp. 221–32.

Lipset, S.M. and Dobson, R.B. (1972) 'The Intellectual as Critic and Rebel: With Special Reference to the United States and the Soviet Union', *Daedalus*, Summer, pp. 137–98.

Litov, N.A. (1966) 'Changes to the Social Nature and Class Character of the Peasantry', G.V. Osipov (ed.), (1966a), Vol. 1, pp. 363–90.

Lubin, Nancy (1981) 'Women in Soviet Central Asia: Progress and Contradictions', *Soviet Studies*, XXXIII, No. 2, pp. 182–203.

Lukács, Georg (1972) 'An Interview', interviewed by Franco Ferrarotti, *Sociological Abstracts*, April–May:

Lytkin, V.A. (1977) 'Critique of Bourgeois Falsification of the Relation between the CPSU and the Intelligentsia', (in Russian), Ch. XII in K.I. Suborov (1977).

McAuley, Alastair (1977) 'The Distribution of Earnings and Income in the Soviet Union', *Soviet Studies*, XXIX, No. 2, pp. 214–37.

McAuley, Alastair (1981a) 'Welfare and Social Security', Ch. 8 in Schapiro and Godson (eds).

McAuley, Alastair (1981b) *Women's Work and Wages in the Soviet Union*, London, Allen & Unwin.

McAuley, Mary (1977) *Politics and the Soviet Union*, London, Penguin.

McClosky, Herbert and Turner, John E. (1960) *The Soviet Dictatorship*, New York, McGraw–Hill.

McNeal, Robert H. (1977) 'Trotskyist Interpretations of Stalinism', in Robert C. Tucker (ed.), pp. 30–52.

Maksimov, G.M. (ed.), (1976) *Vsesoyuznaya perepis naseleniya 1970 goda*, Moscow.

Male, Beverley (1982) *Revolutionary Afghanistan*, London and Canberra, Croom Helm.

Mandel, Ernest (1968) *Marxist Economic Theory*, London, Merlin.

Mandel, Ernest (1974) 'Ten Theses on the Social and Economic Laws Governing the Society Transitional Between Capitalism and Socialism', *Critique*, No. 3, pp. 5–21.

Mandel, Ernest (1978a) 'On the Nature of the Soviet State', *New Left Review*, No. 108, March–April, pp. 3–21.

Mandel, Ernest (1978b) *From Stalinism to Eurocommunism*, London, NLB.

Mandel, Ernest (1979) *Trotsky: A Study in the Dynamics of his Thought*, London, NLB.

Mandel, William M. (1975) *Soviet Women*, New York, Anchor.

Markovic, Mihailo (1977) 'Stalinism and Marxism', R.C. Tucker (ed.), pp. 299–319.

Maslin, A.N. (1966) 'Trends Towards the Combination of Intellectual and Manual Labour', Ch. 12 in V. Osipov (1966a).

Matthews, Mervyn (1972) *Class and Society in Soviet Russia*, London, Allen Lane, the Penguin Press.

Matthews, Mervyn (1975) 'Soviet Students – Some Sociological Perspectives', *Soviet Studies*, XXVII, January, pp. 86–108.

Matthews, Mervyn (1978) *Privilege in the Soviet Union*, London, Allen & Unwin.

Matthews, Mervyn (1982) *Education in the Soviet Union*, London, Allen & Unwin.

Maxwell, B.W. (1935) *The Soviet State*, London, Selwyn Blount.

Medvedev, Roy A. (1971) *Let History Judge: The Origins and Consequences of Stalinism*, New York, Macmillan.

Medvedev, Roy A. (1975) *On Socialist Democracy*, London, Macmillan.

Menon, Rajan (1982) 'The Soviet Union, the Arms Trade and the Third World', *Soviet Studies*, XXXIV, No. 3, July, pp. 377–96.

Merton, Robert K. (ed.), *Reader in Bureaucracy*, New York, The Free Press.

Meyer, Alfred G. (1967) 'The Comparative Study of Communist Political Systems', *Slavic Review*, XXVI, 1, pp. 3–28.

Meyer, Alfred G. (1965) *The Soviet Political System*, New York.

Miller, John H. (1977) 'Cadres Policy in Nationality Areas – Recruitment of CPSU First and Second Secretaries in Non-Russian Republics of the USSR', *Soviet Studies*, XXIX, No. 1, pp. 3–36.

Mills, C. Wright (1957) *The Power Elite*, New York, Oxford University Press.

Mills, C. Wright (1959) *The Causes of World War Three*, London, Secker & Warburg.

Mirsky, G.I. (1970) *Armia i politika v stranakh Azii i Afriki*, Moscow, Nauka.

Monich, Z.I. (1971) *Intelligentsia v struktura selskovo naselenia*, Minsk.

Morton, Henry W. (1983) 'Local Soviets and the Attempt to Rationalize the Delivery of Urban Services: The Case of Housing', Ch. 11, Everett M. Jacobs (ed.).

Morton, H.W. and Tokes, R.L. (eds), (1974) *Soviet Politics and Society in the 1970s*, New York, Free Press/Collier-Macmillan.

Mosca, Gaetano (1965) *The Ruling Class*, New York, McGraw-Hill, third edn.

*Moskva v tsifrakh 1980* (1980) Moscow.

Mowat, Farley (1970) *The Siberians*, Boston, Little, Brown & Co.

Muminov, I.M. *et al.* (1979) *Sovetskaya intelligentsia Uzbekistana*, Tashkent.

Murphy, Paul J. (1981) *Brezhnev: Soviet Politician*, Jefferson, NC: McFarland & Co.

*Narodnoe khozyaistvo SSSR 1922–1972* (1972) Moscow.

*Narodnoe khozyaistvo SSSR za 60 let* (1977) Moscow.

*Narodnoe khozyaistvo SSSR v 1979g.* (1980) Moscow.

*Narodnoe khozyaistvo SSSR v 1980g.* (1981) Moscow.

*Narodnoe khozyaistvo SSSR 1922–1982* (1982) Moscow.

*Narodnoe khozyaistvo SSSR v 1984g.* (1985) Moscow.

Nasyrkhaev, S.N. (1972) *Intelligentsia Uzbekistana i ee rol v stroitelstve kommunizma*, Tashkent.

Nelson, Daniel N. (ed.), (1980) *Local Politics in Communist Countries*, University of Kentucky.

Neumann, Franz (1942) *Behemoth: The Structure and Practice of National Socialism*, London, Gollancz.

Nicolaus, Martin (1976) *The Restoration of Capitalism in the USSR*, Chicago.

Nolutshungu, Sam C. (1982) 'African Interests and Soviet Power: The Local Context of Soviet Policy', *Soviet Studies*, XXXIV, No. 3, July, pp. 397–417.

Norr, Henry (1986) 'Shchekino: Another Look', *Soviet Studies*, XXXVIII, No. 2, April, pp. 141–69.

Nove, Alec (1964) *Was Stalin Really Necessary?*, London, Allen & Unwin.

Nove, Alec (1969) 'History, Hierarchy and Nationalities: Some Observations on the Soviet Social Structure', *Soviet Studies*, XXI, pp. 71–92.

Nove, Alec (1975a) *Stalinism and After*, London, Allen & Unwin.

Nove, Alec (1975b) 'Is There a Ruling Class in the USSR?', *Soviet Studies*, XXVII, Oct., pp. 615–38.

Nove, Alec (1977) *The Soviet Economic System*, London, Allen & Unwin.

Nove, Alec (1982) 'Soviet Agriculture: New Data', *Soviet Studies*, XXXIV, No. 1, pp. 118–22.

Nove, Alec (1983a) *The Economics of Feasible Socialism*, London, Allen & Unwin.

Nove, Alec (1983b) 'The Class Nature of the Soviet Union Revisited', *Soviet Studies*, XXXV, No. 3, July, pp. 298–312.

Nove, Alec and Newth, J.A. (1967) *The Soviet Middle East*, London, Allen & Unwin.

O'Hearn, Dennis (1980) 'The Consumer Second Economy: Size and Effects', *Soviet Studies*, XXXII, No. 2, pp. 218–34.

Oiserman, T.I. (1965) 'Marxism and the Individual', Ch. VII in Aptheker.

Osipov, A.P. (1966) 'Technical Progress and the Changing Professional Structure of the Working Class', (in Russian), included in Osipov (ed.), (1966), vol. 2, pp. 10–27.

Osipov, G.V. (ed.), (1966a) *Sotsiologia v SSSR*, 2 vols, Moscow.

Osipov, G.V. (ed.), (1966b) *Industry and Labour in the USSR*, London, Tavistock.
Osipov, G.V. (ed.), (1969) *Town, Country and People*, London, Tavistock.
Ossowski, S. (1963) *Class Structure and the Social Consciousness*, London, Routledge & Kegan Paul.
Pareto, Vilfredo (1966) *Sociological Writings*, London, Pall Mall.
Parry, Geraint (1969) *Political Elites*, London, Allen & Unwin.
Ponomarev, B.N. (ed.), (1970) *Istoria Kommunisticheskoi Partii Sovetskovo Soyuza*, Moscow.
Ponomaryov, B.N. (ed.), (1960) *History of the Communist Party of the Soviet Union*, Moscow, FLPH.
Presthus, Robert (1962) *The Organizational Society*, New York, Vintage Books.
Rakovsky, Christian (1980) *Selected Writings on Opposition in the USSR 1923–30*, London, Allison & Bushby.
Remnek, Richard B. (ed.), (1977) *Social Scientists and Policy Making in the USSR*, New York and London, Praeger.
Reshetar, Jr., John S. (1971) *The Soviet Polity: Government and Politics in the USSR*, New York and Toronto, Dodd-Mead.
Rigby, T.H. (1964) 'Traditional, Market and Organizational Societies and the USSR', *World Politics*, XVI, No. 4, pp. 539–57.
Rigby, T.H. (ed.), (1966) *Stalin*, New Jersey, Prentice-Hall.
Rigby, T.H. (ed.), (1968) *The Stalin Dictatorship*, Sydney University Press.
Rigby, T.H. (1969) *Communist Party Membership in the USSR 1917–1967*, New Jersey, Princeton University Press.
Rigby, T.H. (1970) 'The Soviet Leadership: Towards a Self-Stabilizing Oligarchy?', *Soviet Studies*, XXII, pp. 167–91.
Rigby, T.H. (1972a) 'Totalitarianism and Change in Communist Systems', *Comparative Politics*, April, pp. 433–53.
Rigby, T.H. (1972b) 'Birth of the Soviet Bureaucracy', *Politics*, VII, pp. 121–35.
Rigby, T.H. (1976) 'Hough on Political Participation in the Soviet Union', *Soviet Studies*, XXVIII, No. 2, April, pp. 257–61.
Rigby, T.H. (1977) 'Stalinism and the Mono-Organizational Society', in Robert C. Tucker (ed.), pp. 53–76.
Rigby, T.H. (1978) 'The Soviet Regional Leadership: The Brezhnev Generation', *Slavic Review*, 37, March, pp. 1–24.
Rigby, T.H. (1986) 'Was Stalin a Disloyal Patron?', *Soviet Studies*, XXXVIII, No. 3, July, pp. 311–24.
Rigby, T.H. and Miller, R.F. (1976) *Political and Administrative Aspects of the Scientific and Technical Revolution in the USSR*, Canberra, Australian National University.
Rodionov, M. (ed.), (1970) *Struktura sovetskoi intelligentsii*, Minsk.
Rosefielde, Steven (1981) 'Assessment of the Sources and Uses of Gulag: Forced Labour 1929–1956', *Soviet Studies*, XXXIII, No. 1, pp. 51–87.
Rosefielde, Steven (1983) 'Excess Mortality in the Soviet Union: Reconsideration of the Demographic Consequences of Forced Industrialization

1929–1949', *Soviet Studies*, XXXV, No. 3, pp. 385–409.

Rosenbaum, Yu. and Sergienko, L. (1972) 'The Organization of Labour of Workers of the *apparat*', (in Russian), *Sovety deputatov trudyashchikhsya*, No. 11, pp. 83–6.

Rothenberg, Morris (1983) 'Latin America in Soviet Eyes', *Problems of Communism*, XXXII, Oct., pp. 1–18.

Rubinstein, Alvin Z. (1977) *Red Star on the Nile*, Princeton University Press.

Rumer, Boris (1981) 'The "Second" Agriculture in the USSR', *Soviet Studies*, XXXIII, No. 4, pp. 560–72.

Rumyantsev, A.M. (ed.), (1963) *Structure of the Working Class*, New Delhi, People's Publishing House.

Rutkevich, M.N. (1966) 'Changes to the Social Structure of Soviet Society and the Intelligentsia', (in Russian), included in G.V. Osipov (ed.), (1966a) Vol. 1, pp. 391–413.

Rutkevich, M. (1974) 'The Social Structure of Developed Socialist Society', (in Russian), *Kommunist*, No. 2, pp. 77–87.

Rutkevich, M.N. (1977) *Intelligentsia v razvitom sotsialisticheskom obshchestve*, Moscow.

Rutkevich, M.N. and Filippov, F.R. (1978) *Vysshaya Shkola kak faktor izmenenia sotsialnoi struktury razvitovo sotsialisticheskovo obshchestva*, Moscow, USSR Academy of Sciences.

Sapilnikov, E.N. (1971) 'The Social Structure of the Rural Population and the Path of its Development', (in Russian), *Voprosy filosofii*, No. 11, pp. 27–39.

Schapiro, Leonard (1965) *The Government and Politics of the Soviet Union*, London, Hutchinson.

Schapiro, Leonard (1970) *The Communist Party of the Soviet Union*, second edn, London, Associated Book Publishers.

Schapiro, Leonard (1972) *Totalitarianism*, London, Macmillan.

Schapiro, Leonard and Godson, Joseph (1981) *The Soviet Worker: Illusions and Realities*, London, Macmillan.

Schlesinger, Rudolf (1947) *The Spirit of Post-War Russia*, London, Dennis Dobson.

Schlesinger, Rudolf (1977) *History of the Communist Party of the USSR*, Calcutta, South Asia Books.

Schneider, Eberhard (1979) 'The Discussion of the New All-Union Constitution of the USSR', *Soviet Studies*, XXXI, No. 4, Oct., pp. 523–41.

Scott, Derek J.R. (1958) *Russian Political Institutions*, London, Allen & Unwin.

Selunskaya, V.M. (ed.), (1982) *Izmenenie sotsialnoi struktury narodov SSSR*, Moscow.

Semenov, V.S. et al., (1968) *Klassy, sotsialnye sloi i gruppy v SSSR*, Moscow.

Semyonov, V.S. (1976) 'Soviet Intellectuals and White Collar Workers', Ch. 9 in G.V. Osipov (1966a), Vol. 1.

Semyonov, V.S. (1979) *Nations and Nationalism*, Moscow, Progress Publishers.

Senyasky, S.L. (1973) 'Changes in the Social Structure of Soviet Society (1938–1970)', (in Russian), *Voprosy istorii*, No. 4, pp. 3–17.

Shedrik, M.P. (1970) *Obshchenarodnoe gosudarstvo – novy etap v razvitii sotsialisticheskoi gosudarstvennosti*, Lvov.

Shkaratan, O.I. (1967) 'The Social Structure of the Soviet Working Class', (in Russian), *Voprosy filosofii*, No. 1, pp. 28–39.

Silver, Brian D. (1974a) 'The State of the National Minority Languages in Soviet Education: An Assessment of Recent Changes', *Soviet Studies*, XXVI, Jan., pp. 28–46.

Silver, Brian (1974b) 'Social Mobilization and the Russification of Soviet Nationalities', *Am. Pol. Sc. Rev.*, LXVIII, March, pp. 45–66.

Silver, Brian (1978) 'Ethnic Intermarriage and Ethnic Consciousness Among Soviet Nationalities', *Soviet Studies*, XXX, No. 1, pp. 107–16.

Skilling, H. Gordon (1966) 'Interest Groups and Communist Politics', *World Politics*, XVIII, 3, pp. 435–51.

Skilling, H. Gordon and Griffiths, Franklyn (eds), (1971) *Interest Groups and Soviet Politics*, Princeton University Press.

Smirnov, G.L. (1966) 'The Rate of Growth of the Soviet Working Class and Changes in its Composition with Respect to Occupation and Skill', Ch. 2 in G.V. Osipov (1966a).

Soktoev, I.A. (1969) *Partinoe rukovodstvo formirovaniem intelligentsii*, Frunze.

Solomon, Susan G. (ed.), (1983) *Pluralism in the Soviet Union*, London, Macmillan.

Solzhenitsyn, Alexander (1974) *The Gulag Archipelago 1918–1956*, Melbourne, Collins/Fontana.

Stalin, J. (ed.) (1944) *History of the Communist Party of the Soviet Union (Bolsheviks)*, Sydney, Current Book Distributors.

Stalin, J. (1945) *Problems of Leninism*, Moscow, FLPH.

Stalin, J.V. (1950) *Marxism and Linguistics*, London, Soviet News.

Stalin, J. (1952) *Economic Problems of Socialism in the USSR*, Moscow, FLPH.

Stalin, J. (1952–55) *Works*, 13 vols, Moscow, FLPH.

Sternheimer, Stephen (1983) 'Communications and Power in Soviet Urban Politics', Ch. 8 in Everett M. Jacobs (ed.).

Strmiska, Zdenek (1976) *Programme socialiste et rapports sociaux en URSS et dans les pays socialistes*, Paris.

Strong, Anna Louise (1957) *The Stalin Era*, New York, Mainstream Publications.

Suborov, K.I. *et al.* (1977) *Partia i intelligentsia v usloviyakh razvitovo sotsializma*, Moscow, Mysl Press.

Suny, Ronald G. (1983) 'Towards a Social History of the October Revolution', *American Historical Review*, Feb., pp. 31–52.

Szelenyi, Ivan (1978) 'The Position of the Intelligentsia in the Class Structure of State-Socialist Societies', included in Marian Sawer (ed.), *Socialism and the New Class*, APSA Monograph 19, Sydney, 1978.

Szymanski, Albert (1979) *Is the Red Flag Flying? The Political Economy of the Soviet Union Today*, London, Zed Press.

Tadevosyan, G.V. (1964) 'V.I. Lenin on the State Form of the Socialist Resolution of the National Question', (in Russian), *Voprosy filosofii*, No.

4, pp. 27–37.

Tarabrin, E.A. (ed.), (1980) *USSR and Countries of Africa*, Moscow, Progress Publishers.

Taubman, William (1973) *Governing Soviet Cities: Bureaucratic Politics and Urban Development in the USSR*, New York and London, Praeger.

Teckenberg, Wolfgang (1978) 'Labour Turnover and Job Satisfaction: Indicators of Industrial Conflict in the USSR', *Soviet Studies*, XXX, No. 2, pp. 192–211.

*The Anti-Stalin Campaign and International Communism* (1956) New York, Columbia University Press.

*The Suppressed Testament of Lenin with 'On Lenin's Testament' by Leon Trotsky* (1946) New York, Pioneer Publishers.

*The USSR Economy: A Statistical Abstract* (1957) London, Lawrence & Wishart.

Ticktin, H.H. (1973a) 'Towards a Political Economy of the USSR', *Critique*, No. 1, pp. 20–44.

Ticktin, H.H. (1973b) 'Political Economy of the Soviet Intelligentsia', *Critique*, No. 2, pp. 5–21.

Titma, M. Kh. (1975) *Vybor professii kak sotsialnaya problema*, Moscow.

Togliatti, Palmiro (1956) '9 Domande sullo Stalinismo'. *The Anti-Stalin Campaign and International Communism*, pp. 97–139.

Towster, Julian (1948) *Political Power in the USSR 1917–1947*, New York, Oxford University Press.

Trotsky, Leon (1923, 1943) *The New Course*, USA, New Park Publications.

Trotsky, Leon (1937, 1965) *The Revolution Betrayed*, New York, Merit Publishers.

Tsokhas, Kosmas (1977) 'A New Imperialism: The Soviet Union in the Middle East', *Melbourne Journal of Politics*, No. 9, pp. 30–57.

Tsokhas, Kosmas (1980) 'The Political Economy of Cuban Dependence on the Soviet Union', *Theory and Society*, 9, pp. 319–62.

Tucker, Robert C. (1963, 1972) *The Soviet Political Mind*, revised edition, London, Allen & Unwin.

Tucker, Robert C. (1967) 'On the Comparative Study of Communism', *World Politics*, XIX, 2, pp. 242–57.

Tucker, Robert C. (ed.), (1977) *Stalinism: Essays in Historical Interpretation*, New York, Norton.

Tyagunenko, V.L. (1969) *Problemy sovremennykh osvoboditelnykh revolyutsii*, Moscow, Nauka.

Ulyanovsky, R.A. (1963) *Neokolonializm S.Sh.A. i slaborazvitye stranny Azii*, Moscow.

Ulyanovsky, R.A. (1965) *The Dollar and Asia: U.S. Neocolonialist Policy in Action*, Moscow, Nauka.

Unger, Aryeh I. (1981) 'Political Participation in the USSR: YCL and CPSU', *Soviet Studies*, XXXII, No. 1, pp. 107–24.

Valiev, A.K. (1969) *Sovetskaya natsionalnaya intelligentsia i ee sotsialnaya rol*, Tashkent.

Vinogradov, N.N. (1980) 'The Soviet Conception of Party Leadership of Soviets', (in Russian), *Sovetskoe gosudarstvo i pravo*, No. 4, April, pp. 13–21.

Vlasov, V.A. (1959) *Sovetsky gosudarstvenny apparat*, Moscow.
Volkov, M. (1973) 'The Scientific-Technological Revolution and the Foundation of the Material Basis of Communism', (in Russian), *Kommunist*, No. 5, pp. 62–75.
Volkov, V.S. and Mukhin, A.A. (eds), (1977) *Sovetskaya intelligentsia: kratkii ocherk istorii (1917–1975)*, Moscow.
Voslensky, Michael (1980) *La Nomenklatura: Les Privilégiés en URSS*, Paris.
Vyltsan, M.A. (1967) 'Composition and Structure of the Rural Population of the USSR over 50 years', (in Russian), *Istoria SSSR*, No. 6, pp. 43–63.
Wädekin, Eugen (1975) 'Income Distribution in Soviet Agriculture', *Soviet Studies*, XXVII, No. 1, pp. 3–26.
Wallace, William V. (1983) 'Sino-Soviet Relations: An Interpretation', *Soviet Studies*, XXXV, No. 4, Oct., pp. 457–70.
Webb, S. and B. (1937) *Soviet Communism: A New Civilisation*, second edn, London, Longman, Green & Co.
Weber, Max (1962) *Basic Concepts in Sociology*, New York, Citadel.
Weinberg, Elizabeth Ann (1974) *The Development of Sociology in the Soviet Union*, London, Routledge & Kegan Paul.
Wesson, Robert G. (1964) 'Volunteers and Soviets', *Soviet Studies*, XV, No. 3, pp. 231–49.
Wheatcroft, Stephen G. (1981) 'On Assessing the Size of Forced Concentration Camp Labour in the Soviet Union 1929–56', *Soviet Studies*, XXXIII, No. 2, pp. 265–95.
Wheatcroft, Stephen G. (1983) 'Towards a Thorough Analysis of Soviet Forced Labour Statistics', *Soviet Studies*, XXXV, No. 2, April, pp. 223–37.
White, Stephen (1979) *Political Culture and Soviet Politics*, London, Macmillan.
White, Stephen *et al.*, (1982) *Communist Political Systems: An Introduction*, London, Macmillan.
Yankova, Z.A. (1978) *Sovetskaya zhenshchina*, Moscow.
Yanowitch, Murray (1977) *Social and Economic Inequality in the Soviet Union*, London, Martin Robertson.
Yanowitch, Murray (1981) 'Schooling and Inequality', Ch. 6 in Schapiro and Godson (eds.), (1981).
Yanowitch, Murray and Dodge, N.T. (1969) 'The Social Evaluation of Occupation in the Soviet Union', *Slavic Review*, Vol. 28, pp. 619–43.
Yevtushenko, Yevgeny (1963) *A Precocious Autobiography*, London, Collins & Harvill Press.
Zagoria, Donald S. (1967) *Vietnam Triangle*, New York.
Zamostny, Thomas J. (1984) 'Moscow and the Third World: Recent Trends in Soviet Thinking', *Soviet Studies*, XXXVI, No. 2, April, pp. 223–35.
Zaslavsky, Victor (1982) *The Neo-Stalinist State: Class, Ethnicity and Consensus in Soviet Society*, New York, M.E. Sharpe.
Zezina, M.R. (1982a) 'The General Composition and Social Development of the Intelligentsia of the Soviet Union Republics', (in Russian), included in V.M. Selunskaya (ed.), 1982, pp. 110–26.
Zezina, M.R. (1982b) *Sovetskaya intelligentsia v usloviyakh razvitovo*

*sotsializma*, Moscow University Press.

Zhdanov, A. (1947) *The International Situation*, Moscow, FLPH.

*Zhenshchiny v SSSR: statisticheskie materialy* (1982) Moscow.

Zhilinsky, S.E. (1980) 'Functions of the CPSU and the Government in the Political System: their Relations', (in Russian), *Sovetskoe gosudarstvo i pravo*, No. 4, April, pp. 131–41.

# INDEX